Prais
Assassin and
the Therapist

"Kottler has done a masterful job in writing a book that is not just about a person, but is rather about us as persons. [It] is a deft treatment of human nature and the nature of living. It goes beyond 'therapy' to the essence of life."

"I read *The Assassin and the Therapist* in two sittings. The first sitting ended at 3 A.M. when I reluctantly forced myself to stop. That alone should answer the question of whether this book is a good read."

"WOW! What a book! What I always appreciate about Kottler's writing is his ability to say what we all (counselors and counselor educators) think but are afraid to admit: that we don't know why counseling works; that we often feel stumped about how to help people; that sometimes our colleagues need more help than our clients; and that sometimes we feel burned out, tired, and fed up with the people who seek help from us. It brings me great relief to read these things. Kottler's words make me feel less alone as a professional."

Cynthia Briggs, PhD, NCC, LPC, DCC
Assistant Professor of Counselor Education, Winona State University; Coauthor of Women, Girls, and Addiction

"One part adventure thriller, one part clinical case study, and one part sage counsel on the practice of psychotherapy, *The Assassin and the Therapist* offers a unique and unflinching examination of the subject of truth and trust in the counseling relationship, and indeed, in everyday life. Kottler's magnetic meditation on the nature of narrative in the construction of our life stories makes for riveting reading, as instructive for the seasoned practitioner as for the novice therapist. I recommend it to every clinician who strives to listen both credulously and critically to client accounts, and to forge a way forward in the slippery terrain of the formulation and reformulation of a client's self-narrative."

Robert A. Neimeyer, PhD
Professor of Psychology, The University of Memphis; Author of Constructivist Psychotherapy

"It may well be the most honest and powerful book on psychotherapy ever written..."

Howard Rosenthal, EdD
Professor and Coordinator of the Human Services Program, St. Louis Community College at Florissant Valley; Author of the Encyclopedia of Counseling: Special 15th Anniversary Edition

"This remarkable story, told by a master storyteller, is destined to be a psychotherapy classic. Fasten your seat belts as Kottler shares a captivating tale that will impact all of your relationships."

Jon Carlson, PsyD, EdD
*Distinguished Professor of Psychology and
Counseling, Governors State University*

"In addition to being an amazing story that is as good as any historical fiction, the book has a great deal of meaning, especially for those of us who are experienced in the art, and sometimes science, of therapy. Unlike so much of the current writing that is either for the novice, or introduces a new twist on a well-used approach, this book will engender many smiles and 'recognition reflexes' by those of us who will identify with Kottler's dilemmas and conclusions throughout his career as a therapist. I believe the readers, like myself, will also appreciate Kottler's humble sharing of mistakes, blunders, or heartbreaking conclusions that come from years of experience as a therapist. He makes us think and reflect about this crazy world of counseling that we embrace as sacred and, in the end, by which we define ourselves and from which we earn our livelihood. I especially appreciate the last chapter which goes to the heart of who we are as therapists, as we struggle with our 'constant companions' of hope and despair because, as the author states, 'deep down inside we really do want to save people; on a good day we actually believe this is possible.'"

Lynn K. Hall, EdD, LPC, NCC, ACS
*Professor, Counselor Education, School of Education, Western
New Mexico University; Author of* Counseling Military Families

The Assassin and the Therapist

AN EXPLORATION OF TRUTH IN PSYCHOTHERAPY AND IN LIFE

The Assassin and the Therapist

by jeffrey kottler

Routledge
Taylor & Francis Group
New York   London

Routledge
Taylor & Francis Group
270 Madison Avenue
New York, NY 10016

Routledge
Taylor & Francis Group
27 Church Road
Hove, East Sussex BN3 2FA

© 2010 by Taylor and Francis Group, LLC
Routledge is an imprint of Taylor & Francis Group, an Informa business

Printed in the United States of America on acid-free paper
10 9 8 7 6 5 4 3 2 1

International Standard Book Number: 978-0-415-80064-8 (Hardback) 978-0-415-80065-5 (Paperback)

Library of Congress Cataloging-in-Publication Data

Kottler, Jeffrey A.
  The assassin and the therapist : an exploration of truth in psychotherapy and in life / Jeffrey Kottler.
    p. ; cm.
  Includes bibliographical references and index.
  ISBN 978-0-415-80064-8 (hardcover : alk. paper) -- ISBN 978-0-415-80065-5 (pbk. : alk. paper)
    1. Psychotherapy. 2. Truth. 3. Psychotherapist and patient. I. Title.
  [DNLM: 1. Psychotherapy--Israel. 2. Deception--Israel. 3. Homicide--psychology--Israel. 4. Physician-Patient Relations--Israel. 5. Politics--Israel. WM 420 K865a 2010]
  RC480.5.K678 2010
  616.89'14--dc22
                                                                                2009030085

Visit the Taylor & Francis Web site at
http://www.taylorandfrancis.com

and the Routledge Web site at
http://www.routledgementalhealth.com

Contents

SECTION I An Assassin's Story

SECTION II   A Therapist's Story

Preface

This may be one of the most unusual books you will ever read, not only about psychotherapy, but about the very foundation of what you think you know and understand. On one level this is an honest and provocative study of a therapist's struggle with doubt and uncertainty, as well as issues that are imperfectly understood and rarely discussed. It tells the story of how I have been questioning the very foundation of what I do as a therapist, teacher, and writer after more than three decades of practice.

There are two parallel narratives in this book. The first tells the story of Jacob, a man in his seventies, who lived through one of the most remarkable periods in history and actually altered those events through his acts of violence. It is a tale of intrigue, of adventure, and of courage, but it is also filled with a number of thorny, moral issues. It is a story of despair, but also of hope.

After joining me on Jacob's journey from his childhood to his recruitment, training, and preparation as an assassin, we will end by looking at some quite unexpected themes that crop up, some of which have a significant impact on the ways we think about our work as therapists and our relationships with clients. We will explore the nature of truth in psychotherapy and in the clinician's life, examining some of the things that we often deny, or at least rarely speak about.

It has been more than a decade since I was approached by an elderly man, obviously distressed, who wanted me to tell the story of his life, a tale that was so secret and potentially explosive that he had kept it to himself for the past 50 years, literally fearing lethal retribution if he revealed what had happened. Five decades later he was still demonstrating symptoms of posttraumatic stress disorder that disrupted his sleep with nightmares. I spent a year interviewing Jacob, then another year doing background and contextual research and writing the story. The manuscript has never been published for a variety of reasons that will eventually become clear. What happened with Jacob and his story is complicated, with many implications that led me to worry about my physical safety, as well as my sanity, or at least my sense of self.

Although, technically, Jacob was not my client in formal psychotherapy, but rather a collaborator in the telling of his story, many of the events that transpired took place within a similar context in which I not only met with him in weekly sessions to hear and document his narrative, but I offered support and guidance along the way. You may never have a client exactly like Jacob, but assuredly you have faced similar dilemmas that have led you into frightening territory from which you tried hard to escape, or at least make more familiar. There have likely been times that a particular client worked on issues that you have not fully resolved, or confronted your most cherished beliefs, or changed you in ways that forever altered the way you do therapy, look at the world, or see yourself. Throughout most of my career I have made a personal study of this phenomenon, exploring how therapists are personally and professionally influenced by their clients. I had hoped that interviewing prominent theorists about their own experiences might help me to make better sense of my own confusion. Alas, collecting those stories only intensified my search to dig deeper for "truth."

The second narrative of this book follows the struggles of a therapist trying to make sense of his doubt, imperfections, and self-deceptions. Yet this turns out to be a tale far different from what I could have ever imagined, filled with twists and a surprise ending that is not to be believed. I must ask you to be patient as you follow my journey that will parallel your own as a reader. Ultimately, you may experience many of the same reactions that I did—shock, confusion, uncertainty, doubt—and I hope you will be intrigued by the revelations that unfold.

What began as a task to simply chronicle Jacob's story of heroic courage turned into quite a different moral fable filled with lies, deceit, and betrayal. This is not only a story of intrigue, mystery, and adventure, a thriller that keeps you on the edge of your seat, but it is also a writer's journey and a psychotherapist's search for truth. The case described becomes an object lesson for digging deep into the complex and ambiguous nature of what we do as therapists and what we think we learn in our work.

Hang onto your chair and be prepared for a quite unexpected ride.

Acknowledgments

Usually the job of an acquisition editor is to recruit an author, sign a book, and shepherd it through the approval process before handing it over to production specialists. My editor, Dana Bliss, and I envisioned a very different book when we first began discussing this project, one that was about the secret and forbidden in a therapist's life. It was through a long series of discussions and dialogues that one small part of that original idea blossomed into the manuscript you will read. In that sense, Bliss was a collaborator on this book who encouraged me to explore some very unknown and frightening territory, offering support, critical feedback, and incisive advice through every step of the process.

I am also grateful to a number of colleagues and reviewers who read and reacted to early drafts of this story. As a result of their input, the book you will read has developed into something quite different from what was originally intended. Sincere gratitude is expressed to the following individuals who reviewed the manuscript and offered valuable feedback: Sam Gladding, Robert Neimeyer, Lynn Hall, Howie Kirschenbaum, Cyndi Briggs, Barry McCarthy, Howard Rosenthal, and Theresa Kellam. Finally, I wish to thank my development editor, Patricia Connolly, who helped refine the flow of a very complex structure into a coherent manuscript that I hope you will find both interesting and engaging.

Chapter **1**

How This Story Came to Be Told

I met Jacob for coffee in a sports bar near his house. I had been asked to see him by a mutual acquaintance who was certain that he had an interesting tale to tell, perhaps one I might be interested in writing about. Reluctantly, I agreed to the meeting, figuring I would get in and out of there as soon as possible.

There were a dozen or more televisions configured in a circle along the ceiling of the establishment. Most of the screens displayed different sporting events. The place was dark, mostly lit up by neon beer signs hung on the walls—Michelob, Molson, Double Diamond, Coors, Fosters, Miller, and Budweiser. Jacob liked the place because a $1.99 breakfast special was offered—two eggs, any style, with bacon, home fries, toast and jelly, and coffee.

Even before we sat down, Jacob launched into his story in a strong Bronx accent. He was a man who, in the parlance of our profession, looked older than his stated age. He was heavyset, with white hair circling the crown of his balding head. I noticed that he walked with a pronounced limp, and as he eased himself into the chair opposite me, he let out a huge sigh as if the effort tested him. In some ways, he reminded me of my grandfather, if not in his manner, then in his dress and appearance. He also struck me as hungry for company and perhaps a bit depressed.

I learned in the first few minutes of our conversation that Jacob was a retired pharmacist who, later in life, worked for the state drug enforcement agency. Apparently, his job had been to investigate drug abuses by doctors and nurses, a career that he felt merited treatment as a tale of intrigue and adventure.

I could tell that Jacob was a bit haunted with an obvious need to unload. As I listened to him ramble on about the high percentage of doctors who were addicted to prescription drugs, I plotted the most expeditious way to untangle myself from this relationship and get out of there. If he had been a client in therapy, I considered and rejected several possible diagnoses, concluding that he just seemed like a lonely, old man who wanted someone to talk to.

I politely informed Jacob that I really did not think there was a book to be done but that I was pleased to have met him. He nodded his head, thanked me for my attention, and then mentioned casually, "It's too bad I can't tell you the *real* story of my early life." He then explained that as much as he wanted to tell me the "other" story, it was just something that he could not do. "It's too dangerous," he added, reeling me in.

By now, of course, even if I wasn't going to write about whatever he was hiding, I had to know what he was holding back. After another hour of pleading, and finally promising confidentiality, I invited him to tell me his "other story" just to get it off his chest. Jacob insisted that nobody knew about his secret life—not his deceased wife to whom he had been married for over 40 years, not his three adult children, and not his best friends. His parents and sister had known only the barest outline of what he had been doing, but not the details.

Anyone who manages to successfully bury a secret for this long usually gets to take it to the grave, so why was Jacob itching to talk about his hidden past only now?

When I asked him this question, he nodded and explained that his first wife had worked as a nurse on the night shift. During all the years of their marriage, he and his wife rarely slept in bed at the same time. When he was working during the day, she was sleeping. They would spend time together for dinner and afterward, and then she would head off to the hospital while he went to sleep. They probably spent the same amount of quality time together as most couples; they just did not sleep together.

He explained that his wife had died a few years ago, and he had recently married again—to a drug counselor. It seemed that for practically the first time in his life, Jacob was sleeping with someone in the same bed. He said that his wife was often awakened in the middle of the night by his thrashing around and screaming out in a strange language. He had no idea what she was talking about and could not offer a reason to account for the night terrors. Finally, the two of them agreed that she would try to write down some of the things he was yelling.

During a lengthy process of translation, both of them realized that whatever was going on during his nightmares, he was talking in Arabic. Jacob's wife was a trained counselor and so she encouraged him to talk about the dreams that so disturbed him. For the first time in his life, he admitted that as a teenager he had been recruited by the Haganah—the Jewish defense force in Palestine that had been founded in the 1920s and after 1948 became the Israeli Defense Force—to fight in the war that eventually led to the establishment of the state of Israel.

I wondered, just as his wife must have done, what the big deal was—surely it was a reason to be proud. But Jacob pointed out quite correctly that it was, and is, illegal for Americans to fight in foreign wars. The U.S. volunteers were told that they could lose their citizenship. They even had to use forged documents to travel to Palestine.

You've got to be kidding, I thought. This old man honestly thought the U.S. government was going to prosecute him for fighting in a foreign war 60 years ago? "So, what's with the Arabic?" I asked him. "What's that got to do with things?"

"I didn't exactly fight as a soldier in the war," he said hesitantly. "I did other things, awful things, that I've never told anyone about."

It was then, in a torrent, that I learned what he recently confessed to his wife. As a youngster growing up in the Bronx, his rabbi taught him conversational Arabic as well as Hebrew. The rabbi had worked in Palestine and claimed that because his students might someday want to settle there, they should be prepared.

Only in retrospect did Jacob now realize that he was groomed for a role long before he understood what it would involve.

By the time Jacob graduated from high school at age 17, he was formally recruited by a representative of the Haganah, to fight in the coming war. The Jews were surrounded on all sides, outnumbered 20 to 1, and knew they were about to be invaded from Lebanon, Syria, Jordan, and Egypt. They were desperate to recruit people to fight, even young idealistic boys from the United States. As Jacob later learned, over a thousand such young men from North America joined the war effort.

During his army training, it was discovered that Jacob had a real talent for marksmanship despite the fact that he had never handled a firearm prior to arriving in Palestine. It turned out that he was particularly adept with handguns.

Although Jacob had thought he had joined the Army, he soon learned that he had been recruited for a very special job. He would be teamed with several other Americans, several of whom, like Jacob, were fluent in both Arabic and Hebrew, and he would become part of a commando team that would infiltrate Arab countries in plain clothes and then kill assigned targets at close range. Because he was both conversant in Arabic and an expert shot, it was decided that Jacob would be the hit man of the team—the one who would fire a .22 Beretta into the target's head.

During the almost two years that Jacob spent fighting this secret war behind enemy lines, operating without official sanction and told very clearly that he and his team members would be disowned by their handlers if they were ever caught, he was sent on over 16 successful missions before he was done. His toll was impressive: he personally killed close to two dozen high-ranking enemy officers and prominent politicians, almost all of them at very close range.

Moral Conundrums

Although Jacob was describing what he portrayed as a heroic and exciting war story from another era, the political and moral climate of the times had changed considerably, not only throughout the world but in my own personal experience. I have great sympathy for the Palestinian cause and feel that many injustices have been directed against the people who were displaced and subjected to oppression. I am disturbed by the rigid positions taken by political figures on all sides, leaving people in Palestine to face starvation and discrimination and to become victims of collateral damage.

Many of the students I now work with are of Middle Eastern background from Iran, Iraq, Lebanon, Pakistan, Israel, and Afghanistan. One of the courses I teach regularly is about the impact of culture on client experiences in psychotherapy. My students are among the most diverse group in the world, many of them Middle Eastern immigrants. I remember feeling so gratified by one recent class in which three women would always sit together in the back of the room, sharing food and whispering secrets. They were best friends—an Iranian, a Palestinian refugee, and an Iraqi Jew who had immigrated to Israel before coming to the United States. I felt such hope watching the three of them interact, having bonded because of what they had in common. Each time I would see them hanging out together, it reminded me that maybe reconciliation between warring tribes was possible.

As fascinated as I was by Jacob's life, as interested as I was in delving into this historical time, I felt uncomfortable stirring up issues that portray Arabs and Jews as enemies rather than as cooperative tribes that lived together peacefully for thousands of years. What kind of moral responsibility do I have to take actions that promote peace rather than rehash the violence of the past?

I have spent the past decade working in civil war-torn Nepal, providing educational opportunities for lower-caste girls who would otherwise not be able to attend school. During my visits to remote villages where we distribute scholarships, I would frequently pass through both government-controlled and Maoist territory. There were times soldiers on one side of a bridge would ask us to pay "tourist fees" in order to pass through, and guerillas on the other side of the bridge would extort money from us in order to proceed. Each time I paid these bribes, I knew the money was being used to buy more weapons and explosives to kill more innocent people. If my conscience was bothered by these side effects of trying to do good, then how could I justify revisiting history that might very well open old wounds?

Ultimately, I decided that the responsibility of any historian and storyteller is to present the events as accurately and honestly as possible, to be fair and impartial, and to take full responsibility for this decision. I acknowledge that I was looking for reasons to justify my choice to go ahead with this story, but I truly felt (and still feel) that the questions and issues raised by this narrative are well worth the suffering of war that it brings back into focus. The setting for this story is one in which one group of oppressed people, victims of the Holocaust, returned to their homeland, but at the price of another group of people who were set adrift.

The Plot Thickens

Once I decided that I would tell Jacob's story, I was also torn by doubt and skepticism. I wondered, could this story possibly be true? And then, how could any of this be documented and confirmed? If Jacob were my client in therapy, I would simply take him at his word, knowing that at some point we would get to some semblance of "truth." But my role was now very different from that of a therapist. If I was going to tell Jacob's story, I knew that attacks on his credibility would come from all sides.

The details that flooded out of Jacob during our initial meeting were staggering in their richness. I determined first of all to consult some history books on the subject to see how much of this could be accurate. I could contact the American volunteer organizations whose members fought in the 1948 Arab–Israeli War. I could recruit researchers in Israel to check some facts before I would go there myself to follow the trail. My mind was racing with possibilities. I did not even hear him when he said for the second time, "So that's why this story can never be told."

"What? Are you kidding me? This story has *got* to be told!" I said.

"Haven't you been listening to me?" he replied. "Do you understand what we did? These weren't just acts of war. These were murders!"

I marshaled my arguments, relying on the little I already knew about Israeli history. "What about Begin? What about Barak?" I shot back, referring to the former Prime Minister of Israel,

Menachem Begin, who had killed dozens of people with his own hands and ordered hundreds more to die—many of them other Jews and British soldiers.

And the then Prime Minister of Israel, Ehud Barak, had made a name for himself after a spectacular mission in which he had done *exactly* the same sort of thing that Jacob had been involved in. He, too, had sneaked into Arab countries and killed enemies who were plotting attacks against Israel.

"Hell," I told him, "you're afraid that Syria or Lebanon will extradite you for murder even though these acts took place during war. More likely, you'll get elected Prime Minister of Israel when this gets out."

It took several more meetings before we decided to go ahead with the project. I agreed to change his name to "Jacob" and to not give any identifying details. If there would be any vengeful retribution, it could be directed toward me. At this point, I was convinced that he was being unduly paranoid, exaggerating any risks for the sake of greater drama.

Over the course of the next year, I spent hundreds of hours interviewing Jacob and recording his narrative, as much time as I have spent with any client in therapy. Each week we met for several hours at the same sports bar, sitting in the same booth, always with Jacob having a clear view of the door. I got the impression that at any moment he fully expected an assassination team would bust in through the door and start shooting. I must admit that I kept looking over my shoulder whenever I heard someone new enter the establishment.

These conversations required every therapeutic skill I had to keep Jacob focused, to keep him on track, and to draw out elaborations. Much of the time he just preferred to complain about his various physical ailments; only when my frustration would reach a boiling point would he reward me with another tantalizing anecdote about one of his missions. And so the year went by, and each week we met until the story was completed.

By the end of the year we spent together, I had written a 400-page manuscript telling the most amazing tales of courage and resourcefulness. I documented carefully each of Jacob's missions (only a few of which are described in this book). Jacob was as proud of the effort as I was, and he made copies of the manuscript for his family members, finally relieved that he could tell his children and friends about his hidden past. We congratulated one another for our partnership, and I even began to forget how challenging the whole process had been.

If only I had realized then that there was an unknown set of forces operating about which I had no idea. Writing this book would change me in ways I could never have anticipated. My whole world would be turned upside down. Everything I knew and understood about helping relationships, or *thought* I understood, would be thrown into chaos.

I know I'm getting ahead of myself. Perhaps I should start at the beginning—of Jacob's story anyway. We will get back to my own personal crisis soon enough, including implications for practicing psychotherapy. To fully appreciate the depth of the pain, confusion, frustration, and danger that I encountered as a result of narrating Jacob's biography, first you have to follow the same path that I traveled along the way. I will tell you a little about how he was recruited and trained for his rather unusual job, describe a few of the missions that he completed, and then talk about the aftermath and its consequences—not only for Jacob and myself, but for others who populate this story. As Jacob began his tale, I sat entranced as he went back a long, long time ago, in a desolate part of Arab-occupied territory in Palestine.

Section I

An Assassin's Story

Chapter 2

First Mission
Tyre, Palestine, March 1947

The pistol was so warm to the touch Jacob could only hold it for a minute or two before he tucked it back into the folds of his robe. With each careful step, he felt the reassuring hot metal digging into his stomach. He started to reach out to touch the .22 Beretta through the fabric of his robe, but then checked himself, remembering his training. He moved his hand casually back to his side, squinted into the blazing hot sun of the desert, and pulled the edges of his *khaffiya* down over his eyes. For a blessed instant, it felt as if he could almost hide inside and forget where he was headed.

"Over there," his companion said as he pointed in the direction of a narrow alley that ran in a zigzag line off the main street. The two teens were dressed identically in white robes that matched those of the townspeople.

They slipped into the shadows, backs pressed against the wall. Each of the young men was breathing heavily although little physical exertion had been needed to reach this point. One of the boys looked sick.

Jacob, the one in the lead, touched the pistol again nervously. "You okay?" he asked his partner. "You look terrible."

Morris nodded his head, looked up for a moment, staring at Jacob's chest but unwilling to meet his eyes. "Yeah, sure, I'll be okay. Just give me a minute. It's so damn hot in this place."

Jacob looked at his watch, staring at the face as if he could see their future. He did not look happy.

"Look," he said in English, then remembered to switch to Arabic. "We've got, what, five minutes to make this work. Either we do it, get the heck out of here, or we face Mordechai when we get back."

Morris just stared at him, not saying a word. He did not seem to be thinking, making any kind of a decision, just waiting—for courage or inspiration? Or was he just biding his time? He reached into the pocket of his robe and pulled out his own pistol, examining it carefully, as if for the first time. The Beretta was such a little thing, like a child's toy that fit in the palm of his hand.

"Put that away," Jacob whispered urgently. "Somebody'll see it."

Morris ignored him, squatted down, with his hand on his knee. The gun was pointed carelessly toward the ground.

Jacob looked around frantically in both directions, but they were completely alone. Just a few hundred feet outside their alley, practically the whole small town was going about its business. In about, three, no, four more minutes, their target would be open. They could see his shadow near the well, surrounded by the dancing shadows of other people.

There were actually three wells in the village, one on each side of the street and a larger one in the middle. The mayor lived across from the main water source.

"You'll find the *mukhtar* doing business right outside his front door," their contact had briefed Jacob. "People come to him with their complaints all day long. Since he is located so conveniently near the water, they just stop by at all hours when they refill their buckets."

Jacob was trying to forget much of what he knew about this guy. Their contact, Mordechai, had told them far more than Jacob wished to know, not only about his location and habits, but personal things about him and his family. How the hell did the Haganah learn so much about these people?

This *mukhtar* was real trouble, stirring up his people as well as those in neighboring villages and towns to strike out at Jews who lived anywhere in the vicinity. He gave impassioned speeches that sounded frighteningly similar to the things Hitler had preached just a few years earlier. "The Jews are vermin," he would often begin. "They breed like rats. They will swarm through our land and consume us unless we exterminate them first. There is no living in peace with these people."

This was rhetoric familiar to the members of Haganah, many of whom either escaped from Nazi-occupied territory or lost their families there. They also knew that people like this *mukhtar* could be very dangerous stirring up trouble. In the Arab rebellions of the preceding years, hundreds of Jews were beaten and murdered as a result of inflammatory speeches. In fact, this whole operation was formed because of a very real fear that wholesale slaughter of the *sabras*, the native Palestinian Jews, would begin very shortly unless preemptive action was taken.

"This first one will be a piece of cake," Mordechai had told them. "There will be no guards. The guy won't be expecting a thing."

Mordechai could be so convincing, so persuasive in explaining how important their job would be. "Maybe it would even change the course of the war," he told them in his East European accent. "It's like a snake," he continued, gesturing, "If you cut off the head of the snake, then it will just thrash around until it dies." Then he waited with a dramatic pause. "Your job, boys, will be to kill the snake. And there is no more important mission in this coming war."

To these boys in their late teens, Mordechai was a father figure, and an impressive one at that. He was a big man in his early forties with a pot belly. Although he never smiled, Jacob was impressed with the size of his teeth. He had a bulbous, W. C. Field's nose and streaks of gray in his hair. When he pointed at things on the map, his fat, stubby fingers looked a bit like sausages. When Jacob thought of this image, it made him feel even queasier.

Mordechai was the liaison between their team and the rest of the Haganah, the freedom fighters. It was rumored that he reported directly to Ben-Gurion. He never actually told them to go out and kill this poor guy. He just stated what the problem was and asked them what should be done. He always made it seem like the mission, and the way it was planned, was their idea. Only afterward did they realize how skillfully he had guided them.

Although Jacob was the youngest on the team, he had been selected to be the leader because he seemed to have a cool head. There was also something in his eyes that said he wasn't to be messed with. He seemed scrawny compared to the others, and so painfully young, not even full grown with a wispy mustache, but he carried himself with authority and confidence. He was only 17 years old, recently graduated from high school in the Bronx, and weighed not more than 135 pounds. It struck him as ironic that although Morris was four years older and a veteran of the world war that had just ended, he still deferred to Jacob.

There were five of them altogether, all Americans from New York who had joined up to fight for the Jewish state in Palestine. None of them had any idea that because of their special skills and fluency in Arabic and Hebrew, they would be chosen as part of a commando team rather than fight in the army.

Morris was the other shooter on the team besides Jacob. He came from the East Bronx and spoke fluent Arabic that he learned from his Christian Lebanese father. He learned Hebrew from his Jewish mother and at *shul* and also spoke a little German and Italian he had picked up while fighting in Italy during World War II.

Unlike Mordechai, Morris always seemed to smile a lot, which got on Jacob's nerves because he could never see what was so amusing. Morris had a gold tooth in the upper right corner of his mouth that gleamed in the desert sun. He was also a blonde, which presented a bit of a problem for them to blend in.

Time to get to work, Jacob thought as he nudged his partner and gestured with his head in the direction of the shadows that were now dispersing. The first thing they had to do was to make sure that this was their target. They had a physical description, and the guy sure looked like he was in charge, but they did not want to make a mistake and kill the wrong man.

When his parents approved, even encouraged him to fight for the birth of Israel, he had imagined himself in uniform, fighting in trenches with comrades from around the world. He had pictured them charging against the Arab Legion, driving them back out of Jewish land.

Because he had learned Arabic along with Hebrew when he was studying for his Bar Mitzvah, and continued the language lessons with his rabbi for some time afterward, Jacob was approached one day by Mordechai to volunteer for a special assignment. The next thing he knew there were five of them in a room together, teamed together as some sort of experiment. After about 30 minutes, they were asked to pick their own leader. They were told that most of their assignments would involve going after heavily guarded military figures. They would probably not survive their first real operation, so this mission was sort of a gift, a dry run to give them a chance to work together.

In addition to the two triggermen, there was Rudy, the radioman. He was the same average height as Jacob but outweighed him by 30 pounds. With his big ears and premature balding, he looked much older than his 19 years. Rudy's parents were Lebanese Jews, both of whom were born in Beirut and later immigrated to America, and he spoke perfect Arabic. He was particularly valuable to the team, code-named *Gimmel*, because of his experience working as a radio repairman in a store while he was still in school.

Sal was from Little Italy, the only non-Jew in their group. His father was from Sicily and his mother from East Harlem. Sal had been incensed at the way the Jews had been treated, especially after learning about the Holocaust. Like Jacob, he had immediately signed up after high school in order to fight against injustice. He was their mechanic and driver, and the only one who could not speak Hebrew and Arabic. Even his English was a little hard to understand at times.

The last one in the bunch, Sammy, was the backup, the understudy. If anyone got hurt, or could not do his job, he was the one who would fill in. He had been trained to operate the radio, could drive fairly well, and at times might be called on to help more directly with an assassination. He was especially helpful in interpreting situations and reading between the lines when instructions were somewhat vague.

As the three of them waited in the jeep, Jacob and Morris walked out into the sun in a direct path toward the mayor. Because he was still chatting with an old lady who was gesturing wildly about something that bothered her, the two of them leaned on the well waiting their turn.

The moment the woman finished her harangue, Morris pushed off the stone rim of the well and took a few quick strides toward the mayor. Jacob was momentarily shocked at his companion's resolve and poise, immediately following him a step behind.

"*Salam alaykum,*" Morris greeted the *mukhtar* formally.

"*Wa alaykum as-salam,*" he answered automatically.

"Are you Salem Ben Yeguda?" Morris asked him in a challenging voice.

"Who wants to know?" he answered, not recognizing the two strangers in his village.

Morris ignored his question and asked again, "Are you the mayor here?"

"Why of course," he replied with a smile. "What can I do for you?"

"Nothing," Morris mumbled. "We just wanted to know." With that, be abruptly turned and started walking away from the well toward the multicolored buildings along the square, each one painted in shades of yellow, orange, and pink. Jacob had no choice but to follow. He smiled sickly at the mayor as he turned away.

"Okay," Morris said in rapid English, "here's what we do."

"We had our chance," Jacob interrupted, "why didn't we take it?" His heart was pounding so hard in his chest he could barely breathe. For a moment, he stooped over trying to force in a little more of the hot, still air. He wanted to just get the hell out of there. The longer they hung around, the greater the chance was that they would be discovered. Even though he spoke passable Arabic, and Morris was fluent in the language, he knew they stood out as strangers in Tyre.

"Here's the deal," Morris explained. "We do it together. Both of us. At the same time. That was the original plan."

Jacob nodded, not wanting to start an argument, but he was angry. Morris had been right next to the guy. It would have been so easy for him to take care of things right then and there.

Jacob casually scanned the area to see who might be watching. Everything looked okay. The mayor was still in place, this time talking to a family who seemed to be having some dispute. The father was yelling at his teenage son while his wife and younger daughter looked on. The mayor seemed to be trying to mediate the conflict, apparently without much success.

"We go up to the guy," Morris continued, "Count to three. Then we do him. One on each side."

"Okay. Okay. Let's just get this over with and get out of here." Jacob could feel his stomach churning although he noticed that both of his hands were steady. He reached into his robe and palmed the small pistol.

They waited in silence for what seemed like 10 minutes, maybe longer. Jacob was amazed that it could be so hot outside, that you could feel so whipped by the sun, but there was never any sweat. It would evaporate as fast as the moisture would form on your skin. He thought for a minute about how good it would feel to drop himself down the well to the cold water below.

Jacob wondered if somebody so young could have a heart attack. For a moment, he looked down at his chest, imagining that he would see his heart thumping visibly through the robe. It was as if he could feel the pulse of his blood in every part of his body, behind his knees, at his wrists, snaking up his neck. He had never in his life felt so terrified.

When he looked over at his partner, he could not believe how calm Morris appeared. It was like he was just going for a stroll without a care in the world. Jacob knew his friend well, and about the only sign he recognized that there was some churning going on inside him as well was a little twitch above his left eye. It was fluttering of its own accord.

The boys approached the mayor once again, and this time he looked suspicious. "*Min wayn inta?*" [Where did you say you were from?] he asked them.

Jacob wanted to reply, but when he opened his mouth to speak, it felt like it was filled with dry, gritty sand. "*Ta'al ya gama'a!*" [Hurry up!] he whispered urgently to his partner to answer for both of them.

"Up north," Morris answered quickly, looking in that direction toward the far well on the other side of the village. "My people are from Beirut."

The mayor waited to see what these young men wanted. Probably some business they wanted to conduct. There was a lot of money to be made during these times of coming war.

"There's something I'd like you to listen to," Morris said and drew a step closer standing to the side of him as Jacob approached him from the other side.

"*Ma bif-ham*" [I don't understand], he said with confusion, turning his head awkwardly from one to the other.

"*One*," Morris said softly, and the mayor leaned forward to hear better.

Oh, God no, thought Jacob. Here it comes. Here it comes. His chest squeezed impossibly tighter, and he could feel himself start to pass out in the hot sun. He felt immobilized by fear. He was afraid that he would not have the guts to go through with this, that he would let his partner down. Then he was afraid that he *would* do it. He could not quite say "kill," could not quite accept that he was about to take a human life. Wasn't there another way they could do this?

"Two," he heard Morris say and knew that he would do as he had been trained. Fear or no fear, it was too late to back out. It was as if someone else was controlling his body.

The Beretta was now palmed in Jacob's hand, just a little, bitty thing that felt heavy like a rock. It was perfect for a mission like this—quiet, easy to conceal, reliable, and although it did not have much knockdown power with its .25-caliber long-rifle loads, it would bounce around a lot inside a body before it came to rest. The barrel of the blue-cast pistol barely extended behind the trigger guard. It was single action, seven bullets in the clip, one in the chamber, so he pulled back the trigger and heard an audible, metallic click.

"Three," Morris said in a whisper.

Just as he counted the last number, both Morris and Jacob raised their arms as if they were both pointing at something on the side of the mayor's head. They placed the muzzles of the blue-steel Beretta against each side of his face, just in front of his ear, so when the gun kicked the bullet would pierce the brain.

There were two loud popping noises, echoing across the square, so close together you could not be sure they were not one sound.

Jacob's bullet hit a bone and did not exit the other side, but Morris's shot splattered Jacob with blood, brain matter, and bone chips.

They both heard the mayor sigh as he exhaled and collapsed to the ground. "Ahhhhhhh," he whispered, then trailed off at the end.

Then there was complete silence. Everything in the village seemed to stop as if all the activity was part of a recording after the pause button had been pushed.

The two boys made eye contact for a second, stunned at what they had done, but for a second unable to move. They just stood there frozen, until Jacob started to stumble. For a panicky moment, he thought he might fall right on top of the mayor's body. He looked down and saw a pool of blood seeping into the ground.

Morris could see his friend swaying and wondered if somehow he had been wounded. He was sickened by the mess that now covered the whole side of Jacob's face and shoulder. For a moment, he thought his bullet had destroyed his friend's face as well when it passed through the mayor's skull.

They heard screams sounding across the square and felt the pounding of people running, although they could not tell if they were running toward or away from them. Without saying a word, they looked for their escape route and started quickly in that direction.

Jacob felt something on the corner of his lip and reached out with his tongue to probe it. It was wet and salty.

"Ughhh," he said out loud, horrified by the realization that he was covered in the dead man's brain.

It made no sense to him at the time, but for some reason he absolutely *had* to smoke a cigarette, to get the taste of the mayor out of his mouth. Without breaking stride, he reached into a pocket for his pack and lighter, which caught in the fold of his robe between his legs. He lost his balance and, before he knew it, fell hard to the ground. His heart was pounding so hard that he could no longer hear the screaming or hear Morris urging him to get up and keep running. He rolled over on his side, with the cigarette pack crushed in his hand, and managed to stagger up and stumble on. He could feel himself starting to get sick.

Jacob thought about stopping to vomit. He could feel the nausea rise up in his throat and felt grateful for any moisture whatsoever. But he knew if he stopped, if he even hesitated, he was a dead man.

He had to keep going, keep running to safety. If he could just get to the pick-up point, he was sure everything would be okay.

There was now sand stuck to the blood and brain matter on Jacob's face and side. He could feel the sticky crust crack every time he scrunched his face. His lips felt so dry and parched but there was no way he was going to moisten his lips again and risk tasting the mayor's brain with his tongue.

Jacob and Morris had run in opposite directions, each to an assigned place where they would be retrieved. Right on schedule, the jeep was waiting at the appointed spot, parked underneath the meager shade of a fig tree. As Jacob walked calmly toward the vehicle, he could see Sammy, Sal, and Rudy staring at him. He must have looked like a zombie, covered in sand-crusted blood.

Jacob climbed inside and sat down. None of the boys said a word to him. They just scooted over to make room, looking straight ahead as Sal started up the engine. Jacob leaned over the side of the jeep and watched a stream of vomit erupt out of his mouth.

Sal drove the only way he knew how, fast, as if their lives depended on it. Morris was waiting at the designated pickup area. They could see the gleam of his gold tooth shining through a huge smile. After he climbed in the jeep, Sal accelerated hard, kicking up sand as they headed back to their base.

Jacob leaned against the frame on his clean side, trying to remain as still as possible in the bouncing vehicle so that little dried pieces of the mayor did not fall in his lap. He felt sad. Could this guy have been that bad that he deserved being killed like that? He had no chance to even defend himself. Heck, he had no idea what hit him.

This was far more personal than Jacob had imagined. He did not want to know who these people were, where they lived, and what they did. He thought he had volunteered to fight hordes of screaming Arabs trying to push the Jews into the ocean.

Many years later, as Jacob remembers his first mission, he still hears the long sigh of the mayor's last breath. The other thing that struck him most was how the boys never said a single word to one another during the whole long drive back to Haifa.

Chapter 3

The Bronx, New York

1943 to 1946

"Hey batta, batta, come on batta batta. Can't hit what you can't see batta." With that, Jacob began an exaggerated windmill motion with his arm and pitched the orange, Spaldine rubber ball toward the batter waiting patiently with a broom handle.

Even though it was close to 40 degrees outside, with a drizzling rain, the kids had been playing in the street for hours. They were spread out all over the street in a classic stickball configuration. Mikey, Jacob's best friend, was at bat, standing over the home base sewer with the most menacing look of Buddy Hassett, the first baseman of the Yankees who, even though not nearly as popular as Bill Dickey or Joe DiMaggio, had a far more distinctive stance.

There were about six other kids from the neighborhood, all part of Jacob's gang, who were standing around, shifting from one foot to the other, trying to stay warm. First base was a particularly well-preserved 1929 Buick, second base another sewer with billows of steam that obscured most of the outfield, and third base a rather beat-up old Packard. The few kids waiting their turn at bat were on guard duty, watching out for cops.

Every hour or so, a patrol car would come by, and the police would confiscate their broom handle to prevent any more broken windows in the area. Fortunately, the cop who lived in Jacob's building would give him the supply of sticks that he had captured that same day, so the cache replenished itself. Still, if they could save a particularly lucky bat by hiding it before the police arrived, that was all the better.

"That you, Jacob?" Mrs. Goldberg called out from the front of her candy store. "I see you Jacob. Whadaya think? I gotta message for you."

Goldberg's Candy Store was the hub of this part of Harrison Avenue, between Burnside and Tremont in the Bronx. Besides Pop's, the Chinese hand laundry, and Abe's Grocery next door, the kids hung out at the candy store if they were not sitting on the stoop in front of their building. Goldberg's had a phone, so it became the message center for the residents on the street.

Jacob and his friends loved the place because you could get an egg cream for 4 cents. They had their routine down that if they complained it was either too sweet, or not sweet enough, Mr. Goldberg would replenish their glass with more seltzer, chocolate syrup, and milk.

"Hey Jacob, I see yeh *boychik*."

Jacob tried to duck down, but it was too late.

"Jacob!" she called out again even louder. "Your Aunt Bertie says that you should tell your mother that dinner is at six. And you should pick up a challah."

"Okay, okay, Mrs. Goldberg. Thanks." Then he muttered to himself a Yiddish expression he had heard his parents use around the house—*Drai mir nit kain kop.* "Leave me alone," or literally, "don't twist my head."

It was Jacob's turn to bat next, so he tried to hurry up his usual routine. Any second he would be called home. Even though he was small for his 12 years, he was a two-sewer man, which meant that he could hit the ball way past the second base sewer cover. Jacob loved to see the ball disappear into the rising mist.

Just before he could pick up the stick, he heard one of the watchers call out, "Jeez it's the cops again!" In one smooth motion, he rolled the broom handle underneath a car parked against the curb and leaned up against it nonchalantly.

The police seemed to have other things in mind and so rolled on past them without even glancing their way. They stopped for a moment at Rocco's Fruit Market on the corner, then turned left and pulled in front of Burnside Manor. This was where all the weddings, Bar Mitzvahs, and parties were held, and apparently there was some sort of disturbance. Probably some old fart had a heart attack, Jacob thought as he reached underneath the car to retrieve the stick.

"Hey guys," a voice called out from the mist. "I gotta go home. It's getting late."

"You can't leave," Jacob answered in his most threatening voice, "until I get my chance to bat."

"But I'm all wet," the center fielder whined. "And it's cold. And my mom's going to be mad if I don't get home." They all knew the real reason is that the outfielders would have their work cut out for them chasing down one of Jacob's hits that would inevitably roll underneath a car or into the storm drain. That was a hindoo, meaning a do-over, but it was still a pain to reach underneath a car, especially when it's wet.

Jacob knew it was a losing battle once he saw the other kids drift toward home plate. They had been playing since right after Hebrew school let out at four, and it was now getting close to six.

This was one of the few afternoons that Jacob was free to play stickball. A lot of nights, he would have to babysit his three-year-old sister when his parents went to visit neighbors. On Mondays, Tuesdays, and Thursdays, Jacob had Hebrew lessons in preparation for his Bar Mitzvah, but lately he had been staying most days to talk to the teacher. Rabbi seemed ancient to him with his long, full beard, dark suits, and *yarmulke*. The other kids gave him nothing but trouble in Hebrew class, throwing stuff around the room, passing notes, and never listening to anything he said. And it was boring to listen to him speak in his accented Hebrew about what it means to be a man once they were Bar Mitzvahed. Nobody except Jacob seemed to pay any attention to him.

Jacob had approached him shyly after class one day, intrigued with this wise teacher who had lived in Palestine for many years and only recently immigrated to America.

"Rabbi, what use is this Hebrew once I read the Torah in *shul* for my Bar Mitzvah?"

"What use is any learning?" said the rabbi. "The Torah and Talmud won't answer any questions for you, but studying their wisdom will help you to ask more intelligent questions."

The rabbi rocked back and forth as he spoke, the only sign of the passion he was feeling for his subject. Otherwise, his voice remained perfectly measured and calm. If he was trying to sell his student on any particular idea, it sure was not evident in his voice. This only made Jacob more curious and interested in his teacher. There was something about him that drew Jacob to his study every afternoon after class was over.

Jacob's father was busy in the printing plant where he served as a floor manager. They had spent a lot of time together going to Yankee games, but since Jacob's chin grew above the turnstile, disqualifying him any longer for free admission in the bleachers, they spent less and less time in one another's company.

Jacob hungered for attention and respect from adults, especially this old rabbi who seemed to know so much and had seen so much of the world. Rumor had it that while living in Palestine he had been quite active in the Zionist cause, although you would never know it from their discussions.

There had been a lot of news in the neighborhood lately about what the Nazis were doing in Europe. The German army had invaded Russia, and the battle of Stalingrad, perhaps the most ferocious of the war, was continuing. Rommel had invaded North Africa and was giving the allies terrible trouble. In the Pacific, however, the American Navy had stopped the Japanese in the Coral Sea.

There was a lot of talk in the neighborhood because people's relatives in Romania, Austria, Hungary, Germany, and the Netherlands were no longer heard from. Other family members had managed to escape to Palestine and were telling terrible stories of slave camps in Europe where Jews were forced to work, often dying in the process from starvation and exhaustion.

"Why do you think none of the things are in the papers or on the radio or the newsreels?" the rabbi asked. "Are these people you know just making up these stories?"

Jacob knew that a neighbor, Mrs. Rodofsky, heard from her sister every week. Now she had not heard from her in months. The sister and her family had come to visit the year before.

"You were saying that you believed the stories were true about what the Nazis were doing."

"Oh, yeah," Jacob said.

"So," Rabbi said, changing the subject abruptly. "Do you think what is happening in Europe could happen here?"

"You mean in America? Here in the Bronx?" Jacob asked.

The rabbi just looked at him with a soft smile on his face. He nodded his head and waited.

"Nah," Jacob said with a nervous laugh, "me and the boys would stop 'em before they ever got past Abe's Grocery." Jacob made an imaginary swing of his stickball bat.

"You joke all you want, but I tell you that bad things are happening over there. Very bad things," the rabbi said.

The conversations between them frequently became solemn. They talked a lot about the stories in the Bible and the lessons of the Talmud, but just as often they talked about how the war was going. Jacob asked the rabbi endless questions about his life in Palestine. He pictured him without his beard, wearing the khaki shorts and high socks of the *sabra* soldiers.

"You ask me so many questions about Palestine. Perhaps you will go there one day."

"Maybe," Jacob answered shyly. If the truth be told, he was going to play for the Yankees after he graduated but he did not want to disappoint his teacher.

"Well, then, if you go to the Promised Land you must not only speak perfect Hebrew but you must also know Arabic. That way you can get along with everyone there—both Jews and Arabs."

That very day, they began supplementing their talks not only with extra Hebrew lessons but also instruction in conversational Arabic. Three days a week, sometimes four or five as the date of his Bar Mitzvah approached, Jacob and the rabbi met for their talks.

To Jacob it felt like he was leading a double life. With his friends, he played stickball and hung out along the front steps and at the candy shop. Although Jacob was the leader of his gang, the instigator of its mischief, and the best stickball player for his age, he led a secret life with the rabbi. If the other kids knew about his extra-curricular studies, they would have teased him mercilessly. They were all going to Hebrew lessons to mark their transition to manhood in the Jewish faith, but none of them took it very seriously. It was mostly about getting presents and having a party where you could invite girls and stuff.

Jacob did not care that much about Hebrew and certainly did not see much use for Arabic either, but the lessons gave him an excuse to talk to the rabbi. For the first time in his life, he felt an adult was treating him with respect. At home, he felt his only purpose in life was to serve as a babysitter for his little sister.

It was actually during an errand for his parents to pick up something for his sister that Jacob's final conversion to Zionism took place. His cousin's family lived about a half hour walk away, and Jacob had been sent over there to borrow some clothes for little Linda that no longer fit their own daughter. There was a park behind Bronx Hospital, and Jacob decided to take a shortcut home that would shave about 10 minutes off the trip. As it was, he was going to be late for supper.

Jacob loped across the park with an easy stride. He was a gifted athlete and especially quick on his feet. If he had not been rehearsing his *haftorah*, the portion of the Bible he would be expected to read at his Bar Mitzvah just a few weeks hence, he would have noticed the boys following close behind him. After they beat him up and stripped him of his clothes, he had to run 10 blocks home wearing only his underpants. The gang beat him up because he was crossing "their" park, and Jews were not "allowed" there.

"Watcha doin' here, kid?" a tall, red-headed boy challenged him as he jumped out of the bushes.

Jacob was stunned for a moment, mesmerized by the number of freckles on the guy's face. For some reason he could not understand, he started counting as many of them as he could see.

"Lookee what we got here," another boy called out from behind. "We got us a yid."

"Forty four. Forty five. Forty six. Forty seven." Jacob kept staring at the red-haired boy, counting the spots on his face.

Third, fourth, and fifth boys appeared out from behind the trees so that they surrounded him in a circle.

"Watcha lookin' at Jewboy?" the freckled kid asked him, as he gave him a push toward the other boys, who pushed him back.

"Damn it!" Jacob thought to himself. "Lost count. Got to start again. One. Two. Three. Four." He never got any further. One second he was staring at the Irish kid's nose, and the next moment he was looking at shoes all around him. Moving shoes. Hurting shoes. Hard shoes. He noticed that they were worn and had holes, some of them were even stuffed with thick socks, some with no socks at all. He tried to count the shoes, but they kept changing, and hurting. It was getting hard to keep focused.

Strong arms lifted him into a standing position and held him in place. Jacob wanted to grab his sides. He could feel his shin was bleeding and looked down to see blood seeping through his pants. His mother was going to kill him when she saw that he ruined his best pair.

"Hey Kike," the freckled kid, obviously the leader, looked down at him. "I asked you a question. Don't you know you yids are supposed to stay away from our park?"

Jacob just stared at him, wondering what he was supposed to say. For the first time, he realized the trouble he was in and berated himself for failing to fight back. He started to squirm but the boys behind him just held him harder. He felt a punch to his kidney that almost collapsed him to the ground.

"I hear you kikes got some weird cocks. Is it true that you get circumscribed?"

The freckled leader started to laugh. "It's circumcised you idiot! They cut off part of their dicks."

"Jesus Mary! Why would they want to go and do a thing like that?"

"Good question. Hey. I got an idea. Let's take us a look."

All the boys started to laugh. Jacob started to fight with all his strength but it did no good. The more he struggled, the more firmly the boys behind held him in place.

"Well boys," freckle face said, "let's see what we got here."

He undid Jacob's belt, unhooked the clasp of his pants, and pulled them down to his ankles. Jacob started to fight as if he would explode. It took all five of the boys to wrestle him back to the ground where they stripped off all his clothes—his shirt, shoes, socks, and last, his undershorts.

"Look at that little thing," one of the boys started giggling. "He ain't even got much hair down there yet."

"Yeah," another one jumped in, "look at the tip of the thing. Looks like a mushroom. How's he gonna screw anyone with that and make little kike babies?"

The boys all had a good laugh at that. When they were done with their fun, or more likely bored because Jacob had now become completely still and passive, they gathered up his clothes into a pile. The leader pulled out his underpants with a stick, holding his nose between two fingers.

"The Jewboy almost shit his pants. Look here." He then tossed the shorts on top of his prone body.

"You better get outta here Jewboy. Real quick too. Before we change our minds."

Jacob just looked up at him, holding his underpants tightly in his hands.

"You hear me! I said get your ass outta here. Now!"

Jacob stood creakily and pulled on his shorts, all the time looking wearily at his adversaries. He tensed himself, waiting for their next attack. He knew there was some kind of trick they had in mind.

"Run now, Jew boy. Run on home." On the last syllable, the leader threw the stick at Jacob and made a move toward chasing him.

Jacob turned and ran as fast as he could on his bare feet.

It was 10 blocks to his building, and he had to run the whole thing in his underwear. He was a 12-year-old boy, just a month away from his 13th birthday, his Bar Mitzvah, and he was forced to run through his neighborhood in his underwear. It was the most humiliating moment of his life and the one event that crystallized his feelings that Jews in trouble could never expect any help unless they helped themselves.

The Bar Mitzvah seemed almost anticlimactic by comparison to the rite of passage he had just lived through. The aftermath was almost worse than running the gauntlet home. Neighbors, relatives, and friends all asked what had happened, but Jacob refused to say a word. It would remain a secret.

There were lots of secrets in Jacob's family, so it wasn't surprising that his parents did not ask about what happened. His father ignored the situation altogether, and although he could tell his mother wanted to ask, she just bit her lip and waited for him to say something. He said nothing and never would.

His mother was not actually his real mother, although she was the only one he remembered. When Jacob was five, his mother died. Three years later, his father married Edyth, and a few years later they had their own daughter, Linda. Still, Jacob loved his new mother dearly, and they all lived together in relative peace. It was the secrets, though, that were killing him.

For some reason he could not understand, Edyth pretended that she was always his mother. He once even overheard her telling some of the neighbors how difficult a labor Jacob was, as if she had actually given birth to him. Over time, she actually believed this fiction.

Another secret was that his real mother's family, who had managed to become better off financially during the Depression, now disowned him. After his mother's death, a few of her sisters and cousins and her parents had stayed in contact with him. They invited him and his father to *seders* and family functions. But then, for some reason, they stopped calling. Jacob once asked his dad about that, and, at first, he did not answer. "It's best not to talk about these things," he advised. That was really his answer for most any problem in life—just ignore it and don't talk about it. Eventually, because Jacob kept asking, his father finally told him that it was probably about money. His mother's family had lots of money and they did not want to have to share it with him. Jacob did not know if it was true or not, but that became another of so many family secrets.

After a few weeks, everyone except Jacob forgot about the incident of him running home in his underwear. Life returned to normal, which for Jacob was pretty good. He continued his meetings with Rabbi even though his official Bar Mitzvah was over. He was now learning more practical, conversational Arabic and Hebrew, rather than the more stilted language needed to read the Torah.

The boys also spent a lot of time at the movies. It was about a year after his Bar Mitzvah that Jacob was at the Park Plaza theater one day. He was there with his friends to see *Lassie Come Home*, which they had already seen before, but usually a few of them could sneak in after the first ones paid.

Jacob was at the candy counter, buying some Goobers, when a tall man struck up a conversation.

"You like them better than the Raisinettes, huh?"

Jacob turned and faced one of the darkest men he had ever seen who wasn't a Negro. It looked like it was some kind of sun-tan, because he could see that the insides of his arms were blinding white compared to his brown skin. He had dark hair and a friendly smile.

"Ah, yeah mister. I like Goobers."

"Me too," he said and held out his hand. "I'm Avrim. What's your name?"

For some reason he could not explain, Jacob was not the least bit suspicious of this guy who seemed to be so friendly. There was something about his manner that seemed so open that he did not appear to be the least bit threatening. They talked for a few minutes by the candy counter, and although the movie was about to start, Jacob did not seem particularly anxious to hurry along. He was curious about this strange-looking man who was showing him so much attention. Later, he learned that Avrim had a small office in the movie theater, but it was never clear why, or what he did there.

"Look," Avrim said, "the movie is about to start. If you've got the time, why don't we meet another time for an ice cream and I'll tell you more about what I do. And I'd like to hear more about your life as well. That sounds very interesting that you are still studying Hebrew. What? Are you going to be a rabbi or something?"

"Naw, I just like it. It's kind of fun," he answered, and then thought this sounded like an awfully lame reason to be spending his afternoons in a rabbi's study.

"Well, how about we meet tomorrow at Goldberg's for a soda or something. That's the one on your street, right?"

Jacob nodded, impressed that Avrim knew so much about the best ice cream places in the neighborhood. He also felt safe there.

"*Shalom alachim*," Avrim said in parting and then slipped into the darkness of the theater.

The next day they met at the candy shop where Jacob was offered a vanilla soda. An hour passed quickly as they talked about the neighborhood and the latest news from the war. It turned out that Mrs. Rudofsky's hunches had been correct. More and more news was beginning to leak out about Jews who had been put into camps and then vanished, never to be heard from again. People were worried, but not yet panicked, because there was nothing in the newspapers or on the radio. The only reports were of the Reds who were advancing on the Nazis in Warsaw and the coming Allied invasion in Europe. There was good news about the war with Japan.

It wasn't until their fourth meeting, many weeks later, that Avrim first talked about Palestine. "You know that's where I'm from, don't you?"

"I thought so. Cause you're so sun-tanned and all. Either that, or you spend a lot of time at the beach."

They both laughed, but then Avrim turned serious. "We have a serious situation there."

"Yes, I know," Jacob answered without hesitation. He was gaining more and more confidence in his conversations with this man who showed such an interest in him. "Rabbi and I talk about things there. He used to live there too, you know. I think I told you that."

Avrim nodded and waited. He often did this, rarely lecturing Jacob like most adults did. He just listened a lot and gently guided their discussions.

"Rabbi was saying that more and more Jews are going to Palestine and it's hard for them there, even harder than where they came from."

"That's true," Avrim agreed. "So you know what's happening there? That we are outnumbered? That the Arabs around us are going to attack soon, right after this war ends in Europe. And the English, the damn limeys," he said with disgust. "They're even worse. They pretend to be civilized, pretend that they care about the situation, but it's a toss-up as to who they hate most—us or the Arabs. They'll just sit back and let us kill one another off. They just want to keep the fight fair so that it looks good for the rest of the world."

"Well, what about the freedom fighters, the Haganah?" Lately in the neighborhood, Jacob and his gang had stopped pretending to be American soldiers who were killing Nazis and started imagining they were Jewish commandos fighting for Jewish independence. More and more of the discussions in their home centered on Zionism. Many of the people in the neighborhood had relatives who had immigrated there.

"Yes," Avrim agreed, "we in the Haganah are trying to prepare for the fight but we have no army, very few guns, and your president, Roosevelt, is not being any more helpful than the British. We are alone there."

Jacob noticed that Avrim used the pronoun, "we," when he referred to the Haganah. It had only been a few years since David Ben-Gurion made his fateful proclamation that since the British were not willing to intervene effectively to prevent Jews from being slaughtered in Arab revolts, they would have to protect themselves. "We must prepare ourselves in earnest," Ben-Gurion announced to the Jewish leadership, "to become a substantial force in the country, capable of withstanding massive assault and also able to talk with the English in a different language."

What started initially as an underground resistance movement had now turned into a well-organized military organization with its own intelligence network, army, and commando units. They were not only the largest Jewish fighting unit in Palestine, but also the most popular. Some of the other organizations, the Irgun led by Menachem Begin, and the infamous Stern Gang, were often seen as radical fringe groups that focused their efforts more often on killing obstructive British officers and Jews suspected of collaboration, rather than the real enemy surrounding them.

Throughout the war, the Haganah tried to maintain a more moderate course, enforcing discipline and retaliation against suspected traitors, but at least warning their targets first to give them a chance to change their ways. In spite of their attempts to appear moderate when compared to the other underground resistance groups, the British branded them all stone-cold killers, no better than the Arab terrorists who were burning Jewish settlements.

Lately, there had even been news of Jewish assassins who were killing other Jews as revenge.

"Is it true what they say?" Jacob asked Avrim one day about a recent report that two Jewish officers in the British army had been murdered by other Jews.

"That was not us," Avrim explained. "That was the Lehi, the Stern Gang. They are very dangerous people and not at all good for our people." Indeed, the Haganah considered the Lehi and Irgun to be as detrimental to their cause as the British. People were worried that civil war might soon break out.

"That's one reason why we need more soldiers," Avrim continued, "good boys like you." Then, he playfully punched Jacob in the shoulder and grinned. "Perhaps when you are older, huh?"

Jacob slurped his soda and looked up over his straw. The sound of the empty glass was magnified in the shop that was almost empty this late in the day when most kids had gone home for dinner.

Although they had met occasionally during that year, sometimes in the movie theater, other times at the candy shop, Jacob did not see or hear from Avrim for over a year after that day. He just disappeared. Jacob wondered if he had gone back to Palestine. He worried about whether he had been killed there. But there was no word and no further contact.

Meanwhile, the big news was that the war would soon end. The Nazis were beaten, and the Japanese were on the run in islands all over the Pacific. Soon the soldiers would be returning home and life could truly get back to normal. But Jacob thought about Avrim a lot. Every time he heard anything about Palestine, about the flood of refugees who were trying to get in, about the Arabs stirring up more trouble, he thought about going there to fight. More and more often, when he thought about these things, the language he used was Hebrew.

Chapter **4**

Recruitment
Bronx, New York, January to February 1947

"Rabbi," Jacob started awkwardly, "that thing we were talking about."

"What thing is that, Yankle?" Rabbi said with a knowing smile, using the shortened version of his Hebrew name, Yaacov.

"You know Rabbi, about going to Palestine. I think I'm ready now. I finished school just like you told me. Now I'm ready to go. At least I think I am."

The rabbi looked up from his papers, a little distracted by the manuscript he was studying on his desk. It was an old, beat-up piece of furniture that looked like it had been through a war itself. Its surface was covered with stacks of books and pages of neatly written script. With a sigh, the rabbi closed the book in front of him and folded both his hands on top of it.

"Jacob, my boy, are you sure you want to do such things?"

"I think so Rabbi. It's just that nobody seems to understand. They say that what's happening over there isn't our business. We're Americans first, not Jews."

"Son, there is nobody who will help the Jews unless strong young men like you are willing to do it."

"So, then you're saying that I should go? You give me your blessing?"

The rabbi looked at him, really looked at Jacob like he never had before. He seemed to be studying him, peering deep inside in such a way that Jacob felt he was being scrutinized for some imperfection. Although Jacob was extremely uncomfortable, he made himself calm and faced the rabbi without looking away. Whatever test he was being asked to perform, he was not going to back down now.

Then all of a sudden, an idea occurred to him. At first, it sounded ridiculous to him, but the more he thought about it, the more sense it made. All this time that Rabbi was studying Jacob, he had no choice but to return the gaze in his own form of scrutiny.

Something that never made sense to Jacob was why Avrim, the big-time Haganah recruiter, had first talked to him at the movie theater four years earlier. And why had he spent so much time with him, week after week, meeting with him, talking to him, and telling him about Palestine? Jacob knew that he was fairly bright, and certainly capable, but he wasn't *that* special that a busy man like Avrim would invest so much time in their relationship.

So the question that now occurred to him as he watched Rabbi studying him so closely was why had Avrim settled on recruiting him? Of all the boys in the neighborhood, why was Jacob the chosen one, the soldier who would help the Jews fight for freedom? The thought was now developing that he had been set up by Rabbi. All along, Rabbi was the one who picked him as a good prospect. That was the real reason he had been teaching him Arabic and Hebrew. That was why he had been meeting with him on a regular basis. And that was why Avrim had struck up the friendship. It had never been an accident, their casual meeting in the movie theater where Avrim had an office. If it had not happened there, Avrim would have contrived to meet somewhere else.

Rather than feeling angry at Rabbi for his deception, he looked at him with renewed respect. He knew that the old guy was smart with his knowledge of the Talmud and Torah, plus all his languages, but he never dreamed that he was still operating as part of the Jewish underground. From the time he had been 12 years old, Rabbi had picked him out, groomed him as his special protégé, and then when he thought the time was right, brought in Avrim to close the deal. Well, after five years of work, both of them must be feeling pretty damn proud of themselves that all their efforts were now about to pay off.

Jacob was pleased that he had managed to figure out what was going on behind the scenes. Avrim had recently reappeared after a year's absence. Before he met with Avrim to tell him his final decision, he needed to talk with his parents. By comparison, this conversation was almost anticlimactic. As usual, his mother sat silently as his father talked, mostly to press Jacob to commit himself to go to college when he returned.

"You're nothing," his father told him again, "without an education. If this is what you want, your mother and I support your decision."

Jacob looked over at his mother for a moment, who did not look at all like she agreed with her husband. But she kept her mouth shut and tried to smile reassuringly.

"But," Jacob's father continued, "you've got to promise us you'll go to school when you come back."

"Sure Dad, you know that's what I want to do anyway. I told you I want to go to pharmacy school. This'll just be for a short time anyway. Probably just a few months. The UN will step in for sure and prevent a war. But we have to be ready just in case."

In truth, Jacob was actually hoping for a real war. He and his friends had missed out on the world war that just ended, and they looked with envy at the returning GIs who looked so good in their uniforms and were getting all the best girls.

It was almost a week later before Jacob could find Avrim in his office at the Park Plaza Theater building. It was a shell of a place with nothing but a desk, two chairs, and some boxes of files on the floor. It was obvious that Avrim spent very little time there.

"Look Avrim, I'm ready now. I'm ready to go."

"You know because you're under age, your parents will have to sign for you?"

"*Ayn baayot*," Jacob answered casually in Hebrew. "No problem. They said they would."

"And you know you can lose your citizenship over this? You Americans are not allowed to fight in foreign wars. It's a crazy law, but lately your State Department has been enforcing it to try and stop your people from going over there."

Lately there had been talk of ex-soldiers enlisting in the Israeli military. The first general in the Israeli army was going to be Mickey Marcus, a graduate of West Point. The first commander of their Navy was to be Paul Shulman, an American Jew and Annapolis graduate. More and more fighter pilots had been talking about going over to help build the Israeli Air Force. The U.S. government felt like they had to do something to stop the volunteers or they would jeopardize their alliance with the British who already had their hands full keeping things in that volatile region under control.

"Yeah, you already told me that before." About a dozen times, Jacob thought impatiently, ready to get on with things. Besides, he had a plan to sign up under a false name so that he could protect his citizenship. Rabbi had given him the idea and told him how it could be done.

"Okay, okay. Here's the story. You take these papers to your parents," Avrim instructed as he pushed two sheets across the empty desk. "You bring those back to me as soon as you can."

Jacob nodded with a huge grin on his face. This was the moment he had been waiting for. Although he did not think anything would change Avrim's mind, Jacob was greatly relieved that they now had a deal.

"There's a ship leaving pretty soon. Maybe even next week. So the timing is good. Actually, if I hadn't heard from you soon, I'd have come looking for you. This might be the last chance to get a boat into Haifa for a while."

A week later, Avrim got a message to Jacob that he was to report to a pier on the west side of the Hudson River at four o'clock the following Thursday. That was in just three days!

It struck Jacob as more than a little strange that his parents did not say anything to any of the neighbors. And it was just as peculiar that Jacob's friends, although they knew about his impending departure, treated it just as if he was going away for college and assumed he would be home for the High Holidays. Jacob could not believe how insulated his friends were, as if there was no world outside of the Bronx. All they cared about were the Yankees, the next stickball game, girls, cars, and more girls.

At least he said good-bye to his friends, which was not the case with the people in his building. He did not know if his parents were ashamed or what, but they never told anyone where he was going. It was like, all of a sudden, he would be gone, and that was that. Maybe it was some sort of Jewish tradition that you do not talk about people after they disappear. That sure seemed to make things easier in the concentration camps, and lately, more of the people showing up in the neighborhood had those tattoos on their arms and those haunted looks. They looked like normal people, mostly, but Jacob kept seeing them as skeletons staring through the wire fences.

When Jacob and his parents arrived at the pier, there were dozens of boys the same age, all carrying bags for the long trip. Apparently Avrim and his buddies had been very busy, Jacob thought to himself. He looked around the area and saw the boat that was to be their home for the next few weeks. Cargo was being loaded deep into the open bays of the freighter, huge wooden crates that were marked "foodstuffs." Jacob wondered if that was all they were carrying.

It was a cold, winter afternoon, early dusk already settling in. Although Jacob's mother made him wear his warmest sweater and peacoat, he could already feel himself shivering. His mother leaned against him with an arm around his waist. Jacob looked down as did his mother and felt tears coming to his eyes. He wondered if this was the last time he would ever see her. "Oh Jake," she said, misunderstanding, "don't worry. We'll be okay. You just take care of yourself, okay?"

"Sure Mom," he said, wiping the sleeve of his wool coat across his eyes. He turned to his father, who was standing awkwardly, with his hands shoved into his pockets.

"Well son, I guess this is it. You do what these people tell you. Keep your head down," he added, completely at a loss for words. They shook hands solemnly, and then his father leaned over and kissed him on the cheek. "*Shalom aleichem,* son. We're very proud of you."

"*Aleichem shalom* father," Jacob answered automatically and then added, "*L'shana habah B'yerushalayim.*" This age-old saying is the final blessing to every Passover *seder,* referring to the dream of all Jews to return to the promised land of Palestine.

***

It was just a few hours later that Jacob boarded the freighter en route to Malta. The *John Namin* was designed for carrying cargo, usually heavy machinery crated in large wooden boxes and stored below in the two holds or on the spacious decks. That it wasn't built to hold more than a dozen crew members was rather obvious with the 160 young men aboard, plus the dozen Haganah guides, one of whom was Avrim.

The boys appeared boisterous as they waved gaily to their families and girlfriends still standing on the dock in the soft, early evening light. They jostled one another for the best positions, not only to watch the city lights disappear but also to catch the best view of the Statue of Liberty on the way out of the harbor. Most of these boys had never been away from home, much less on a sea cruise. Although they were excited, there was something else, an almost tangible nervous tension. Their good cheer looked strained and overdone, as if they were playing the part of fellows off on an adventure across the seas.

It took very little time, a matter of minutes actually, for the boys to swap stories about who they were and where they were from. Jacob immediately struck up a friendship with several other boys standing in his vicinity, all of whom reminded him in some way of his friends back home. It was as if by leaving their families behind, there was desperation to form a new one just as quickly as possible. If the truth be told, they were absolutely terrified by the prospect of being on their own for the first time; in some ways, it was even worse than the prospect that within a matter of weeks they might be killed.

Jacob was uncharacteristically quiet among his new friends, most of whom seemed far more comfortable with embarking on this new adventure. They stayed up for hours talking about everything they could think of and were finally asked by one of the Haganah officers to go down to bed. Down in the cargo holds, they had strung up hammocks stacked in threes. Jacob ended up with the top one, which, although difficult to climb into, gave him more air to breathe.

Although Jacob swore there was no way possible he would ever get any sleep that first night, between the excitement of the voyage, the claustrophobic quarters, and the swinging hammocks, he was shocked to find himself shaken awake the next morning by one of the Haganah representatives.

None of the Haganah officers seemed to have any names, or at least any that they ever referred to. They were all in their mid-twenties and sunburned. Jacob was especially impressed with their arms that reminded him of the tapered legs of a mahogany table. They were all extremely polite, friendly, and accommodating, very tolerant of the questions being directed their way by the curious young men in their charge. Although their job was to begin the training for the new recruits, they were able to do so in a way that was more persuasive and encouraging rather than the usual threats issued by boot camp sergeants.

Each of the "suntanned people," as they were called by the boys, was dressed identically in khaki shorts with large pockets. During the warmth of the day, they walked around without shirts, their gold Stars of David gleaming on chains around their necks. These soldiers were not only formidable looking, but they seemed to know everything about anything. Just for fun, the boys would think up hard questions for them but had yet to stump one of them.

For the weeks they remained on board the ship, their routines never varied. The day began with exercise on deck. They would spend an hour working up a frothy sweat doing calisthenics, push-ups, jumping jacks, and running in place. It felt especially good to stand near one of the rails so that ocean spray might occasionally cool them down. These sessions would then be repeated in the afternoon, and then again in the evening after dinner.

The boys were herded into the dining room, which was really just another storage facility lined with benches and long tables. Because they did not yet have their sea legs and were still so excited and nervous with the beginning of this adventure, most of them did not have much of an appetite. They were surprised to discover that along with juice, scrambled eggs, and coffee, there were portions of bacon on each plate. Apparently, this would not be a kosher menu.

The mornings were usually devoted to strategy sessions as well as history lessons. The boys were assigned to groups of 10, each with its own leader who would structure discussions about how to handle certain situations. Rather than instructing the boys on what to do, their leader would draw the ideas out of them, and let them figure out for themselves what to do. This was very different from the history lessons in the afternoon when a few of the officers would inform them about background information they should know.

During their first afternoon on board, the head suntanned guy, about twice the age of the other officers, addressed them in an orientation session. They had all been gathered together on deck for the purpose.

"We're going to be together a little over a week," he began, "maybe longer depending on the weather. And I'm warning you, it can get pretty rough out here."

For the first time, nobody was making wisecracks. The boys were attentive and listening carefully, as this was the first time they were hearing anything other than rumors about where they were headed and what to expect.

"We have some big problems. I can't lie to you. The British have been cracking down on us. Hard. We can't even squeeze a fart through a crack these days."

The boys laughed, but he did not wait for the laughter to die down before he continued.

"Our first stop is Malta. Then. . ."

"Where the hell is *that*?" one of the boys called out from the back. "Is that, like, near Gibraltar or something?"

"No," he answered immediately, looking right at the boy in the back who thought his question had been anonymous. "It's in the Mediterranean, just about 60 miles from the tip of Italy. It's a group of about five small islands, part of a British province actually, which is kind of ironic when you think about it."

Jacob was wondering what was so ironic about that, looking puzzled, until one of the other recruits whispered in his ear, "We're trying to escape the English by hiding in one of their other islands. Get it?"

"You'll be there a week, maybe two weeks, depending."

"Depending on what?" two, or maybe three guys yelled out at the same time, and then they all broke out laughing.

The officer just looked out over the crowd of eager faces. He knew how nervous and frightened they were. He understood that all this laughter and horsing around was just their way of trying to deal with a situation that was completely beyond their comprehension. He wondered if they realized that half of them would be dead before the year was out. Let them enjoy this little Mediterranean cruise.

"It depends on how long it takes us to get some smaller boats to sneak you into Haifa. We can't possibly get in with a boat this big. The British patrols will pick us up right away and that would not be a good thing. Trust me."

He waited for one of them to ask the next question, but since nobody obliged, he continued. "One thing you don't want to do is get caught by the British. If you're lucky, they'll just put you in jail, or deport you to a detention camp."

"What if you're not so lucky?" a boy in the front asked. He looked very sick, and since the seas were quite calm, his uneasiness could not be the result of the slight rocking motion of the ship.

"In large groups, they can't do much other than put you in jail, but in small groups, like in the ones you'll be joining, they could treat you like spies. That means you'd be shot."

He paused and looked around the deck, nodding his head, sure now that the reality of their situation was finally sinking in. This was not just a lark, a school holiday, but serious business in which their lives now depended on how well they listened and learned.

"Well, that's enough for now boys. You'll be meeting with your teams next."

Jacob was assigned to another group for the first history lesson. Their instructor looked nothing like any teacher he had ever seen before. Not only was his appearance fearsome, with a black scraggly beard and longish curls, but he would look more at home on a beach standing barefoot in his shorts.

"Here's our situation," the teacher began. "We've been waging war on four different fronts. First, of course, we're fighting for survival against the Palestinian Arabs. They see us as invaders even though our people have been living there longer than they have. We don't have to worry about them so much. We are neighbors and have been for a hundred generations. Besides, they bicker so much among themselves that many of them see us as allies against the British. You can be sure they will fight but we don't see them as a major threat."

"Then what the hell do you need us for?" one of the boys called out, followed by laughter.

"Easy now young man, I'm not finished," the instructor said, but softened the words with an uneasy smile. It was easy to tell that he was trying to be reassuring but failing to convince even himself.

"Where was I?"

"Four fronts," someone else called out.

"That's right. Four fronts. Second, we will have to deal with the Arab Legion and that's a bit of a worry. We're talking about five countries, maybe six if Iraq joins in, that will have a go at us, using the Palestinians as an excuse. There's King Abdullah of Transjordan, the one with the biggest and best trained army. But the good news is that he doesn't really want the Palestinians to have their own state because he wants their land for himself. Lebanon and Syria will definitely jump in but their troops are weak. Egypt is a bit of a worry for us. But the good news is that none of them trust each other, and they especially don't like Husseini, the Grand Mufti of Jerusalem. He's the guy trying to control things. So you can see what we're up against. We're also fighting the British who are a pain in the ass in their own right. They're supposed to be neutral but there's no doubt where their loyalties lie. They want the Arab oil and they could give a rat's ass about what happens to us. Then finally, there's also the war of public opinion. Soon they're going to vote in the UN to decide whether we get our homeland or not. We are completely dependent on support from the rest of the world and especially from you Yanks."

"The Limeys only came here in the first place after the first war because they wanted to control the Suez Canal and the oil they seem to have in plentiful supply around here. Now all they care about is public opinion and this is one of the last places on Earth which they still think they own. You know, the sun never sets on the British Empire and all that rot.

"The truth is that they can't, or more likely, won't do anything to help us. When the Arabs rioted in the Twenties, the Brits didn't lift a finger to protect us. That's when we started our own defense force, the Haganah."

"Okay," the teacher abruptly switched topics. "The other thing you have to know something about is the immigration situation. This could save your life because when you try to sneak into the country, the British are going to try anything they can to stop you. You need to understand their motives because that will help you work around them if, God forbid, you are captured. Got that?"

A few of the boys had fallen asleep sitting upright. The ones who were left were doing their best trying to pay attention. The teacher shrugged, thinking to himself that he could already predict which ones would be killed first. He had been through this so many times before that he felt sad seeing these bright, eager, innocent faces. These boys had no clue what they were in for.

"In a little more than a decade thousands of Jews immigrated to Palestine, most of them refugees from Europe. As you can imagine, the Arabs aren't too happy about this situation. They're afraid, quite legitimately actually, that through sheer numbers we'll be able to stand up to them; they'll lose influence as well as territory. They know that unless they do something to oppose us, we will have our homeland and they believe it's going to come out of their hide. They're not far wrong."

"So, here's where you come in. We're outnumbered at least 50 to 1—probably more than that when you actually count combatants. The British have 70,000 trained soldiers watching our every move. There are 10 times that many Arabs that can be called into action. In just a few months, the United Nations will be voting on whether to partition Palestine into a Jewish state. We think we have the votes to get it through, but it could be close."

"So, where do we come in?" one boy asked impatiently. He looked ready to resume his nap but wanted to make sure he wouldn't miss anything.

"It's simple. We need you to help us with the first line of defense. We figure in less than six months we're going to be at war, and not just with Egypt and Transjordan. Everyone is going to jump in when we're down and try to get some punches in. You are going to help us hold things together until we can get more reinforcements and arms. Any questions?"

There were a thousand questions, but the boys were too tired to continue. After retiring to their bunks for the night, they awoke to find themselves docked at a pier where they were loaded onto buses. They drove for two hours inland to a camp where temporary barracks had been constructed. There was a tall, lanky officer, deeply tanned of course, who was waiting for them once they lined up in front of the vehicles.

"Glad you made it on your perilous trip," he said in a clipped, British accent.

Everyone laughed. So far, it had been a breeze. But what is with the accent? Was this guy Jewish or what?

"Righto. Now that you've had a little cruise, it's time to go to work. We have a lot to teach you and not much time."

He paced slowly past the boys standing in line, slapping a riding crop against the side of his white knee socks. He was dressed just like a British officer with khaki shorts and shirt and a black Sam Browne belt. The only thing that distinguished him as Jewish was the conspicuous Star of David worn outside the beige shirt, and a blue beret. Not only did his accent signal that he had once been in the British armed services, but also his stance. He stood with his legs apart, hands behind his back, rocking back and forth with the riding crop peeking out of his right hand.

"As you lads were told before, you'll be with us a fortnight. More or less. We don't know exactly how long you'll be here because we have to find enough smaller boats to take you into Palestine."

He paused again and made another round walking down the line looking at each of the boys, sizing them up. Each time he slapped the riding crop against his leg, a few of the boys flinched, wondering if he was going to use it on them. So far, all the officers had been pretty easygoing, but this guy looked like a ball buster.

"Do you have any questions?" he asked, and then before anyone could possibly answer, he said, "Good then. You blokes get squared away and we'll be talking to you again after tea."

They were assigned to rooms that held four bunks. This time, however, the boys tended to keep to themselves. It was as if it was too much trouble to make friends again, knowing they would soon be split up. It seemed there were to be no lingering attachments.

After eating cake, coffee, figs, and Middle-Eastern pastry that was as sweet as the coffee was strong, they were herded into a storage facility that contained an incredible assortment of weapons. It was like a truck had simply dumped them in piles on the floor. Somebody had begun sorting them out, because pistols were laid out on long tables, and rifles and semiautomatic weapons were stacked on the floor or just heaped onto existing piles of ammunition.

Jacob looked around, amazed at all the guns. He had never handled a gun, so he could not identify the Berettas, Colts, and other handguns. He wandered over to a pile of rifles that came from a half dozen different countries that were stacked like firewood. There were Russian SVT 38/40 semiautomatic carbines, American M1 and M2 rifles, German Mausers and Gewehr sniper weapons with long scopes. It was like a whole warehouse of guns that had been smuggled in from all over the world.

"Okay lads," the English guy called them to order, "keep your eyes inside your heads. You won't actually be shooting anything with these weapons while you're here."

A collective groan with disapproving catcalls interrupted him. To the boys' surprise, rather than scolding them, he broke out in an understanding grin. "There'll be plenty of time for that later, I promise you."

He waited for the boys to settle down, swishing his crop back and forth, brushing his leg, then standing at attention with his arms folded behind him so that his elbows formed two triangles. The heels of his black, shined shoes also created a perfect V.

"Our hosts who are kind enough to allow us to train here have an ordinance prohibiting the firing of arms. Since we don't want to risk their goodwill, you'll be doing everything short of actually shooting these guns. But I promise you, before you leave here, you'll know everything you need to know about every one of these weapons." With that, he pivoted as delicately as a ballerina, and strode away. Before he had even closed the door, the dozen suntanned guys had taken over, barking orders, and dividing the boys into teams.

During the next week, they learned the art of desert warfare. They were given lessons in how to navigate and drive vehicles in deep sand. This was especially challenging for Jacob and the others from New York, because they had never learned to drive, and the only navigating they knew was on the subway lines.

They were taught hand-to-hand combat, bayoneting, demolitions, and how to operate a radio. It was as if they were being given three months of basic training squeezed into a single week or two.

Jacob most enjoyed breaking down the weapons, cleaning them, and reassembling them. He found that he was among the fastest in his unit, able to take apart a .45 automatic and put it back together blindfolded in less time than it took the other kids to break the pistol down. Even more to his liking were the smaller handguns they were allowed to work with—especially the Beretta that fit so snugly in his hand it was almost invisible. Unlike the big American automatics made by Colt and Browning, the .22 and .25 Berettas seemed almost like a little toys, not so much lethal as efficient.

By the time their weapons training was over, Jacob had dry-fired each of the handguns, carbines, and sniper rifles so many times he could feel cramps developing in his index finger and the muscles in his neck. Still, he could not wait to try out live ammunition once they arrived at their next training camp.

Ten days after arriving in the camp, the boys were informed that they would be leaving that night for Palestine. Jacob was assigned to an Italian boat captained by its owner who was trying to make some fast money leasing his cruiser to ferry illegal passengers. It was a 42-foot pleasure craft, originally outfitted for fishing, but stripped down to accommodate the 10 boys who were slipped on board for the two-day trip across the Mediterranean.

During the voyage, the captain did not speak to his passengers, perhaps because he did not speak any English, but also because he seemed to want to keep his distance from them. For their part, the boys also kept mostly to themselves, treating one another with careful consideration and politeness. Completely gone were their fun-loving, boisterous spirits that made the previous cruise seem like a summer camp. They now looked like the scared young boys that they were.

Jacob spent most of the voyage riding in the back of the boat, more interested in watching where they had been than where they were going. Seeing the rippling waves reminded him of taking the Dayliner with his folks as they had sailed up the Hudson River for a day's outing. He felt sad watching the wake disappear as it merged with the ocean. There was nothing left to distinguish it from the rest of the water. It was over and gone, and nobody could tell that it ever existed. He wondered if anything he ever did would leave any sort of lasting impression.

At dusk on the second day, they puttered slowly toward the harbor of Haifa on the northern tip of Palestine near the Lebanese border. All the boys were crowded in the bow of the boat watching the lights of the British patrol boats far in the distance crisscrossing back and forth like slow shooting stars in the night. It seemed obvious that they were expecting some sort of trouble with so many gunboats in the vicinity.

Thankfully, it was a cloudy night, so with their running lights out they would be invisible for some distance. Still, the boys were puzzled when their Italian captain started yelling at them and gesturing wildly with his arms. "*Avante,*" he kept shouting at them and making diving motions with his hands, "*Avante. Avante. Tutti i voi ottengono nell' acqua.*"

When the boys stared at him with puzzled expressions, he jabbered even more hysterically. "*Ci e troppo pericolo. Ottenere fuori della mia barca.*"

"He wants us to get off his fuckin' boat," someone yelled out in disgust. "Says it's too dangerous with all the patrols around."

Surely, Jacob thought, the captain could not expect them to jump out here. It looked like they were more than a mile from the spot where they were to be met. There was no way possible they could swim that far, especially trying to dodge all the patrol boats cruising back and forth with their searchlights on.

"Get in the water," the captain kept screaming at them, indicating that he was about to leave one way or the other. "*Ottonere fuori della mia barca maledetta!*"

"He says get off his damn boat," translated the Italian kid.

If they wanted to get off, it was now or never. Without a single word to one another, or even a wave goodbye to their captain, they each slipped into the water and began the swim for shore.

Jacob noticed that some of the boys were strong swimmers, showing freestyle form that looked eerily beautiful in the black water. He could just make out the splashes of their kicks as they continued to progress away from him. Jacob decided he would dog-paddle in, not only to conserve energy, but also because it was the most silent way to proceed.

During the next impossibly long five hours, Jacob slowly made his way toward the twinkling lights of the harbor. Each time a patrol boat would come near, he would stop and tread water, waiting for it to pass. A few times he even had to duck under water and hold his breath until the searchlight passed over him. He felt so terrified that there were times he thought about giving up, just letting go, and slipping under the water. He decided there was no way he was going to surrender to the British, no matter what.

Jacob found that by navigating to a boat that was anchored in the harbor, he could stay under cover until it was safe to move on to the next boat closer to shore. He could hold onto the anchor, or a rope hanging over the side, and catch his breath before he moved on. Several times he could hear British sailors talking right above him. One time, a sailor who had a little too much to drink pissed over the side, sprinkling him with warm urine. Jacob was too tired to care.

Over and over again, he kept whispering to himself like a mantra, "I don't wanna get caught. Don't wanna get caught. Don't wanna die. Gotta keep going." Still he kept paddling closer to the lights, using the parked boats for cover, promising himself that he would just go a little further and then he could rest.

One thing that sustained him above all else were the visible lights of *Eretz Yisroel*. All his life Jacob had heard about the Promised Land, the place where all Jews would someday return. He could feel tears running down his cheeks, more saltwater to taste on his lips. As exhausted and frightened as he felt, this was one of the most important days of his life. It was as if all the dreams and fantasies of his childhood, all the stories he had heard from Rabbi and Avrim, all the tales he had read in the Bible, were now about to come true.

Jacob involuntarily swallowed another mouthful of saltwater from the wake of a British patrol boat that sputtered by. As he treaded water, trying to keep his head above the waves, he stared longingly at the beaches along the coastline. Behind them, he could see the outline of hills and mountains, so different from the Bronx's Orchard Beach, where he and his friends hung out during the summer.

Making such a comparison, Jacob's thoughts drifted back home. He wondered how his parents and little sister were doing without him around. He thought about sitting at Goldberg's candy store, eating his favorite charlotte russe, a sponge cake filled with whipped cream. He pictured himself playing marbles in the street, trying to shoot an inny through a hole in the cottage cheese container. Would anyone besides his family miss him? Did his friends back home think about him? Where were his shipmates swimming in these very waters, fighting for their own lives? Maybe they were within earshot of him at this moment? He felt an irresistible impulse to call out for help. He could not stand being alone in the dark a minute longer.

Jacob was crying now, on and off, telling himself he would never make it, that he was going to die before he ever got to see a naked girl besides his sister, before he would ever see his parents again. Somehow, the worst thought of all was that he would drown before he ever got to fire a shot, or do anything useful. It was like his whole sacrifice had been completely wasted.

By the time he found himself washed up on shore, Jacob was surprised to see a man waiting on the beach with his arms folded, smoking a cigarette. He looked like he was out for a walk and was amused by the strange specie of fish that washed up ashore.

"It's about time you got here," he said with a hoarse laugh. "What took you so long?"

Jacob was about to answer him, to tell him to go screw himself, when his last thought before passing out was that he hoped they would not use torture before killing him. Then he heard the man speak to him in Hebrew and he knew he was safe.

"Welcome to Palestine young man."

5

Training
February to March 1947, Mt. Carmel, Palestine

"Hurry lad, hurry! Come on, come on. We can't wait all night for you. The rest are already loaded up."

Jacob stood up, shaky on his feet, swaying from side to side as if he was still on board the boat. "Are the rest here?" he croaked through salt-crusted lips. "Did they all make it?"

"Yes indeed," the silhouette answered impatiently. "Come on. They're all waiting for you."

Sure enough, Jacob saw the outline of two transport trucks with canvas tops idling nearby. He climbed aboard to find everyone from his boat, plus a few others he did not recognize, all sitting quietly on the bench seats. A few were smoking cigarettes, although Jacob had no idea where they had gotten them. In their hurry to jump off the ship, they had to leave all their personal belongings on board.

The drive took less than an hour, winding its way up curvy roads to the camp at Mt. Carmel, which would be their home for the next several months. This was the major Jewish training facility in Northern Israel, and it was huge. There were neat rows of tents and barracks, glowing pinkly as the orange ball of the sun rose slowly above the horizon. There were four watchtowers set up at each of the corners, facing enemy territory. It was less than 25 miles to the borders of Transjordan, Syria, and Lebanon, and there were the Palestinian Arabs, all of whom were building and training armies set to attack. This did not include the armies mobilizing farther south when Iraq, Egypt, Saudi Arabia, and Yemen were added to the picture.

There were deep washes and gullies that protected the eastern exposure. These dry riverbeds were lined with bottles and cans, designed to act as an early warning system should advance scouts try to use the natural indentations for cover. In all other directions, there was nothing but open desert, sand stretching to the mountains in the distance, the Golan Heights.

The camp was laid out with designated areas for each of the various training activities. Already, thousands of new recruits could be seen wandering around with the characteristic sleepwalk of young people who have just awoken. Some were heading toward the mess tents for breakfast, and others were already organized in squads for practice sessions on one of the ranges.

This was truly an international army. Young men and women were talking in a dozen different languages—mostly German, Russian, Polish, Czech, Italian, and English, using Yiddish and Hebrew as the universal bridges. There were a few sabras—native-born Jews whose families had lived in Palestine for generations—but most of the new recruits seemed to be recent immigrants from Eastern Europe. Some of them, like Jacob, were literally just off the boat.

The outfits people were wearing seemed as diverse as their languages. The standard military uniform seemed to be chocolate brown or khaki pants, shirts, ties, and jackets, although some of the recruits were wearing what looked to be remnants from an assortment of armies—American fatigues or the British African uniform consisting of khaki shorts and a shirt held together by crossed black leather belts. Most surprising were the number of people around who seemed to be wearing Arab garb of flowing robes and keffiyeh, the traditional headgear.

Jacob was also surprised at the number of young women in the camp, many of whom seemed to be involved in the same training exercises as the men. He was uncomfortable with the idea of fighting alongside women at first; the only girls he had ever known were the giggling sort from home who were more interested in finding husbands than doing manual labor or launching careers.

Never having been out of New York before, much less in another culture, Jacob felt overwhelmed by all the strange customs. He had been told that volunteers had been recruited from over 45 different countries to fight in the war. This presented a nightmare for the officers trying to give orders when there was no common language. At this point, Jacob's only interest was to orient himself to his new environment.

The whole camp was encased in gates and fencing, with barbed wire on top. There was a motor pool area and driving range where the soldiers were trained in how to drive various jeeps and armored vehicles in the deep sand. Many of the volunteers were refugees from Europe, and most of them, like the New Yorkers, had never driven before. The results could be quite comical, if not dangerous.

There were areas designated for training in hand-to-hand combat and various shooting ranges for an assortment of weapons from handguns, machine guns, antitank rifles, and heavier artillery. One of the best things about their location seemed to be that they could fire their weapons for miles in any direction without hitting anything.

As Jacob stowed the new gear that was assigned to him and walked around the camp, he looked around to see if he could find anyone he recognized, but the place was so big and everyone was so busy that it was impossible to locate anyone.

During the next few days, Jacob and the other new arrivals were subjected to intense training that reinforced what they had been learning earlier on board ship and in Malta. There were the usual rigorous physical exercises, judo instruction, bayoneting, and small arms training. For the first time, they were using live ammunition that was a true luxury with bullets in such short supply. Rounds had to be smuggled into the country, sometimes a few at a time hidden in pockets and underwear. Young children cruised the streets of Tel Aviv and Jerusalem, their sole jobs being to beg, steal, and buy ammunition from the British soldiers who would soon be leaving.

In addition to the small arms practice, the recruits were taught the basics of assault training, which included map reading, strategic attack, and defensive maneuvers. An hour was spent each day practicing with Sten guns, rifles, and heavy machine guns, familiarizing them with any conceivable weapon that might be found on the battlefield. After lunch, they were drilled in sniper actions, laying mines, firing mortars, and launching grenades.

Jacob loved the shooting ranges stocked with an assortment of interesting targets—pumpkins and oranges set up on posts, as well as paper targets with the silhouette of a human body. The recruits were given an assortment of handguns from Italy, America, Germany, Czechoslovakia, and Belgium, no two of them exactly alike. Jacob found the big Colt .45 automatics to be loud, cumbersome, and almost too big for his hand to hold comfortably. The little Berettas felt like they were almost an extension of him. In no time, he became a remarkable marksman.

One exercise that Jacob found especially fun was shooting at the paper targets at 10 and 25 yards. The instructor would simulate a hostage situation in which an enemy soldier was holding a Jewish girl with a knife to her neck. He would then call out one part of the target's body—"shoulder," "right eye," "pinkie," "left kneecap"—and they would be required to hit that particular spot, firing two quick rounds. To his surprise and the delight of the instructor, Jacob rarely missed.

Frequently, whenever Jacob stopped to reload or change to a different weapon, he would notice a big guy with a potbelly talking to the shooting instructor. They were always whispering about things, and at times, they seemed to be looking his way.

It was after his fourth day in camp that the big guy approached him after practice on the bayonet range. This was a brutal exercise, especially running in the desert heat with heavy, World War I rifles mounted with long knives that they had to stick repeatedly into straw-filled dummies.

"Well young man," the mysterious guy said as he walked up to him. "My name is Mordechai and I've been keeping an eye on you. You're quite a shot with those pistols, aren't you?"

"I guess so," Jacob mumbled, embarrassed at the attention but also secretly pleased he had been noticed.

Mordechai was a very big man, over 6 feet, 3 inches, with a rather large, Semitic nose. His hair was streaked with gray even though he was only in his early forties. He was obviously very important in the camp, although because the Haganah did not use obvious signs of rank, you had to tell more from subtle things rather than symbols on the uniform.

Mordechai always seemed to have a pipe in his hand, although it was rarely lit. He seemed to use it more as a prop than an actual smoking device. He pointed the pipe stem at Jacob's chest. "I have an assignment for you," he said without preamble. "You interested?"

Jacob looked up at him, trying to read his face for some indication of what he had in mind. A mission? Wow, he had been here only a few days and already they had something for him to do.

"Sure," he shrugged. "What do you want me to do?"

"That's what I like to hear! Tell you what. I have some other boys I'd like you to meet. You'll be working as a team, sort of like an experiment."

"An experiment?"

Mordechai nodded, putting a heavy hand on Jacob's small shoulder. "We'll talk later. Then you can meet the other guys on your team."

Wow, Jacob thought. He had already been noticed. Mordechai must have been impressed with my shooting, Jacob thought proudly, admitting that he was quite amazed himself considering he had never even fired a pistol before this week.

***

Later that afternoon, Jacob entered a large classroom with desks scattered around, as well as couches arranged in a U-shaped configuration. There were two windows along one wall, each with wide sills.

Jacob noticed there were already four other boys, about his age, in the room. There was an Italian-looking boy sitting on the windowsill, and two guys sitting on opposite couches, one a blonde and the other appeared Semitic. The fifth member of the team was pacing along the far wall. All of them seemed as ill at ease as he felt, all wondering what the hell they were doing there and what sort of special experiment the big man had in store for them.

"Name's Morris," the blonde guy on the couch broke the silence, looking first to Jacob the newcomer, then to the others. As he spoke, he gestured wildly with his hands, as if he was on stage. He looked older than the other boys, at least 20 by Jacob's guess.

"Hey, howya doin'," Jacob shook his hand. "I'm Jacob. From the Bronx."

"Hey," Morris answered. "We're all New Yawkers," he said, exaggerating the accent.

"I'm Rudy," the Arab-looking guy on the other couch chimed in. It turned out he was Lebanese.

"Glad to meet ya," both Jacob and Morris answered in chorus, giving a salute. They looked in the direction of the real tough-looking kid who had been pacing back and forth and now sat in one of the school desks.

"Hi," he said with an unexpectedly warm smile, taking a mock bow from his seated position. "I'm Sammy." He not only did not look Jewish, but he did not act that way either.

Jacob, never so good at remembering names, was already having a hard time keeping them straight. Morris was the blonde with a gold tooth. He looked All-American. Rudy was the Arab. Then there was Sammy who just needed a leather jacket and a cigarette hanging from his lip to complete the image of a young Marlon Brando.

They all turned toward the boy sitting in the window who looked especially ill at ease. He was obviously Italian looking, and when he opened his mouth, they were sure of it.

"Sal," he said simply. "Been here soon."

Sammy, the tough kid said, "Huh? Whaddya say?"

"*Niente*," Sal said shyly, obviously not very fluent in English. Sal was from Little Italy, recently immigrated to the United States from the old country. It was a mystery what he was doing with the Haganah. Later, he explained in mangled syntax and very creative grammar that he was angry at the way the Jews had been treated. The other boys suspected he was just in search of adventure and did not like living in Little Italy very much.

Although Mordechai had called the meeting for 4 P.M., and it was now close to 4:30 P.M., Jacob believed that it had been arranged this way. Jacob had become accustomed to the idea that nothing these Haganah leaders did was an accident. This gave them a chance to get to know each other first.

Jacob's first impression was that he liked his teammates. They were a serious group, by and large, responsible and mature. If their lives were going to depend on one another in the coming months, maybe even a year or more, it was extremely important that they trust one another. Already he could tell that they were all feeling proud that they had been picked for this assignment, whatever it might be.

"So, what's this all about do you think?" Rudy asked.

Jacob told them he spoke Arabic, as did Morris and Rudy. Perhaps that had something to do with why they were there.

Before they could answer, Mordechai entered the room with the pipe stuck between his teeth and a file folder in his hand.

***

"A few years ago Ben-Gurion authorized a division, the *Shai*, to centralize our intelligence and gather information about Arabs who are most dangerous to us. We've been interested in any Jews who knew, lived, or worked with Arabs, especially in the villages we've identified that are known to be troublespots. And we have been especially interested in any Jews who can speak Arabic." He smiled. "That's why you boys are with us now."

Jacob shifted in his seat and then looked around at his new mates. They were as taken by this charismatic fellow as he was. Mordechai had a way of talking that, while always calm and reasonable, demanded their complete attention.

"So, for many years we've been able to place our people in these towns. They've also managed to infiltrate all the main population centers in Jaffa, Nablus, Hebron, Haifa, and Jerusalem. They know the political situation there. They've been living among them, making friends among them. You must understand: these are very dedicated people, no less so than the rabbis who devote their lives to studying the Talmud. They've been quite systematic about this. And they'll be able to provide you with anything you need to know. Anything."

Now, Jacob asked himself, what the hell did that mean? When was he going to get around to telling them what this was all about?

This history lecture was interesting and all, but he wished the guy would get to the point already.

"A few years ago, during the Nazi war, we tried a little experiment. It was in '43 that we set up an Arab Platoon. They were formed as part of the Palmach, the militia. We had tried something similar in '39 when we'd organized special units, the *Hanokmim*, meaning The Avengers. Their job was to seek revenge against Gestapo officers associated with the extermination camps."

All the boys except Sal seemed to know enough Hebrew to follow Mordechai's allusions. Sal had a permanent frown just trying to grasp English, so it was hard to tell how much of this he was following. Mordechai sensed this and paused occasionally.

Mordechai laid his pipe down on the table, freeing both hands to gesture as the story continued. It was easy to see that this was important to him, and Jacob wondered if he had somehow been involved in this operation.

"We got over 200 of the bastards. At one point we even thought we'd assassinated Eichmann but it turned out we got the wrong guy."

He picked the pipe back up, palming it upside down in his hand. Little tufts of tobacco floated to the floor.

"About this same time, the Haganah also set up special units for Arabs as well. The *Peulot Miuchadot*, the special action group, was designed solely to retaliate against Arab terrorism. We were going to fight back against the Nazis, but also let the Arabs know we hadn't forgotten about them either.

"We trained 10 Arabic-speaking Jews as commandos, not unlike what we are doing with you now. They were used primarily for revenge and retaliation when someone was kidnapped from a kibbutz or a Jewish girl was raped." He looked meaningfully at the boys. "Let me tell you. They were *very* effective," he added, leaving no doubt in their minds that these people knew exactly what they were doing.

So, *this* was what they had in mind for us, Jacob thought to himself. We are not going to be regular army after all, but sort of like a special commando group.

"Recently, Yisrael Galili, he's chief of the Haganah High Command, has authorized us to expand the operations of the Arab Platoon. Ya'akov Dori is the Head of Operations and he has given us limited resources, just enough to recruit you boys and prepare you for the missions we have in mind."

Finally, Jacob could no longer restrain himself. "What sort of missions are you talking about?" he blurted out before he realized he was voicing what he had been thinking.

Mordechai looked at him, or rather *over* him, his eyes acknowledging that he heard the question, but for now, he chose to ignore it and continue with the orientation his own way.

"Basically, there are three kinds of things that must be done. The *hish-bazim*, fast-falcons, are very quick, in-and-out jobs in which we will insert you in a place. You will take care of what we need, and then get out, usually within a few hours."

Jacob wondered what he meant by that ominous phrase, "to take care of what we need." He glanced over and felt reassured that others shared his confusion. Rudy was scowling. Sammy's foot was bobbing up and down nervously. Sal was, of course, looking befuddled. Only Morris seemed still and totally attentive, content to follow along at whatever pace Mordechai wanted to lead.

"The second type of assignment is even more valuable to us, the *tayarim*, or tourists, in which you will spend up to a week in a place. This will give you plenty of time to look around, to confirm what our intelligence has discovered, and most importantly, to observe your target and plan your mission carefully."

Mordechai stopped for a moment, casually crossing his leg while he leaned against the desk. Sticking the pipe stem between his teeth, he scanned the room to check out how the boys had reacted to what he imagined was a fairly overwhelming experience. The only important thing, as far as he was concerned, was to recruit these boys for the team, secure their commitment, and then sit back and observe how they worked together. There were many within the Haganah High Command who thought this whole project was not only foolhardy but dangerous. How could they possibly expect untrained teenagers, Americans yet—who had been coddled in their rich cities—to undertake these suicide missions infiltrating Arab territory, taking out targets, and then come back alive? And what if they were captured? Could they really expect these boys would hold out under torture? Even if Ben-Gurion and the rest would disavow their actions and pretend they had no idea what they were doing, who would really believe this? So much depended on what these young men could do, and with so little time to prepare them for what lay ahead.

"So," Mordechai prompted the boys, pleased to see they were still attentive. "Any questions so far?"

"You said there were three," Sammy said.

"You mentioned there were three kinds of missions," Jacob jumped in to clarify, "but you only told us about two of them."

"Right," Mordechai nodded, pointing the end of the pipe at Sammy as a gesture of acknowledgement. "Glad you were paying attention. The last one doesn't concern you. This is the *mitbasesim*, literally the settlers. These people spend several years in a village establishing their position there. You boys are too impatient for that," he joked, "aren't you?"

Jacob and Sammy nodded their heads, but the others thought that might be a much better idea rather than rushing into a situation before they knew what they were dealing with.

"I mentioned to you that in the past, we have eliminated Arab targets primarily for two reasons. And they were?"

Feeling very much like he was back in school, Jacob fed back what he remembered. "You said for payback when they messed with our people. And then as a warning so they would know we will hit them hard any time they try to hurt us."

"Don't forget," Rudy added, "as a general deterrent and a pre-emptive strike."

"*Che cosa?*" Sal said, increasingly confused by Mordechai's speech in an unfamiliar European accent. Sammy strolled over toward the window, sitting next to the Italian. "He means we're going to kick their ass before they kick ours."

"Exactly," Mordechai agreed. "But for you boys, we have something very different in mind."

Jacob changed positions on the hard desk, thinking it was time to relocate himself to a couch or the windowsill the way Sammy had. So, he wondered, what the hell did Mordechai have in mind for them?

"Your missions will have military objectives," Mordechai quickly got to the point, sensing the boys were becoming restless with all the background and itching to get to the main course.

"You will interrupt enemy plans, disrupt their operations, and most of all, eliminate their most dangerous leaders. Most of the time these will be high-ranking officers in the Arab Legion. For this first operation, though, we want you to take care of a political figure who has been a pain in the ass."

"You're talking about assassinations, aren't you?" Rudy clarified. "You want us to kill people."

There it was. The naked, unadorned truth about what they were expected to do. Up until this point, Jacob felt lulled into Mordechai's poetic speeches and inspiring history lectures. Talk about eliminating targets and all. But there was no way around it. Rudy was right. They would not be shooting at enemy soldiers across battlefields. They would not even be knocking off targets at long distance with sniper rifles. They were expected to go into these places where these bad guys lived, to shoot them right in the open, and then try to get away. The whole thing seemed crazy, more far out than a Hollywood movie. Even Gary Cooper would not do such a thing.

"Look," Mordechai said with greater urgency, sensing they had reached a critical point. "We didn't start this trouble. The Arabs have been harassing us, killing our people. They have vowed to destroy us. We can't just stand by and let this happen, can we? They have vowed to kill every last one of us if we give them a chance. What choice do we have?"

"But," Rudy protested, "to actually kill someone who . . . I mean . . ."

"If you have a problem with this," Mordechai answered him with a surprisingly calm and accepting voice, "you may back out any time you want. Remember, you are volunteers here."

Volunteers. Sure, Jacob thought. We are volunteers alright. But now that we are here, now that we got to this point, we are not going to back out now.

Jacob wondered if Rudy's particular reticence was related to his own Lebanese heritage. Both of his parents had been born here, and although he was a dedicated Zionist, his people had lived with the Arabs for generations. He would be fighting, maybe even killing, people who were practically his neighbors.

Mordechai could not afford to lose any of them so early. If Rudy backed out, maybe the others would lose heart as well. Even though there were hundreds of other boys that he could choose from, his instincts told him that these were the ones who had the best chance not only of doing their job, but of working together as a team until they were either captured or killed. He had few illusions that given the missions they would be assigned, infiltrating deep into enemy territory and taking out the most prominent targets available, these boys would last very long. But even if they could get one of the bastards, one of the Arab Legion's leaders, maybe it would be worth it.

"I know you are uncomfortable with what we are asking you to do. Keep in mind, however, that the very word assassin actually originates from Arabic. During the 11th century, Islamic fanatics were sent to kill anyone one who was deemed an enemy."

"I don't know about the rest of you," Jacob said, voicing Rudy's concerns expressed earlier, "but I signed up because I thought we were going to be. . ."

"You Americans," Mordechai interrupted, shaking his head in amusement. "You think this is going to be a fair fight like your Hollywood movies? Do you honestly think that we can line up against them in neat rows on the battlefield, just like the French and the British?" He laughed hoarsely, trying to picture this scene.

"Do you realize just how few of us there are? We can mobilize, what? Maybe 6,000 troops. We've got people sneaking into the country, but these aren't soldiers! These are people who lost all their families in the war or the concentration camps, everything they have. Most of them have already been through so much with the Nazis they couldn't fight if they wanted to. But we don't have a choice. There is nobody else to fight."

Mordechai was getting himself worked up, his usual calm manner replaced by a passion they had not seen before.

"Even among those who are ready to fight, we don't have enough guns for them. You've seen our arms. And many of them are so old we can't find enough ammunition for them.

"I won't kid you boys. It would be difficult to underestimate the value you could have to us, to our cause. Such acts that we have planned for you can have spectacular effects. When Julius Caesar was eliminated, all of Rome collapsed."

"But would God permit us to do these things?" Jacob asked, remembering what he had learned in school. "Would the rabbis approve. . ."

"What's God got to do with it?" Mordechai said, showing anger for the first time.

Jacob dropped his head in embarrassment. Whatever happened, he did not want to disappoint this man who had put such faith and trust in him.

"Look," Mordechai said more gently, approaching Jacob, "If you question whether the end justifies the means, consider how many more of us would be alive today—how many millions of Russians, Poles, Czechs, even Americans—if Hitler's generals had been successful blowing up his bunker in '44."

Mordechai paused and looked out the window. "In that direction," he indicated with his outstretched arm, holding his pipe by the bowl and using the stem as a pointer, "these very same Egyptians, *and* the Syrians, the Jordanians, the Iraqis, the Lebanese, and our Arab neighbors right here in Palestine, they want to do the very same thing." He withdrew his arm, stuck the pipe between his teeth, and paced along the floor. "Unless," he said suddenly looking up at them, "unless we. . ." He stopped again, slowly making eye contact with each one, and said, "Unless *you* can stop them."

There was a long, uncomfortable silence before Morris finally spoke. "Mordechai's right. It's no different. We're soldiers too, just like the guys who fight in the trenches. We'll just be fighting a different kind of war."

The boys all looked at one another, searching one another's eyes, before nodding.

"So, where do you want us to start?" Jacob asked.

"Well, the first thing you must do is have a leader. I have selected you, Jacob, for that role. Does anyone have an objection?"

Jacob was dumbfounded. Why him? Morris was the obvious choice. He was the only one among them who had ever seen combat in World War II. He was also the oldest. Already though, Jacob could see that Morris was overly cautious. If the two of them approached a puddle on the ground, Morris would walk around it but Jacob would tramp right through it, taking the shortest, most direct route, even though he might get wet. Maybe that is what Mordechai wants in a leader.

"We are a democratic people here in Israel. We have had enough of people telling us what to do so we like to spend our whole lives arguing with one another about who should be in charge. Our leaders don't tell us what to do; they ask us what needs to be done. So I am putting this to you. Are you okay with Jacob as the team leader?"

Nobody said a word, but they all looked at Jacob to see how he was taking the news. It wasn't actually a complete surprise to him, as Mordechai had been spending extra time with him over the previous few days, asking his opinion about things and watching him at the shooting range.

"Okay then. That's settled. Next point. There are several different parts to any operation. First is planning. Second is execution."

The boys laughed at the choice of words. Even Mordechai smiled.

"Okay. Okay. Settle down." While the boys quieted, shifting uneasily in their seats, Mordechai took the pause to refill his pipe with tobacco that smelled sweet like cherries. Jacob stared at his hands, wondering if he would ever light the thing or just play with it. Although Jacob enjoyed cigarettes, as much for the way the habit looked as its taste, he could not imagine smoking a pipe that made anyone look like a British pansy.

"If the planning is done carefully, if you take into consideration every possible thing that can go wrong, if you rehearse your roles and practice as a team. . ."

". . .then we won't fuck up," Sammy inserted with a grin. "Is that what you were going to say?"

Mordechai shook his head sadly. "I wish I could assure you that this is the case. Unfortunately, you will find in these operations that many things can go wrong, none of which are within your control. Guns misfire. Vehicles break down. Weather changes. But my job is to prepare you so that you can adapt to whatever you might face in the field."

Mordechai pushed off from the desk and paced the length of the room. The smoke drifting from his pipe made him look like a steaming locomotive. "So, any questions?"

Of course there were a thousand of them. But the boys were so overwhelmed by what they had just been told that they sat quietly.

"Okay, now the bad news."

They groaned.

"What we are doing together is a bit of a secret. Only the Haganah High Command knows about this little project, and they will deny it if they are ever asked. As a matter of fact, the Haganah will deny that you were ever part of us, as will the Israeli Defense Force."

***

Throughout the next several days, the training schedule for the team (code named *Gimmel*, the third letter of both the Hebrew and Arabic alphabets) was accelerated. They followed the same regimen that other recruits were subjected to, but then met as a team with specialists who prepared them for their unique roles. Each team member was assigned a specific job, although each was prepared to assume the responsibilities of any of the others should they be taken out of action.

Jacob, as team leader, would be the main shooter, working in concert with Morris who was the other expert marksman. The two of them were often taken to the range after hours and drilled in tandem shooting exercises that pitted their competitive abilities against one another. Morris, the bigger man with bigger hands, did better with the larger caliber .45 automatics, whereas Jacob excelled with the smaller pistols. They both became experts at firing any handgun with either hand, from distances up to 25 meters.

Sal was the most proficient among them on the driving ranges, and especially getting around in deep sand. It also helped that he seemed to have some mechanical ability that would be helpful if their escape vehicle ever broke down.

Rudy was to be their communications expert, because he had spent much of his childhood working in the family radio store. He was familiarized with the myriad of radios that they might have to work with in the field, and then his job was to teach the others about the equipment. Each of the team members was molded into a specialist and was then expected to teach the others. This built the type of fluid, cooperative, interdependent unit that would be necessary for their work. It would also make Jacob's job much easier because all decisions could be made cooperatively.

Sammy was the only one among them who was not designated a specialist. Because it was highly likely that one or more of them would be put out of action at one time or another, it was decided that they needed an all-around back-up guy who was familiar enough with everyone else's job that he could step in with a moment's notice. This suited Sammy's street-smart mentality, because he did not like being stuck in one niche.

As the next few weeks passed, Team Gimmel shaped into an impressive fighting unit. The boys had never been in better physical shape. Even more importantly, their confidence grew to the point where they were itching to actually go to work and apply their skills.

Over the previous weeks, the team had been sent on a series of training missions, each one graduated in danger and difficulty. At first, they were sent into an Arab village to retrieve something valuable that was in plain view. This was supposed to be a test of their ingenuity and willingness to operate with the brashness that would be required in later assignments.

Most often, they were sent in to Arab-occupied territory to recruit spies, a mission that turned out to be utterly worthless. Later in the war when these Arab collaborators would attempt to cross Jewish lines to present their intelligence reports, they were almost always shot. If by some miracle they were captured, nobody ever seemed to believe them.

Finally, they were sent into the field to complete a real assignment, one in which their job was to eliminate a dangerous enemy. The mayor of Tyre was one of the most notorious agitators in the area, known for financing the purchase of arms in his village, as well as stirring up his people to raid Jewish settlements. Mordechai believed him to be a good solid target for Team *Gimmel's* first mission. He definitely needed to be neutralized, and he was not well guarded and would not be expecting trouble.

***

On the jeep ride back to camp from Tyre after their first mission killing the town leader, the only conversation was about directions and location. Although Sal was an excellent driver, they became lost several times trying to navigate back home. Sammy tried to give Sal precise directions, but obviously something got lost in the translation. They studiously avoided any mention of the task they had just completed. Jacob noticed that nobody even looked at him, reluctant to see the dried gore on his neck and face.

Once back in their room, cleaned up, and rested, there finally seemed to be some expression of pride in what they had done, even though both Jacob and Morris felt very uneasy about the actual killing.

"We did it!" exalted Sammy. "Can you believe it?"

Jacob, as the designated leader, just kept his thoughts to himself. He was supposed to set an example. Perhaps if he mentioned how upset he felt, they would lose confidence in him. Maybe the whole team would be destabilized. Still, he did feel good that it was over and they came back alive.

The one thing he most wanted to talk about was the way he had gotten splattered by the Arab's brains. He could just as easily have been hit by the bullet himself. They had been taught to shoot at a slightly upward angle, right next to the ear, so the bullet would hit bone, rattling around inside, and do the most damage. Jacob guessed that Morris had aimed level instead, sending the bullet straight through.

"I did shoot too low," Morris agreed. "Guess I got a little nervous."

Jacob nodded and patted Morris on the shoulder. "Hey, we were both pretty nervous. But next time let's do it right."

Chapter 6

Prison
April 1947, Acre, Palestine

Most strange, Jacob thought as he stood by himself under meager shade watching people pass by on the dusty street. He was in the heart of the Acre, northern gateway to Palestine, a place teeming with activity. Looming ahead was the fortress-like complex of the British prison that once served as a walled city in the 16th century. It was an impregnable structure, dating from the time of the Ottoman Empire. On one side was the sea, and the other walls were surrounded by moats and a series of defensive measures that made escape impossible—until recently, that is.

Jacob shook his head in wonderment at the sheer audacity of what had taken place just a few weeks earlier. He must have inadvertently made some kind of gasping sound, because he noticed an old woman staring at him as she shuffled by.

It had been a major coup on the part of the British to find that they had captured Yehoshua Zetler, no less than the Chief of Operations for the Irgun. This was the most militant wing of the Jewish defense forces, a splinter group of the Haganah that had formed an underground organization designed to retaliate against Arab attacks and British meddling in their affairs. In the past 15 years, they had launched their own terror campaign, strategically assassinating British officers, Arab leaders, and even Jewish sympathizers. Even Ben-Gurion and those within the Jewish High Command were appalled at the ruthless tactics employed by Zetler and his boss Menachem Begin.

Once the British placed the trophy prisoner in their most secure prison, they smugly assumed that this was the end of things; they had cut off the head of the scorpion that had been delivering such lethal stings. Unfortunately for them, they sorely underestimated both the resolve of the Irgun operations chief and the strength of his organization. Within days after having arrived in Acre, the Irgun had already begun planning a daring escape that would free not only their leader, but also hundreds of other Irgun and Haganah operatives who had been languishing in despair waiting to be hanged or thrown to the Arab mobs once the British abandoned their positions.

Zetler and his comrades noticed that they could hear street sounds through one of the prison walls, deducing that there must somehow be access to the outside world through the brick and stone. On May 4, an Irgun commando team placed explosive charges next to the wall, blowing a huge crater in the stone blocks that had stood for 400 years. In the ensuing confusion, hundreds of prisoners, including Zetler, were able to escape through the passageway.

If the prison had been escape-proof before this daring rescue, afterward the British locked up the fortress so tight that it could be certain nobody would ever leave again without an appropriate escort to the gallows. This was most unfortunate for one recent arrival who was considered even more valuable than Zetler as a potential source of intelligence. Known only through a code name, this Moroccan Jew was thought to contain within his head the plans for every Haganah operation as well as the names of several spies who were providing crucial information from within British headquarters.

Long before the Mossad ever came to be known as the most effective intelligence-gathering operation in the world, the Haganah managed to place agents, double agents, informers, and deep-cover operatives in almost every segment of the British command. Even the switchboard operators would give reports to the Jews on the most confidential phone calls between Palestine and London, Cairo, or Damascus. Once the British captured the Moroccan, they believed he was a prize that more than made up for the loss of Zetler and the escapees. After all, the Irgun was a fringe group that had been discredited by many among the Jewish High Command. But the Moroccan, he was a different story, privy to the goings-on of all Jewish plans for the coming war.

The British assigned one of their most capable and ruthless interrogators to the case, giving him the task of breaking the prisoner until every last one of his secrets was known. Amazingly, the Moroccan somehow managed to last through a whole week of interviews and torture without revealing anything significant.

Word had recently reached the Haganah that it was only a matter of time before the Moroccan would surely break. After it was discovered that beatings only heightened his resolve, the interrogators attached electric wires to his penis and various parts of his body. After screaming himself hoarse through several of these sessions, the Moroccan thankfully lost his voice so that he could not talk even if he wanted to.

During the time it took for him to regain his ability to speak, the guards forced him to stand continuously without support. They covered his head with a sack so that he lost all sense of time and place, and then screamed at him continuously from all sides. Each time he stumbled, or even swayed, a swift kick or shock from a cattle prod would force compliance. After eight or nine hours standing in place, he would eventually collapse into unconsciousness. But as of yet, he still had not talked.

His hanging was scheduled to take place in one week, and it was inevitable that the guards would accelerate their efforts, knowing that if they were going to get anything valuable from their prisoner, it would have to happen soon. The Moroccan's situation was hopeless, of course, but he still believed that his comrades would not allow him to die. If they had been able to rescue Zetler just a few weeks earlier, surely they could do something for him as well.

The Haganah considered every possible option for rescue but soon realized that with the increased vigilance and security arrangements, there was really nothing that could be done to save him. Of even greater concern was the certainty that eventually the

Moroccan would compromise their future operations. Something had to be done, not only to protect their interests, but also to lend assistance to their courageous comrade.

***

After having spent the past months training with his new friends as a team, learning every way ever invented to take a human life in the most efficient way possible, Jacob was more than a little confused as to why he was standing alone outside of Acre. The rest of the team had escorted him to the general vicinity of the prison entrance but then retreated to a prearranged staging area where they would wait in support. It would be Jacob's job to enter the prison, and to do so alone.

Just three days earlier, Jacob and the rest of the team were sitting in their discreet office with the sign on the door that read, "Outside Activities." The ambiguous wording fooled nobody, as it was pretty obvious that this was a thinly disguised euphemism for "dirty tricks." Because the boys kept mostly to themselves, this only added to the rumors throughout the camp about what sort of outside activities they were involved in.

"What means 'bipod,'" Sal asked, turning the training manual for a Czech ZK/383 light machine gun all around, as if he could somehow decipher its meaning from a different angle.

"Whatsamattayou," Rudy teased him. "Can't you read? It's a stabilizer for the thing because it's so damn heavy you can't keep it steady without support. Especially you with those weak, spindly arms of yours."

"*Sei proprio una faccia di merda,*" Sal muttered under his breath.

"Whaddya say?" Rudy challenged him, enjoying the banter.

"What's wit you? Can't you understand Italian? It means you a sack of shit."

Sammy joined in the laughter, when the jarring sound of the phone interrupted the argument. Although the phone was situated in Jacob's cubicle tucked away in the corner, all conversation stopped so they could hear what was being said, at least from Jacob's side.

"We have a problem," the older man said simply.

"Yes?"

"What's he saying?" Morris whispered into the room. "Does he have something for us?"

The other boys joined Morris at the door, crowding into the space of the cubicle. Jacob's heart was pounding, both with the excitement of what would come next, and the fear that maybe they would be asked to do something that was impossible. With his friends crowding into the small space, it was difficult to breathe.

"We have a man captured by the British," Mordechai explained. "He's been convicted as a spy and sentenced to die."

"So, you want us to go and get him?"

Mordechai laughed. "You are certainly not short of chutzpah."

"I don't understand."

"Jacob, son, it can't be done. After the last escape, they won't even let visitors inside anymore except for immediate family of those who are condemned."

"What's he saying?" Sammy asked urgently. "What's going on?"

"Shut up!" Rudy scolded him. "Can't you see he's talking to the old man." Then he turned around to face the others with a huge grin on his face.

"So," Jacob prompted Mordechai, "I still don't understand." At least phone conversations were mercifully brief and to the point, unlike the whole morning lectures they would endure face to face. Mordechai was absolutely paranoid that someone could be listening in on their conversations; after all, that is what the Jews had been doing for some time with the British communications.

"You can't get him out. There's just no way." Mordechai paused for a moment and then added, "You're going to get him out, but not by helping him escape."

Jacob knew immediately what he meant and he felt sick. "You mean. . . you can't be serious. . . I mean, you. . . ah. . . you want us to kill him?"

"Kill who?" Sammy asked. "Who's he want us to kill?"

Jacob gave Sammy a look that froze not only him in his tracks, but the others as well. Something weird was going on. This was not going to be an ordinary mission, not that any of them were.

"Just listen to me," Mordechai pleaded in his usual calm, soothing voice.

"You gotta be kidding? You want us to kill a Jew?" Jacob shook his head in disbelief but was unwilling to make eye contact with his friends.

"Will you listen to me please? I'm trying to explain."

Jacob sat silently, the phone held to his head but resting on his cheek rather than near his ear. It was as if he wanted to put more distance between himself and the voice on the other end of the line.

"Look, you're not going to kill him. You're not going to kill anyone. For God's sake, the man's a hero. You can't believe how he has suffered. I'm just asking you to help him."

Five seconds. Ten more. Complete silence on the phone. Everyone was quiet, waiting. Even Sammy would not have dreamed of interrupting whatever was going on.

"What else?" Jacob prompted. "What do you want us to do?"

"It's not 'us.' This one is for one man. In and out. Just delivering a package. A very small package."

***

Jacob looked at his watch one more time, making certain that he timed his approach to arrive at the prison gate exactly as scheduled. The prison administrator had been adamant about the time for the appointment. As the prisoner's supposed brother, Jacob would be allowed to visit for 10 minutes. Not one minute more. The arrogant son of a bitch acted as if he was doing the family some kind of favor because one representative would be permitted to bid the condemned man a last goodbye. Jacob wasn't even sure what a Moroccan fellow looked like and so wondered if there would be any resemblance. Although Jacob's skin had now darkened to the color of all native *sabras* in the desert sun, he just hoped they could pass for brothers.

After signing in and showing the required identification that had been expertly forged, Jacob was escorted by two guards into a holding area where he was asked to remove all his clothes. A burly sergeant with a Scottish accent was less than delicate doing the strip search, peering into his ears and nostrils and poking into his mouth with a pencil.

"Bend over. Spread your cheeks," the sergeant said, obviously as disgusted with this assignment as Jacob felt. "Come on now. Hurry it up!"

Jacob felt like he was going to faint. He seriously wondered if he bent over whether he would be able to stand up again. Please God, he prayed silently. Please, if you will just let me out of here.

Jacob left the thought unfinished as he felt the sergeant stick the pencil into his anus, probing roughly, and not without some enjoyment of Jacob's discomfort.

If they caught him, Jacob realized that he would hang alongside his comrade, but not before first being subjected to the same kind of interrogation. Without a doubt, he was convinced he could never last more than a few hours. Even the thought of what they might do to him made him rethink whether he might announce that he had changed his mind and preferred to leave. But he knew that now he was committed. If they found the package, he was dead. End of story. Nothing he could do about it.

"All right lad, put yer clothes back on and then follow me."

"Ah, yes sir. Right away sir. Thank you sir."

It worked. They had not found it. From reports about previous dry runs into the prison, Mordechai had learned that although the British conducted very thorough body searches, there was one part of the anatomy they would not touch. The homophobia of the prison guards permitted them to probe every orifice with a pencil, but they were very reluctant to touch a man's penis with their bare hands. That was a line that would not be crossed. And after all, what could be hidden in that small place between the underside of the penis and the testicles?

Before being led into the examining room, Jacob had first excused himself to use the toilet. While left alone, he took the four pills—the package—and taped them to his very flaccid penis using clear, adhesive tape. Once the search was over, Jacob surreptitiously scratched his balls as he tucked in his shirt, palming the pills in his hand. As he and the sergeant walked down the dark corridor to where his "brother" was waiting in the death-watch cell, Jacob pressed the sticky part of the tape into his palm with his thumb so that he might relax his arm in a more natural position.

Jacob now rehearsed in his head what he would say to the Moroccan. His job was to hand over the package and explain what it meant. Mordechai had stressed that, ultimately, it was the condemned man's own choice what he wanted to do and how he wanted to die. All they could do was provide him with the means to follow through on his intentions. Among the four pills in his sweaty hand, three were identical, all strong sedatives that might bring relief of the constant pain he was suffering. The fourth pill was cyanide.

When Jacob approached the cell, the Moroccan looked up in fear, anticipating the next interrogation session.

"Shalom my brother," Jacob said to him through the bars in Hebrew, "our mother sends her love."

"Speak only English!" the sergeant ordered. "None of your Jew talk." Because he had turned to face Jacob when he spoke, he did not notice the look of confusion on the Moroccan's face, and he did not wonder why they had greeted one another in Hebrew instead of their native language.

The Moroccan continued to stare at Jacob, completely at a loss as to what was going on. Then recognition slowly occurred to him and he replied in heavily accented English, "Hello my brother. It is good to see you again."

Once the cell door was opened and Jacob was allowed to enter the holding area, the two young men embraced and Jacob kissed the side of his neck. As he held this brave man in his arms, this broken man who had held out against interrogation and torture for six excruciating days and nights, it felt as if he really was his brother. They were both soldiers who were fighting this war behind enemy lines.

***

When Mordechai first explained what was intended, that Jacob would smuggle into the prison some pills that would bring relief, and ultimately death, he was absolutely appalled.

"But why?" Jacob stuttered. "Why not get him a weapon?" By this point the other boys retreated to their own desks. They could see how upset Jacob was, that what Mordechai had in mind was by no means the noble mission they anticipated.

"You don't understand son," Mordechai explained patiently, using his softest voice. "There's no way to get a weapon inside. They will search you everywhere. And once they find the gun—and believe me, they *will* find it—you will find yourself in the same situation as our Moroccan friend."

Mordechai paused for a moment. "And we wouldn't want that now, would we?"

"But there must be *something* we can do for him. There must be. . ."

"Even if we could get a weapon in," Mordechai interrupted more harshly than he intended, "what then? He might shoot a few guards but then the few hundred who are left would shoot him. And you."

Mordechai waited for his words to sink in and then continued in his infuriatingly logical way. "You must realize there *is* something we can do. Only one thing, but a very important thing. The only weapon the man has is his own choice. Do you understand that? It is important to explain to him that there will be no rescue attempt. There is no hope. The only thing waiting for him is more pain, and then death on the British gallows. But if he chooses—and it can only be his choice—he can die on his own terms." Mordechai paused meaningfully, then added, "And cheat the enemy of what they want so dearly."

Remembering this conversation, Jacob held his brother and felt him trembling. The poor man could barely stand without support. They looked at one another in the eyes and then Jacob smiled shyly.

"So," the Moroccan asked his guest as he shuffled back to his bunk where he could rest from the exertion of standing up. "What news from home?"

Jacob examined the prisoner as objectively as he could. The man was gone, already dead on his feet. Mordechai had been right after all; there really was no hope. But then he realized that the hardest part of his mission was about to begin, in which he was the one assigned to deliver the final sentence of death. He was to take away this desperate man's last shred of hope.

"Well, you know," Jacob said with a shrug, looking toward the guards, "much the same."

"They'll back away," whispered the Moroccan in Hebrew. "Just wait a minute."

Jacob glanced once more over his shoulder and then carefully reached out and held the prisoner's hand in a firm embrace, pressing his palm and the little package into the flesh. The Moroccan deftly withdrew the pills and tucked them into the folds of his bedding. He looked quizzically at Jacob, unsure of what he had been passed but, perhaps, sensing what this meeting was about.

The Moroccan looked at Jacob, speaking no words. It was an imploring look, one that required no words. Jacob just shook his head and smiled sadly.

"Nothing?" the prisoner asked in a voice that was hoarse and strained.

"I'm sorry my brother. But after the last escape. . ." He left the thought unfinished.

"I understand," the Moroccan said, straightening his posture as best he could. Sometime later, Jacob realized that the really strange thing about this interaction was that it had seemed as if *he* was the one who was being given comfort rather than the other way around.

"They considered everything they possibly could," Jacob explained. "They. . ."

The Moroccan held up his hand, the same one that had held the pills just a minute ago. Jacob noticed that while the rest of the man's body seemed to be trembling, his hand remained still. He smiled for a moment at Jacob, a warm smile as if to show that he was genuinely grateful for the visit. Then he turned serious. "Will it hurt?" he asked.

"I won't lie to you, brother. Thirty seconds and it's over. No more pain."

The Moroccan nodded his head in understanding. "And the other pills?"

"They're for the pain."

He nodded again. They both looked at the ground and sat in silence.

"Do they know that I haven't talked, that I haven't told them a thing?" The Moroccan said this fiercely, proudly, as if this was the single most important point he wanted to make in this conversation. "You tell them that, do you hear? You tell them."

"They know already my brother. That's why they sent me here to help you, to give you a way out. You are a hero. And some day all of Israel will say a *kaddish* for you and the sacrifices you made."

They both knew that nobody would ever hear about the work they had done, but the lie felt comforting for Jacob to say and, he suspected, for the Moroccan to hear out loud. Just as the words left his mouth, Jacob realized that he was speaking as much to himself as the other man. If he should die in this prison, or in some other tiny Arab village stomped to death by a mob, he just hoped that someone would find out what he had tried to do.

"This is some kind of war," the Moroccan said softly, shaking his head. Tears were pooling in his eyes and a single tear snaked its way down his cheek, moving so slowly it was as if he did not even have enough energy to cry properly. Jacob did not have the same problem: he was now crying freely. He realized that he was not only crying for this brave man, this brother, but also for himself. How long would it be before he ended up in the same place? And would he be offered the same kind of deliverance?

"It is time for you to go now," the Moroccan said gently. He tried to stand up to escort his guest to the door but realized that even with Jacob's help, he could not quite manage to rise.

"That's okay," Jacob reassured him. "You just rest for awhile." He then leaned over and embraced his brother, hugging him fiercely.

The Moroccan gently pushed him away and looked one last time into his eyes. "See you on the other side." Then he was gone, just like that, retreating inside himself.

As Jacob walked away from the cell, he heard a hoarse voice singing: *Od lo avda tikvatenou* [Our hope is not lost], *hatikva ba shnot alpayim* [our hope of 2,000 years]. He recognized it immediately as the *Hatikva*, the prayer that would someday become the Jewish National Anthem.

Chapter 7

Parade
March to May 1948

Things were not going well in the struggle. People in the south were starving, completely cut off from the world. Jerusalem was in a state of siege and about to fall at any time. The roads into the city had been blockaded. In the worst defeat the Jews had suffered since Masada—the mountain fortress where a thousand people died opposing the Romans in the year AD 73—a convoy on its way back from a kibbutz had been attacked and destroyed. Most of the Haganah's pitiful supply of armored vehicles was now in the hands of their enemies.

Arab guerrillas had mounted successful attacks within the Jewish stronghold, blowing up critical buildings. The office of the *Palestine Post* had been destroyed. The Arabs even had the audacity to strike at the headquarters of the Jewish leadership. There was little food, few serviceable weapons, and almost no ammunition. Meanwhile, the Arab armies were growing bigger, stronger, and better equipped by the day. Things were looking increasingly hopeless.

To make matters even more bleak, there had been a crushing blow to morale during the last session of the United Nations. Even though President Truman had promised that the United States would support the establishment of a Jewish nation after the original partition vote, his administration was now balking. In a speech to the General Assembly, the U.S. representative announced that the United States would be withdrawing their support and were recommending that partition be postponed indefinitely. To Ben-Gurion, Golda Meir, Chaim Weizmann, and the other Jewish leaders, this felt like the ultimate betrayal. They could expect even less help from the outside than they were already getting.

***

"We must go on the attack," Mordechai explained to Jacob and the team during one of their routine briefing sessions. "All we are doing is defending ourselves. It's like we're trying to hold on with broken fingernails." Mordechai was referring to the general strategy that Ben-Gurion had been employing up to this point. Still, Jacob could not help but feel slighted. During the past year, they *had* gone on the attack, hitting the Arabs hard where it hurt the most. They had successfully completed several missions without a hitch, including traveling to Belgium to take out an arms dealer and participating in an ambush along with a regular army unit to open up a blockade along the road to Jerusalem. Most importantly, they brought back critical information on troop deployments along the border, which they realized were more training exercises and feints rather than genuine threats.

Mordechai smiled. "No Jacob, I don't mean you. You boys have done a marvelous job. If I had a hundred more like you, we could win this war on our own."

"We're losing people," Mordechai said, shaking his head in disgust. "We're losing a lot of our people, and we don't have that many to spare. It's time we hit them hard," Mordechai said, smacking his fist against his other hand, "harder than we ever have before. Enough of this playing around."

Jacob could feel excitement building. The team members were frustrated and restless, having been kept out of major battles so as to keep them fresh and out of harm's way until they were needed most. Or at least that was the explanation they had been given for remaining in camp when everyone else had gone to fight. From their viewpoint in the mountains, they watched the action with mounting anger, spectators in the most important actions of the war. Jacob had also spent enough time with this man to know when something important was brewing.

Sal, in particular, was livid about their relative inactivity (they had been sent on several reconnaissance missions). He kept muttering to himself as they waited for Mordechai to finish a phone call, ending each declaration with a hearty *Figlio di puttana* (son of a bitch). Except for the convoy ambush, Sal, Rudy, and Sammy had been relegated solely to supporting roles.

"Excuse me?" Mordechai addressed the mumbling Italian, who seemed to be having a complete conversation with himself while the others looked on in amusement.

"Nothing Signore," Sal answered, looking down and shaking his head.

"Look," Mordechai said in a soothing, placating voice, "if it's about being left at home. . ."

"Well come on!" Sammy interrupted. "What are we here for if you're not going to let us fight?"

"Oh? So you don't think we're putting you to good use? You know damn well that you've done more for this war than any other bunch of guys we've got. You're just too valuable to risk in an all-out assault. The Arabs have snipers sitting on every rooftop."

"Okay. Okay." Sammy said holding his hands up, palms forward in surrender. It was obvious that he did not agree with Mordechai, but he knew that he could not win the argument. It was best to let the old man get to the point so they could find out why they had been held in reserve.

"As you know, we trounced them pretty good during the past week. In fact, we beat them so badly that almost the whole Old City was completely abandoned."

Rudy and Sal looked at one another and smiled.

"No guys," Mordechai commented as he saw their expression of jubilance, "that isn't a reason to celebrate. We've lived here with the Arabs for many years. They have been our neighbors and friends. It is a sad day indeed to see them leave. Yes, it is true that we must control this sector, but it is not with the people who we wish to fight. It is with the Legion and their leaders."

"So, what do you want us to do?" Sammy asked impatiently. He was the one member of the team who seemed to become exasperated by Mordechai's indirect, methodical way of getting to the point. By contrast, Jacob loved the clever ways that their leader guided them in the directions he wished them to go. Even when Jacob knew what to watch for, it wasn't until many days later that he and Morris could figure out what Mordechai was really after. Even then, they could only guess, never certain if the conclusion they came to was what had been intended.

"As you know," Mordechai continued, ignoring Sammy's outburst, "the Arabs have been in retreat. But they can't afford to leave altogether. They've got to keep us busy up here so they can strike elsewhere with less resistance."

Jacob and Morris looked at one another meaningfully, knowing that something big was coming. This was not so much revealed in what Mordechai was saying but rather in the pace in which he was saying it. Over the past half year, they had come to learn that the slower and more methodically Mordechai briefed them, the more dangerous the assignment. This one was going to be a "whopper."

"We happen to know that a very high ranking officer in the Arab Legion is planning a demonstration in the Old City. He is talking about leading a parade right through the Arab sector—or at least that's what our sources tell us. If he can manage to show them displays of power, he can convince them to keep fighting, to stick around and make trouble for us rather than settle into peace."

Mordechai held out his arms, wiggling his fingers to invite a response. "So? What do you think?"

Jacob sat for a moment, looking for the trap. He knew this was a trick question. Mordechai already had a definite plan for what he wanted them to do, but rather than telling them directly, he would draw it out of them. Instead of resenting this manipulation, Jacob and the others actually appreciated that the Haganah at least involved them in the decision making rather than giving direct orders.

Jacob wondered what he and the others would do if they were given a mission that they knew would lead to certain death. Surely, they had close calls before, but there was always at least the illusion of getting out alive.

While Mordechai took the long, slow, indirect path to whatever devious plan he had in mind, Jacob drifted back to the time spent in Malta many months earlier. He remembered it was the second day after they had been off the ship when they were administered the oath of allegiance:

> As long as I assist as a volunteer in the War of Liberation of the nation of Israel, I hereby swear on my word of honor, to accept unconditionally and without reservation, the rules and discipline of the Israeli Defense Army, to obey all its orders and instructions given by the authorized commanders and to do all in my power, and even to sacrifice my life in the defense of the freedom of Israel.

"To sacrifice my life," Jacob recalled. Just how far would I go to face certain death on one of these crazy missions? Jacob had a feeling he was about to find out.

"So," Morris was saying, "why don't we just take this guy out?" Until that point, he had been quiet and reflective, completely still in his seat while the others moved around restlessly.

"Yeah?" Sammy challenged him. "How we gonna do that? The guy is marching in the middle of a fucking army, for Christ's sake! What are we gonna do, just walk up to the guy and pop him?"

"First of all," Morris replied, "it isn't going to be *us*, it's going to be Jacob and me." As soon as he saw Sammy's hurt look, he regretted his outburst. "What I mean is, just like we've done before, when two of us can get in and out quickly, we are invisible to them. They don't see us until it's too late."

For Morris, this was a rather long speech. He did not like to speak up at these meetings, preferring to work things out with Jacob and the others in private. "Isn't that right, Jake?" he said to move the focus away from himself.

"It's possible," Jacob said noncommittally, remembering once again the words of his oath, to sacrifice his life. He tried to picture Morris and himself strolling up to this general at the head of his army, taking him out, and then. . . well, then. . . he just could not imagine any other ending to the story except being torn apart by the enraged crowd of thousands who watched the spectacle. And if by some chance they should survive their initial capture with all their limbs intact, once the Arabs figured out that this was the same team who had killed their militia commander, well, it was too horrible to even consider the fate that would await them.

"Let's back up a little," Mordechai interjected. "Before we get to the details of a plan, do you agree that eliminating this general—if it was possible—would be a tremendous embarrassment for them?"

"Well, sure it would," agreed Sammy, who had been full of bravado a few minutes earlier but now was having second and third thoughts about the wisdom of such a mission. "But why send us in? I mean, wouldn't it be easier to use a bomb or something, like what they've been doing in Jerusalem?"

Mordechai shook his head. "Too messy. Too many civilians would get hurt. Besides, there's no guarantee a bomb would take him out."

Sal nodded his head thoughtfully and then raised his hand just like an eager student in class. "What about sneeper?"

Everyone looked puzzled for a moment, then Sammy, who seemed to understand the mangled English better than anyone else, interpreted: "He means a sniper."

Sal nodded his head enthusiastically.

"That's an excellent idea," Mordechai acknowledged. Sal broke out in a grin and looked proudly at the others, as if he had gotten the gold star for the day. "That would definitely do the job, and do it cleanly. But can anyone guess why that would not be preferred?"

Jacob could now see where this was going, and what Mordechai had in mind all along. "You want to stick it in their faces. You want us to show them that we can hit them any time we want, wherever we want. You want them so afraid of us that they'll never sleep soundly until they leave us alone." As he listed each of these reasons, and saw Mordechai nod his head each time, he then made the final point: "This is to be a symbolic action. You want us to get up close to him, just like we do, and take him out right in front of his whole army and the whole city watching. They'll be talking about this one for years."

Mordechai looked at Jacob but did not answer right away. He might have nodded his head, but if he did, it was so subtle that it could have been just his chin dropping a little in thought. Before he had a chance to answer, Jacob answered for the team. "We'll do it. I think we can do it."

"Are you fucking nuts?" Rudy jumped in, until this time a spectator to this conversation. "You're saying that you and Morris are going to go after this guy in front of his whole army? And you think you've got a prayer of getting out of there alive?"

"Wait a minute," Morris defended his partner. "I agree that it would be very difficult to get close to the guy, but under the right circumstances it could be done."

"Right circumstances?" Rudy said incredulously, shocked at how the most level-headed among them was actually contemplating this suicide mission. "You gotta be kidding me."

"What if," Morris continued speculatively, "what if we were in Legion uniforms, dressed just like they were?"

"Could this be done?" Rudy looked toward Mordechai, hoping the only real grown-up in the room would somehow intervene and talk them out of this crazy stunt.

Mordechai looked at Rudy and smiled, but he refused to answer. He was going to let the team work it out. In fact, if he could have walked unobtrusively out of the room at that point, he would have. He knew he was no longer needed. He had seen this process work enough times to know that the five of them would eventually fashion a workable plan. His job at this point was to act as consultant and provide whatever further information and resources they needed.

"Yes," Jacob answered for Mordechai, convinced that the die had been cast and this would be their fate. "If we can dress ourselves in Legion uniforms, we can march right along next to the guy. Nobody will even notice us. There will be lots of music blaring and people screaming. If we're lucky, they might not even hear the shots."

"Yeah?" Rudy said, still skeptical. "But as soon as the guy hits the ground, you're going to have an angry mob and army all over your ass."

"What if we propped him up?" Morris said in soft voice and then realized with surprise that he had spoken his thought out loud.

"What the hell are you talking about?" Rudy asked him in a voice that was becoming less shrill and more calm, as if even he could picture it now.

"If Jacob and I come at him from different sides, kind of hook his arms like this," Morris said in an excited voice as he made a "V" with his arm just like a gentleman would escort a lady. "Then when we pop him, if we both suspend him between our arms, we can carry him along, marching between us, until we get to a good spot to drop him and run."

Jacob thought about it for a minute, trying to picture it in his mind. It could work, it really could. He turned to look at Mordechai. "You said he was a little guy, right?"

"Yes, our sources tell us he is very slight, about 5 feet 4. He weighs about 135 pounds."

"Thatta smaller than you," Sal teased him.

"*Pisciati in bocca!*" Jacob said automatically. Lately, Sal had been teaching them all how to swear in Italian and this was one of their favorites, which directed the person to urinate in his own mouth. "We can do this Morris. If you stand on one side and I hold him up on the other, we can lift him up off the ground and keep him going until we can dump him."

"If you boys will excuse me," Mordechai interrupted, "I've got to be at another meeting. Why don't you discuss it further, make your plans, and tell me what you need. We have about three days before the operation, which doesn't give you a lot of time to rehearse your plans before you have to go in. Let's plan to meet again tomorrow."

***

It wasn't often that they had free time to roam around Haifa, and this was a particularly opportune time to do so. For the first time, all except the Arab Quarter was completely in Haganah hands. There was rejoicing in the streets, with people excited about their victory. For the first time in 2,000 years, since the Jews had been thrown out by the Phoenicians, Egyptians, Persians, and Spanish, and more recently by the Germans, Russians, Italians, and then the Arabs in collaboration with the British, they now controlled a part of their ancient homeland.

They found a corner table in a *qahwa*, a formerly Arab café that was just a room open to the street. There was sawdust on the floor and roughly constructed tables where Jews, and even a few Arabs, were playing backgammon and dominoes and drinking strong, black coffee. They sat and talked further about the mission and how they would pull it off. They were particularly puzzled about how they would manage to secure the uniforms they would need. There was no time for any other operatives to get what they would need, so they would have to do it themselves, the night before the parade was to begin. This would require them to actually infiltrate the Legion camp and spend the night there, a prospect that seemed even more dangerous than the mission.

In their previous assignments, they had all been amazed how if they walked around as if they belonged and knew what they were doing, everyone pretty much ignored them. Even with Morris's blonde hair and blue eyes and Sal and Sammy's nonexistent Arabic, they remained invisible or, more likely, seemed to fit into the scenery as if they belonged there. The more confident and experienced they had become over time, the more comfortable they became in Arab clothes, and the less often they were noticed in the places they visited. People would glance at them, see they were strangers, but then continue about their business with almost no curiosity. It was a phenomenon that the boys did not begin to understand, especially during this time of war. But it was something they accepted as part of their continuing good fortune.

Back in the camp, Morris and Jacob had practiced carrying Sal between them, imitating the goose step march of the Arab Legion soldiers. They found that they could easily balance their friend between them if Jacob, the smaller one, lifted Sal higher to balance Morris's height. The hardest part was trying to swing their outside arms in cadence while holding the extra weight. This would take some practice.

Now relaxing at their table, eating the last crumbs of *baklava* and *asabeeh*, pastries made from phyllo dough, nuts, and honey, the boys continued their usual complaints about the ways they were isolated, ignored, and occasionally even ridiculed by the *sabras,* the native Israelis.

"What the hell is a *machalnik* anyway?" asked Sammy, often puzzled by Hebrew words that had not been part of his Bar Mitzvah training.

"They're initials," answered Jacob with a full mouth of chewy honeyed dates that were sticking to the roof of his mouth.

"Say what?"

"Initials. For *Mitnadveh Hutz La'Aretz*. It's the name they've given to the volunteers, the *Machal*."

Sammy nodded his head thoughtfully and then seemed to change the subject, although he was really pursuing the same theme in a different way. "Did you hear they made ole Mickey a general, the first Jewish general in 2,000 years?"

Mickey Marcus was a New Yorker just like the boys. He had served on Eisenhower's staff during World War II, and then later in the Pentagon. He had been recruited about the same time that Jacob and the others had come over, but unlike the other *machalniks* who were treated with grudging acceptance by the *sabras*, Marcus was enjoying tremendous respect from Ben-Gurion and the Jewish leadership. He was writing their training manuals, planning strategy for the High Command, and leading successful commando raids with the Palmach into Arab territory. He was an endless topic of conversation among the team members because he represented the valuable role that Americans could play in the war. Israelis were always griping about Truman having abandoned them.

When the conversation lapsed into silence, Morris pulled out a wrinkled letter that he smoothed out in front of him. "Amy asked me. . ."

The boys groaned. Morris's fiancée wrote him every week, without fail, not only sharing news of things back in New York, but also complaining constantly about how lonely she was and how much she missed him.

"Why are you there, my darling?" she wrote. "You just finished fighting one war, and now you are fighting another. What are you doing there? And what do you hope to prove?"

They were good questions, the same ones that each of them had been asking themselves since the day they first boarded the ship for Palestine. Again they responded with a collective shrug. They seemed to reach an unspoken agreement that they would never press one another too hard about their motives. They might tease on occasion, and sometimes even become angry, but they would never push. Especially after a mission was over, when Jacob and Morris first climbed back into the jeep with soiled clothes and dazed eyes, they never asked about what happened. And they never told, never even talked about it between themselves except for the very first time when Morris had splattered Jacob by shooting at the wrong angle.

There was some discussion about whether the whole team was even needed for the mission in the Legion camp where they would get uniforms. Jacob felt it was too dangerous to risk all their lives, that perhaps he and Morris might have a better chance if the two of them went in alone, and came out alone.

Rudy, the one who had initially been the most hesitant, was now the one who was most insistent that they stick together as a team. "Who knows what might go wrong?" he pressed Jacob, the one who ultimately had final authority. "You might need me to radio for help. If one of you gets caught or hurt, Sammy'll be there to back you up. And you sure as shit need Sal to get you the hell out of there after things get going."

The reasoning did not make sense to Jacob. He knew that the more of them who tried to infiltrate the Arab camp the next night, the greater their chances were they would be spotted. But he was unwilling to break up the team, even for a single mission. For moral support more than anything else, they would stick together.

***

The Arab camp was completely different from their own base. There were the expected tents set up everywhere, but the energy was so different. There were men walking around dressed in an assortment of clothes—some in robes that had once been white but were now streaked in gray, British-type military uniforms, or loose-fitting pants and blouses crossed with bandoliers of ammunition. About the only things they had in common were the almost universal thick, black mustaches and long, curved knives at their sides.

Rather than being drilled and trained, the soldiers were sitting around in small groups playing dominoes, smoking *sheeshas*, Arabic water pipes, and talking. They were surprised to see some groups were even drinking beer, which was forbidden to observant Muslims. The whole place smelled of fish, which seemed to be the main staple of their diet.

It was surprising as well how easy it had been to enter the camp. There was no real security and very few guards along the perimeter. If there was some sort of password, the team had managed to avoid being challenged by simply walking through an area that was uninhabited. As they wandered around the place, nobody even looked at them, much less asked them what they were doing there. They just stayed together as a unit, keeping Sal on the inside so if any communication was required, Morris and Rudy, the two native Arabic speakers, could do the talking. As it turned out, the precautions were hardly necessary.

Even at dinner, they sat undisturbed and unmolested at a circle of their own. It was while slurping up the rich custard for dessert that they heard an announcement that special parade uniforms would be distributed by the tailor at the far end of the camp. Without seeming to rush, they made their way to the line as fast as they could, wanting to make sure they got what they came for.

Things proceeded smoothly as each man was distributed practically brand new, polished boots, a freshly laundered uniform, and a colorful *khaffiya* in hues of green, yellow, or black. They knew that each man in line would be asked the sizes of his clothes and boots, so they had rehearsed with Sal the Arabic numbers they would need.

When his turn came, Sal stood calmly in front of the tailor, answering *ashra*, his boot size of 10, when he had just been asked his waist size. When the tailor looked at him in confusion, and then yelled at him in a torrent of Arabic, Sal just shrugged and smiled, uttering the only other phrase he knew, "*Ma bif-ham,*" I don't understand. Morris quickly jumped in and explained that Sal spoke Farsi and had come all the way from Iran to fight the Jews. The tailor smiled in appreciation and handed Sal a brand new uniform in his size.

As soon as the uniforms were dispersed, the soldiers made their way back to their tents to relax and sleep. Because Jacob and the others had no tent to return to, they casually made their way back to the jeep to spend the night. So far the plan had gone better than they had any right to expect.

Morris and Jacob showed up back in camp just after breakfast so they would not have to risk lengthy interactions with their fellow soldiers. They were loaded onto lorries loaned to the Legion by the British, along with some impressive artillery pieces—75-mm and 105-mm howitzers. Jacob and Morris looked at one another in amazement, because these guns were so much more impressive than the homemade *davidka* used by their own army.

As soon as the trucks were unloaded in the central square, Jacob and Morris made a quick exit toward their preplanned staging areas. They located the first bend in the street where they could surreptitiously join the parade in the front without drawing attention to themselves. Further intelligence reports had indicated that the general would be marching in front with his staff officers, followed by several hundred infantry, then the cavalry mounted on both horses and camels, and then finally the mechanized unit. It would be an impressive display of pageantry and force, with the soldiers decked out in parade uniforms, marching in goose-stepped formation, colorful banners flying, and haunting, martial drumbeats signaling the power of the Arab Legion.

As Jacob stood in the shadows, listening to the drums get louder as the parade approached, he kept thinking about what could happen in the next few minutes. It wasn't the actual shooting that worried him; it was what would occur afterwards. Jacob knew that if he was detained by the soldiers, or worse yet by the screaming crowd, he would be lucky if he died swiftly. He just hoped that he would have time to place the gun to his own head, just in front of his ear, and take his own life before the mob had a chance to take their revenge.

Nobody had ever attempted anything like this, such a reckless strike at the heart of the enemy. He wondered if that was because nobody had ever thought of doing something this crazy, or because it could not be done. Either way, he would soon know.

The drums were getting louder, deep, rhythmic pounding that was oddly hypnotic, producing exactly the intended effect of an army on the march. He saw the first colorful banners fluttering in the slight wind. One last time he looked across the street to see his partner leaning casually against a wall, half hidden in his own shadow.

The women along the street made the distinctive, high-pitched noises in which they fluttered their tongues inside their mouths. The eerie trilled cheers were mixed with the screams of children on the sidewalks, working the crowd into a fevered pitch. When Jacob saw the goose-stepping Legion soldiers, he was reminded of old movies he had seen of the Nazis on parade in Berlin. Holding on to that image, he realized that killing this guy was going to be the easiest one yet. All he had to do was picture Hitler leading the SS.

Sure enough, the short general was at the head of the parade, grinning and waving like he had just won the greatest victory for his people instead of having failed them by arriving too late. This was all for show, all to communicate the message that we are omnipotent, that nobody can stand in Allah's way—certainly not these infidel Jews who will be crushed by the force of our cannons and brave soldiers. The crowd loved it.

Deep breath. Jacob pushed away from the wall, as if some magnetic force was holding him there. Once he took his first step toward the marching soldiers about a dozen rows back from his target, it was as if his brain shut off completely and he was functioning automatically. He concentrated only on timing his steps to those of the row he joined. Raise his right arm and left leg, then left arm and right leg. Keep in cadence. Look to his left, his new companions did not even register his presence. They were checking out the crowd, looking for loved ones or pretty girls.

A curve in the street to the right allowed Jacob and Morris to close the distance to their target, taking double strides on a straight trajectory rather than staying with their row. There was only one line that now separated them from their prey, a row of soldiers holding banners. These would be the only ones they would have to worry about because they had a clear view of their general ahead. Even so, Jacob and Morris knew that the only ones who carried loaded weapons during parades were the officers. If they moved quickly enough, they would be gone before the colonels even knew what happened.

One more quick glance to his left, meeting Morris's eyes, and then they both skipped ahead at a jogging pace, pulling alongside the general. The drums were deafening now, or at least they sounded that way to Jacob. Perhaps it was the sound of blood pumping in his ears. In either case, he looked around for a moment and could see lips moving, women's mouths fluttering, but could hear nothing but the sound of drums.

Jacob hooked his left arm through the general's, while Morris mirrored the same movement on his right. The little man, so arrogant and self-assured just a moment earlier, started to yell out just as the two pistols were placed on each side of head. The gunshots were thankfully buried in the shrill yells from the crowd and the booming echoes of the drums. The general shuddered once, twice, kicking his legs and emptying his bowels as he was dragged along by his executioners.

"Higher!" Morris urged his shorter partner. "Lift him higher. You're dragging his feet!"

They resumed their march, almost without breaking stride. They could see funny looks on the faces of the crowd, as if they knew something was terribly wrong, but nobody was saying or doing anything to intervene. As long as the drumbeats continued and the parade moved forward, the spectators seemed reassured that everything was going as planned. That their general had blood dripping on his face and shit running down his pant leg seemed more like an illusion than real.

Jacob could hear urgent whispers behind him and knew that the soldiers holding the banners could tell their leader was in trouble. They seemed to be deciding what to do about it, unsure whether it was their place to disturb the great general. Surely, if he was really ill or injured, his staff officers would take care of matters. But they were blithely marching just ahead, basking in the glory of the people's affection.

"Ready?" Jacob whispered to Morris as they approached the steepest bend in the road, the place they had planned to make their getaway. Although Morris was staring straight ahead, concentrating on his goose steps and holding the general upright, Jacob knew he had heard the signal.

Just before they reached the appointed spot, Jacob heard screams from the crowd, quite a different noise than the cheers that provided background noise. Jacob looked up and saw two women pointing at him with savage looks on their faces. The whole rhythm of the parade seemed to stutter.

"Shit," Jacob yelled, "Let go! Let's get out of here!"

They let go of the general's arms, and he fell straight to the ground, tripping the next row of marchers, finally grinding the parade to a ragged halt. The drums kept beating, driving the soldiers forward until they piled into those in front who had stopped.

Morris took off to the left, while Jacob bolted to the right. Unfortunately, he had to run right by the two women who had first noticed that something was wrong. They reached out with their hands to grab him, screaming for help to capture the killer. There was chaos everywhere, people running in different directions believing they were under renewed attack. The two women held on tightly, one with a solid hold on his gun-belt, screaming with all their might for help to subdue their prisoner. While one held on, the other reached up to try and scratch his eyes.

Jacob could see others running toward him and knew that time was running out. He realized that he still held the pistol in his hand and thought about using it first on his attackers, and then, for a moment, considered turning it on himself. One last attempt to free himself: he raised his hands, brandishing the pistol and ordering the women to back away. To his surprise, they did just that, retreating, and even holding their tongues for the moment.

Without a second's pause, he made a dash for the crowd gathering around the body, using the chaos for cover and then melting into the throng of like-dressed soldiers milling around in confusion. The next thing he did was dump the brightly colored head covering that instantly identified him.

Walking slower, so as to not draw attention to himself, he backed into a side street, only turning when he was certain nobody was following him. The one thing he must absolutely avoid at all costs was leading the avengers back to his own team who were waiting to pick him up around the corner.

Bless his heart, there was Sal waiting calmly in the driver's seat of the beat-up jeep. Sammy was riding shotgun, holding tightly onto a prized Sturmgewehr 44 machine gun that he managed to borrow from the Arab camp they visited the previous evening. The German assault rifle had been outfitted with a grenade launcher that Sammy was pointing in the direction of the crowd that was now chasing Jacob, but falling farther behind as he lengthened his stride.

"Come on!" Rudy urged him from the back seat. "Move your ass!"

Jacob placed his right hand on the side of the vehicle and used it to hurdle over, landing with an awkward thud onto the seat. Before he had a chance to steady himself, Sal took off in the direction of the next pick up point where Morris was found waiting as calmly as if for a taxi. It was at this point that the three of them turned to look at Jacob and Morris, checking them out for wounds or injuries. Their glances lingered a moment longer than necessary, waiting for the simple nods of their heads, indicating that they had indeed gotten their man.

Chapter 8

Truce
June 1948

On June 11, a truce was called by the United Nations to negotiate a settlement that neither party had any intention of agreeing to. The Arabs still had visions of pushing the Jews all the way back into the Mediterranean. The Israelis still hoped that if they could stop the momentum of the Arab Legion, they might even expand their present territorial boundaries. As the borders now stood, the Jews had little hope they could effectively defend their country against future attacks.

Although much of the shooting ceased during this first truce in the war, there would be welcome time to rearm for the next stage of battle. Both sides wanted to sneak in one last campaign but were like punch-drunk boxers—exhausted, delirious, but unwilling to sit down at the end of the round.

The Haganah wanted to use the downtime to hit some strategic targets in the quietest way possible without violating the truce agreement, or at least being caught doing so. This was where Team *Gimmel* would continue to play a significant role, operating without official sanction and as an independent unit. If they were caught during the truce, nobody would acknowledge them.

If they were tortured, they knew nothing they could reveal. They were perfectly suited to continue the war while everyone else was supposedly taking a break.

Morris and Jacob were strolling casually down the dusty main street of a town in the Golan Heights across the Syrian border. A traditional stopping point for nomads and caravans since Byzantine times, it was now a cultural and administrative center for the area with almost 20,000 inhabitants. With its strategic location poised over Israel in the valley below, the town was now a major staging area for troops set to continue the invasion that began a month earlier.

The road was lined with shops, food stalls, and open cafes. During late morning, there was a busy stream of traffic proceeding through town—a few old, rusty cars, but mostly camels, oxen, and mules. People were drinking glasses of sweetened tea, or tiny cups of strong coffee, talking in small groups around small tables. On the street, children played while their mothers shopped for food. Occasionally, soldiers could be found walking in pairs, lending the only modern touch to what could otherwise have been a village from a hundred or a thousand years ago.

"No way," Morris said to Jacob as they walked on the shady side of the street. While they walked, he shook his head back and forth, far more times than was needed to make his point. "It just can't be done."

"I agree," Jacob answered, unwilling to contradict his friend directly, "but what if we waited until he leaves the compound." Seeing that Morris was about to interrupt, he held up his hand. "Wait. Hear me out. The guy can't stay with his guards forever. I mean, he's gotta have a girlfriend or something. Maybe he sneaks away."

"Nope," Morris insisted. "How long do we have to watch this guy? He's been trained by the British. He's practically one of them, for God's sake! He doesn't make mistakes and he's very, very careful. We had no idea just how careful until these past days. Shit, I'm tired of hanging around here. Let's just go back."

Before Jacob could answer, he noticed two soldiers approaching them on the same side of the street. They had noticed all morning that people were being stopped and detained, particularly since there seemed to be so many strangers around—businessmen, reporters, smugglers, shady characters, even tourists. That latter role is exactly the identity that the two were traveling under at that moment. Four days earlier, the whole team had driven across the border to scout out a prospective mission that would involve knocking off the leader of the Syrian militia for this area. While Sammy, Sal, and Rudy used the jeep to scout out escape routes and survey enemy troop deployments, Morris and Jacob used the time to keep an eye on their prospective target. After a few days of surveillance, they now concluded that he was just too well protected to get close to him. As always, Mordechai would defer to their judgment: if they did not think the job could be done, then that was that. They would return to camp and plan for another assignment.

"*Sabah al-khayr,*" one of the soldiers addressed the two of them. "*Min wayn inta?*"

Although they well understood that they had just been offered a good morning and asked where they were from, the two boys just smiled and shrugged their ignorance of the language. They were posing as tourists and dressed the part in baggy pants, open-necked shirts, and linen jackets.

"Your papers please," the soldier tried again in heavily accented English, extending his hand.

Although they knew they were hardly being picked on because they could see most of the foreigners in the town were being watched, they were still feeling nervous about the quality of their identity papers. The American passports were excellent forgeries, the same ones supplied by the Haganah to get them into the country under false names in the first place. But the entry visas could be a problem because they depended on an Arab contact to supply them with the necessary documents. They had no idea how good they were as they had yet to be tested.

"Is there a problem?" Jacob asked in his most authoritative, arrogant tourist tone.

Either the soldier had a very limited mastery of the English language, or he simply chose to ignore the challenge, but he repeated again in a bored voice, "Your papers please."

As the soldier's hand was still extended, Jacob had the mischievous idea of seeing how long he could stall until the man's arm got so tired he had to retrieve it. When he saw the look of open hostility in the other soldier's face, he thought it wiser to appear as cooperative as possible.

"Sure," Jacob said amiably, "I've got them right here." He reached inside his jacket, feeling the weight of the Beretta in the outside pocket of the same side. He glanced over at Morris and saw him nod acquiescently, so he pulled out their passports and handed them over.

The soldier glanced through the passports first, unimpressed with the American eagle on the front, and then studied the entry visas suspiciously, as if he was determined to find something wrong. Jacob wondered what about them was inviting such scrutiny.

"May I ask where you are from?" the lead soldier asked politely, still holding the documents in his hand.

"New York. In America."

"And you?" the soldier asked Morris.

"Same. From the Bronx. It's. . ."

"I know where the Bronx is," the soldier said with some formality. "I lived in your country for one year, in the state of Maryland. That is where I learned to speak English."

"Yes," Jacob smiled, "and you speak very well."

If the intent of the flattery was to put the soldier at ease, it had the opposite effect; he now seemed even more suspicious. "I'm afraid you must come with us. There seems to be some irregularity with your papers."

"May I ask what the problem is?" Morris asked, casually slipping his hand into the coat pocket that held his pistol. When he saw Jacob shake his head, he relaxed and removed his hand.

"Nothing that I'm sure can't be straightened out. It's just that I don't recognize the signature on your visa." As he explained this last part, he studied the American faces intently, looking for signs of nervousness or deception. He seemed disappointed that the two tourists were so cooperative.

They followed the two soldiers down the end of the street where the commercial area ended, and up the road to the headquarters of the military command for Southern Syria. The building was somewhat isolated from the rest of the town, but with its elevated position, it had a grand view of the whole area. There were a number of military vehicles coming and going, soldiers standing around, and others engaged in some sort of training exercise. There could not have been a worse place for the two of them to be taken. Even if they somehow managed to elude their captors, there was no way that Sal could maneuver their jeep in close enough proximity for them to escape several hundred armed guards. Somehow, they would have to talk their way out of this mess.

As soon as they entered the main headquarters, they heard a voice from inside ask their escort what these people were doing here. The soldier responded in rapid Arabic to his superior that these two strangers seemed suspicious and that their visas appeared irregular. The officer nodded his head and directed the arresting soldier to bring the prisoners into the interrogation room. This was a very spacious facility with a long wooden table in the middle and two narrow tables along the walls. The back wall was dominated by a huge picture window that opened up onto a garden and open field that was bordered by a high hedge. In addition to the door they entered, they saw another door leading to another room, or perhaps a possible exit.

Morris and Jacob were directed to sit on opposite sides of the table, with the English-speaking guard at the end. Jacob glanced over his shoulder toward the window and noticed that the officer was sitting behind him, making it awkward for him to see what was going on. Spaced at equal intervals around the room were four other armed guards who, while not exactly pointing their weapons at the prisoners, still wore sidearms with their holsters easily accessible.

Speaking in rapid Arabic, the officer ordered the arresting guard to act as interpreter. Throughout the duration of the interrogation, he would direct his questions to the solider, who then translated them into English, as well as converting their answers into English.

"Who are you?" the officer began abruptly. "What are you doing here?"

Morris had to bite his tongue for a moment, tempted to answer the question in Arabic until he remembered that they were only ignorant American tourists. Nevertheless, both he and Jacob were grateful for the extra time they had to prepare their answers, waiting for the soldier to translate.

"I already told this fellow here," Morris said, pointing toward the translator, "we're just looking around. Taking some time off before we go back to university in New York. I go to Queens College and my friend here goes to NYU. That's. . ."

The officer spewed a flurry of Arabic toward his subordinate, revealing not only his impatience, but also that both sides were pretending they did not understand the other's language. Jacob and Morris now understood that they were in the hands of professional intelligence officers, clearly well trained by the British. With no possibility of escape or rescue, they realized that in a matter of hours they would end up either hung as spies or, most likely, thrown to a mob for more prolonged execution. Of their own accord, Jacob could feel the bottoms of his feet burning and his scrota retract.

"Enough!" the translator said with surprising anger. "We asked you what you were doing here."

"I already told you," Morris said wearily. "We're just visiting here on holiday."

"On holiday?" the soldier said incredulously, without waiting for his superior to continue the questioning. "In the middle of a war, you come to our country on vacation?"

"Well, it's not exactly a war now, is it?" Jacob pointed out, unable to resist the tease. "We thought there was a truce going on."

As the soldier whispered to his officer, Jacob understood that they both believed he was lying. Real tourists would be terrified at this point, but these two arrogant Americans were acting as if this was all an inconvenient lark.

"Where are you staying?" the officer asked next.

"At the hotel," Morris answered, before realizing that they could easily check this detail. In fact, they had been sleeping in their own camp outside of town.

"Yes? Then where may I ask is your key?"

"At the hotel," Morris said with a shrug. "We left it with the clerk."

Then, with no transition, the next question came out of nowhere. "Do you have sunglasses?"

"Sunglasses?" Morris asked. "You want to know if we have sunglasses?" He wondered what the hell that was all about. Was there some trick here he was missing? "Ah," he said hesitantly, "no, I guess we don't."

"You are tourists," the soldier said with a knowing smile, as if he had just caught them in a carefully laid trap, "but you don't have sunglasses."

Jacob and Morris looked at one another in confusion. Were they missing something here? What the hell did not having sunglasses have to do with being a spy? They thought it best to just keep their mouths shut.

Over a period of two hours, the officer continued to pepper them with questions about the most obscure, unusual subjects—what they had for breakfast, whether they knew how full the moon had been the previous night, what they thought of the capital city of Damascus. If this was some secret interrogation technique taught to them by the British military intelligence, it only succeeded in making the prisoners more frustrated and impatient.

"We demand to see a representative from our embassy," Jacob finally blurted out. "Enough of this shit! You've got no reason to hold us. We told you that we are just tourists. If you don't want us around, then fine, we'll leave. I'd have thought you'd want a little business around here with. . ."

Jacob stopped when he saw the expression on Morris's face. He turned around in his chair to see the officer holding out both his palms. In each hand he held one of their pistols. Looking directly at the two of them, he asked them in Arabic what they were doing walking around the town carrying the weapons of assassins. His look signaled that they had better be very careful not only with what they said, but how they said it.

Jacob looked toward the interpreter, waiting for him to translate the question that was already quite self-evident. "Hey," he said with a disarming smile, "you'd have to be crazy to walk round this place without some kind of self-defense. As you said, there's a war going on. And then there's bandits and killers too."

"And may I ask," the officer said slowly and calmly, "when was the last time you fired this pistol?"

"Oh, gee, I don't know. I'd say about. . ."

"A week ago," Morris finished the sentence, suddenly realizing where things were going. "It was a week ago, wasn't it Jacob? We were practicing in a field, shooting at lizards and sand rats."

"You're sure it was a week ago?" the officer asked again, this time bringing the pistol in his right hand up to his nose and smelling like a connoisseur with a fine wine.

"I don't know," Morris said hesitantly. "Could have been sooner. What do you think Jacob, what, four, five days ago?"

"Could be right," he said absentmindedly. He was staring at the two doors, wondering if they might somehow make a break for it. At least if they were shot escaping it would be far better than anything else these people had in mind for them. He would not see his family again. They would never even know what happened to him. He would just disappear, probably end up chopped into a dozen pieces. He wondered what his rabbi would say about not being buried in hallowed ground as a good Jew. Would God understand the circumstances? Would God forgive him for these things he had done?

Jacob looked up from his chair to see the officer standing over him screaming something. He could not actually hear the screaming—for some reason, the sound seemed to be blocked out for a moment, as if he was gone from the room although his body remained present—but he could see everyone else in the room flinch, and he could see the cords in the man's neck standing out—definitely angry, verging on out of control.

For some reason, once the officer started yelling at them, the rest of the soldiers joined in, screaming in Arabic that they were liars and spies. The thing they could not figure out, and the one reason they seemed to be holding back from shooting them on the spot, was that the two of them did not appear to be Jewish. Morris, in particular, really confused them because of his blonde hair and blue eyes.

Just when it seemed the officer was about to grab Jacob around the neck and pull him out of the chair, the mystery door opened up with a bang and a figure appeared. He was a small man, obviously of some importance and rank, and extremely well built. When Jacob noticed his muscular arms, barrel chest, and thick neck, he recognized with a start that this was the same man they had been sent to kill, or at least to assess the possibility of such a mission.

The colonel was known all over Syria as an accomplished wrestler who still competed in tournaments. Like many of the best

Arab officers, he was a British trained professional, highly disciplined and fastidiously dressed. He wore his gray hair in a short brush cut, as uncharacteristic for an Arab as his clean-shaven face and perfect teeth. Along with his brightly shined knee-high boots, he wore a Sam Browne belt that held a holster at his side. With professional interest, Jacob noticed he carried a Webley, Mark 6 revolver, heavy for an officer's sidearm but also quite accurate with a 6-inch barrel. This was a man who obviously knew his business and probably accounted for the high level of training that they had encountered so far in his staff.

"What's going on here?" the colonel asked his officer, obviously irritated by the interruption in his office.

"We caught these spies, Sir," the officer explained in Arabic as he came to attention.

When the colonel turned to examine the two prisoners, Jacob and Morris smiled as disarmingly as possible. They sure did not look like dangerous spies but indeed resembled harmless American college students with their slouching posture and easy-going nature. He studied them for a moment, then called out to the officer in charge, directing him to lead the Americans into his office. He then turned and marched back through the door.

With surprising courtesy, the English-speaking soldier escorted them inside the office, followed by four of the guards. The colonel was sitting behind his desk, flanked by a large window overlooking the gardens leading up to the hedge. Once Jacob and Morris were seated in the two chairs before the desk, the colonel resumed the questioning with exaggerated politeness. Even when they replied evasively and with largely unsatisfactory answers, the colonel remained calm and unflappable, as if he had all the time in the world to chat with these Americans. Whether he was tired of staring at the soldiers, shifting their weight from one foot to another as they waited impatiently for their colonel to allow them to shoot these infidels, or he decided to try a different interrogation strategy, the guards were dismissed from the room with a wave of the hand and barked orders. They were told to wait outside the door until they were needed. Apparently, they were used to such an arrangement because they trotted out of the office without a look back. Just as the door closed, Jacob noticed that they stationed themselves on either side of the door, while there was still a crowd of soldiers sitting around the table apparently discussing their case.

"So, if I understand you, what you are saying is that you are just visiting our town, on holiday. You happen to be carrying pistols for your own protection. And the reason your visas are not signed properly. . ." The colonel looked up from the identity papers sitting on the desk, shaking his head, "They are poor forgeries by the way."

Morris started to protest, but the colonel ignored him and continued. "I just don't know what to do with you."

Morris started to speak again but stopped when he saw the colonel rise from his seat and stare out the window to the garden below. There were flowers blooming in the beds that ran along the perimeter. The bit of greenery and color was a welcome relief from the grays and beiges that dominated the landscape in the front of the building.

"So," the colonel said with his back to the prisoners, "may I ask you again why you have decided to visit us in the middle of a war?" He glanced over his shoulder for a moment but then continued looking out the window.

"Well," Jacob answered, "as we told your guys out there, we were just looking for a little excitement so we've been traveling around the area. A lot of times people go to the beach to watch a typhoon, don't they?"

The colonel remained perfectly still as he stood there, speaking slowly and softly, yet with an undercurrent of menace. "You think our little war is a joke, is that it? You think this is all for your entertainment, you Americans who are sending money and guns to our enemies?"

"Colonel," Morris said as he rose from his seat and walked over to the window, "would it be possible for us to meet with a representative of our embassy? I'm sure he could straighten this out."

What the hell is Morris doing? Jacob thought in a panic. They had to be very careful not to do anything to antagonize this guy. They were completely at his mercy. The best they could hope for is that they would be treated as prisoners of war, and perhaps sent to prison in Damascus. Just as he thought this, he realized how unlikely this fate would be. But it was important to hold on to some thread of hope. It was taking every ounce of his resolve to stop himself from breaking into tears. He had never been so scared and helpless in his life.

Morris and the colonel were standing about four feet apart, both enjoying the view as they chatted about the fictitious travel itinerary that the boys had supposedly been following during their school summer holiday. Jacob was no longer listening to the conversation but was instead fascinated by the subtle dance that seemed to be going on between the two of them. He noticed that Morris maintained a careful distance between the two of them, but then would take a small, almost imperceptible step in the direction away from the officer. Then the colonel would unconsciously follow Morris's lead, taking a step to the right as well. After another minute of idle conversation, Morris would again shift his weight first to the left foot, then as he leaned to the right, he took another small step. Again, the colonel also moved in that direction, but closing the distance a few inches at a time. Within the course of 10 minutes or so that Jacob had been watching this interaction, he noticed that the two of them were now standing side by side not more than a foot separating them.

Again, Jacob wondered what the hell Morris was doing. Just when he thought about interrupting this little chat, he was horrified to see Morris suddenly turn and grab the colonel in a bear hug from behind. Not at all a smart thing to do, Jacob thought, as he jumped out of his chair to try and lend some help to his struggling partner who was thrown off by the bull of a man as if he was just an annoying insect. Jacob was still circling around the desk when he saw Morris duck under the man's outstretched arms that had been used to break the hold—it looked like some sort of instinctual wrestling maneuver. With a smooth motion, as if he had been practicing this exact move all his life, Morris reached under the colonel's arm, lifted up the flap of his holster and grabbed the Webley.

When Jacob saw Morris bringing the huge pistol up to the colonel's face, he took cover behind the desk. It was a good thing, too, because the large-caliber weapon took out a very large chunk of his head. The explosion in the small room was so loud that Jacob could hear nothing except for a high-pitched ringing in his ears. When they had practiced firing these weapons at the range, they had always used ear protectors of some sort. He could not imagine that anything could be so painfully loud. He was stunned by the sheer volume of the noise, but even more so by Morris's unexpected action. They had never talked about doing such a thing; Jacob never had an inkling that his partner was even thinking about such a crazy stunt.

When Jacob peeked above the desk, he saw Morris yelling something at him but still could not hear a thing. It was easy enough to figure out what they had to do next. The door was already opening and some very angry soldiers were about to shoot them dead. Morris had pushed the windows outward and was half crawling through the narrow opening when the first soldier appeared through the door. Using all his weight, and a running start, Jacob launched himself at the door, closing it painfully against the leg of the first man. He then pivoted, running back toward the window, and leaped through the narrow space that Morris had opened. Bullets were kicking up clods of the rich soil at their feet. For some reason, they were aiming low, trying to hit their legs and somehow take them alive. Or maybe they were just terrible shots, Jacob considered gratefully as they approached the protective hedge along the outside perimeter.

Once they started to scale the wall of foliage, and heard bullets whizzing above and to the side of their heads, Jacob decided they must indeed have been lousy marksmen, or at least so shocked by the murder of their leader that they could not draw a proper bead on their fast-scurrying targets. As they reached the top of the hedge, Jacob looked back and saw a dozen or more soldiers running across the garden in their direction. In seconds they would be upon them.

There seemed to be screaming everywhere. People were running. Shots were fired. In a part of his mind, Jacob recognized not only the sound of small arms, but somebody was firing a machine gun in controlled bursts. Must be somebody on the roof, Jacob thought as he finally joined Morris at the top of the hedge and flipped himself recklessly over the other side.

Pain. Terrible pain. Was he hit? Couldn't be dead. Too much pain. Jacob was lying on his back, the breath knocked out of him, tangled with Morris. They both looked up and saw that whereas the hedge had been only about six feet high on the one side, it was almost twice that high as it dropped into a ditch on the edge of a back alley. The good news is that the bullets now perforating the hedge were going comfortably over their heads.

It was a miracle that they had not broken any bones, although Morris was moving with a pronounced limp. Jacob thought that he might have cracked some ribs, but otherwise, he considered himself in reasonably good shape—except for the fact that he still could not hear very much. For now, he considered that a blessing, as he was already so terrified he would rather not know the full extent of their pursuit.

Jacob and Morris hobbled down the alley that ran behind the building. They had no clear idea of an escape plan, except to try and stay ahead of the soldiers who were now cresting the hedge, but taking their time to climb down the other side. Between Morris's groans over the pain in his injured ankle, and Jacob's jagged breaths, they certainly would not be making a silent exit. It hardly mattered anyway, because there was really only one way they could go, and that was out the alley to the front of the building.

Expecting to find a whole company of enemy soldiers poised at the alley exit, they were positively shocked to see the familiar jeep idling in front. Somehow, Sal, Rudy, and Sammy had followed them to the command headquarters when they saw they had been captured. They must have waited under cover until they heard the gunfire, positioning themselves to provide support. Both Sammy and Sal were laying down suppressing fire with Sten guns, keeping any of the soldiers inside the building from pursuing them out the door. Because of where they were parked along the side, the only soldiers who had a direct line of fire were the ones on the roof.

"Come on!" Rudy yelled encouragement to Morris and Jacob. The two of them were obviously having difficulty moving all that quickly. "Get your asses moving!"

Sal backed the jeep up a hundred yards, bringing it closer to the hobbling team members who were breathing raggedly. Morris and Jacob climbed gingerly into the vehicle, and before they could even close the door, Sal took off spraying up sand from the back wheels. Both Sammy and Sal continued shooting the machine pistols, aiming for the tires of the vehicles that would most likely be pursuing them.

"Are you okay?" Sammy asked from the front seat. "What happened?"

Jacob just nodded his head, still unable to hear all that well. It took too much energy just to breathe without adding to his discomfort. Each bump in the road seemed to send a jolt of agony into his side from the bruised or cracked ribs.

By now, they were moving so quickly that further conversation was impossible. Each of the boys held on tightly as Sal pressed the jeep as fast as it would barrel down the dirt road. When they looked behind them, they could not see pursuit following through the limited visibility. It would not be long before the whole damn Syrian army would be following.

They came to a fork in the road with one sign pointing south down the Golan Heights toward the valley in Palestine below, and the other going due west deep into the interior of Syria. Sammy, acting as navigator, pointed toward the west fork, telling Sal to go left heading in the opposite direction from where their pursuers would ever expect. Although they had no way of confirming that their feint worked, in the two hours they proceeded along the deserted road, they never noticed anyone following.

Following Sammy's directions, Sal worked his way around back roads, at times even going cross-country across desert, until they circled around back to the road that headed down the Golan Heights. Once they could resume a reasonable speed limit, Sal followed up on Sammy's original question.

"What the hell was that all about?" he asked with genuine relief in his voice, amazed they had been able to escape.

"Oh," Morris answered casually, "just a little misunderstanding about some paperwork."

"Yeah? I bet," Sal said with a laugh. "So, were you at least able to scout things out so we can get the guy? We might as well salvage something from this disaster."

"Don't worry," Morris answered, nudging Jacob sitting next to him. He cried out in pain with his ribs poked. "We took care of it," Morris said simply.

"What? You gotta plan?"

"I told you. We took care of it."

"Whatta ya mean, you took care of it? What's that supposed to mean?"

"Just what I said," Morris laughed again, turning to see how Jacob was doing. As much as it hurt, Jacob could not help but laugh either.

When Morris told the story of what happened, and how they ended up alone in the office with the same guy they had been sent to kill, everyone in the jeep laughed hysterically. They could not stop. Just as one of them would begin to calm down, another would start up again, setting them all off in a fit of hysteria.

Part of their laughter was certainly an expression of relief, but another part was far more disturbing. Whereas just months earlier, they had all been so horrified at taking a human life, it had now become so routine that the escapades struck them as comical. It had now become a matter of just crossing another target off the list and moving on to the next one.

As Jacob sat in the jeep with his friends, thinking about what a miraculous escape they had made, he could not help but compare how different this was from the times he would get into fights back home. It scared him how much he was enjoying himself.

Chapter 9

Capture
September to December 1948

The atmosphere in the training camp, and in the whole city of Haifa, was jubilant. The Israelis now seemed to have the war won, or at least fought to a draw. They had rebuffed Arab invasions and even attacked successfully against occupied territory. It seemed that they would now take advantage of the disarray and chaos among the Arabs, blaming one another for their defeats, and so hoped to expand the borders of their tiny country. The main problem they faced was the race against the clock before the British–Arab coalition called another cease-fire just when the Jews gained momentum.

Troops were redeployed and resupplied. Fresh guns and ammunition were brought into play. And anytime UN observers looked the other way, limited operations were mounted. Assassinations were particularly suitable operations during this time until the Israelis would be permitted to mount their next offensive. At this point, the whole Arab union started to unravel, each country now negotiating separately with Israel for the most favorable terms. Except for a few pockets of resistance in Southern Lebanon and in Egypt, the Arabs had lost their taste for war.

These days, it was unusual for Mordechai to visit the team at the camp. He preferred to conduct business and issue orders via couriers or the telephone. He seemed to be preoccupied with other responsibilities, perhaps those related to negotiating the coming peace and preparing to govern a new country. Once he had assembled the team in the briefing room, he took more time than usual, even for him, to get to the point.

"I can't tell you how proud I am of you boys and what you've done here," he began his talk. He then recited a list of all the missions the team had completed, including even the minor actions in which they had been sent into villages to do reconnaissance.

Rather than having the intended effect of showing Jacob and the others how appreciative he was, Mordechai was instead making them all very nervous. This was so unlike him, and they just wished that he would get to the point. After a talk they had the previous night in a bar, which had touched upon death, they were all feeling more than a little homesick and ready to go home. Not only was the war in its last stage, but the missions were becoming more and more dangerous. After dozens of forays into parts of Southern Lebanon and Jordan, they could no longer operate quite so anonymously. The bounty on their heads had been raised to a substantial sum, especially during these times, and they could easily be recognized if anyone had a decent description of them.

"I have one more job for you boys," Mordechai finally mentioned, and then you can all take a little vacation. Thirty days leave, even time to visit home if you like."

Now that struck Jacob as *really* strange. Mordechai had to know that if they left, not all of them would return. After all, they were volunteers, in no way compelled to remain in the Israeli Defense Forces. Jacob just had a bad feeling about what was coming.

"Compared to what you've already done, this will be a cakewalk."

Rolled eyes and groans all around. That was what Mordechai always said before he presented them with some ridiculously impossible mission. After all, the only assignments they ever brought to this group were the ones that could not be handled any other way.

"I want you to go into Lebanon."

More groans. "That's where you want us to go for a holiday?" Rudy called out.

"Not that far. Just across the border. There's a village in the area that is about to hold an election, or at least the kind of election they have there where they will choose their leader from among several men. There is one guy who, if he gets in power, is going to make trouble at a time when everything is just starting to settle down. Most of the Lebanese have accepted that we will be their neighbors. Many of the people don't even mind the arrangement since they have been living, trading, and working with us for centuries."

They had all heard this lecture before many times. It was a mystery, in a way, what this war was really all about. Arabs and Jews had indeed been coexisting for thousands of years. They even descended from the same tribes at one point, even though their religious convictions evolved in different directions.

"This one troublemaker is saying that we will work to make Southern Lebanon a Christian country, to convert all the people so as to provide a buffer between us and the Muslims. While it would certainly be in our interest if some of the more radical Lebanese did adopt a more Christian spirit of forgiveness, don't they realize that Christians have been killing one another just as long as we have? But the main thing. . ."

"What do you want us to do, Mordechai?"

Everyone turned to stare at Morris. This was so unlike him to show impatience. He was the one who was most consistently tolerant and indulgent. During missions, he could stand in place for hours and not do anything more than blink and breathe. During the long-winded briefings, he was the one who would sit most quietly, rarely interrupting the proceedings to even ask a question.

"I'm getting to that, Morris."

"Just tell us what you want us to do," he answered him in a challenging voice. The whole atmosphere in the room was charged with tension, not only because of Morris's remarks but also because of the residue of the previous night during which they had articulated for the first time that they wanted out. They had regrets about some of the things they had done. They had even started to wonder if any of their actions made any kind of difference.

"Okay," Mordechai said, looking directly at Morris. "I want you to stop the discussion in this village."

As usual, he neglected to say how he wanted the job done. Increasingly, as the team's successes mounted up, he left more and more of the operational details to the boys, letting them handle things any way they preferred. Mordechai's job now involved telling the team what he wanted, and then providing any logistical support or backup that might be requested. This was a perfect arrangement for him because not only did he have plausible deniability if the team was captured and their activities came to public eye, but the Haganah would be insulated from direct involvement.

The mission sounded simple enough. They would ride up to the village, using the main highway north, and take the guy out. They had operated in this vicinity many times before, so they did not even see the point of scouting the area. They could be there and back in a day, and then start to head home.

***

The open jeep made prolonged conversations difficult, but Jacob and Morris were so excited about their upcoming leave that they could not stop talking to one another about their plans. Morris confided that he was going to take the next available ship home to be with his fiancée, and he was not going to be returning. Immediately after returning to the East Bronx, he planned to be married and start a family. He talked about going into business with an enthusiasm that surprised the others who had no idea about his plans for the future. He was certain his father would help him get started, provide a little seed money.

"Hey," Sal chimed in. "Me too."

"Me too what?" Morris teased him, knowing where the conversation was leading because Sal had not stopped talking about the subject for months.

"You know. The pizza joint. I've learned a lot about getting along with different kinds of people just from hanging out with you guys and all. Having a successful restaurant just ain't about making good food. You gotta be charming too."

Jacob kept his thoughts to himself, but he could not stop thinking that their most successful skills these past years had been directed toward killing people without getting caught.

"So," Sal continued, his voice rising louder so the guys up front in the open jeep could hear him as well, "I was thinking that maybe I've been thinking too small. I was thinking maybe I could open up a few stores, maybe one over in the Bronx so you guys could enjoy my cooking. And then maybe one in Westchester too."

"You'll be a regular franchise, won't you?" Jacob prompted him, trying to get in before Morris made another wisecrack. He realized how important this conversation was to all of them. It was like with the prospect of going home, they were finally talking about themselves at a much deeper level. Or maybe it was the prospect of facing danger again.

"And maybe I'll do some racing too while I'm at it." Sal listed all the different tracks in the area where he might do some driving. He was very pleased with himself that he had a definite plan.

Not to be outdone, Rudy felt strongly that with all his experience with radios and electrical equipment, especially the on-the-job training he had these last few years under the most stressful circumstances imaginable, he would have no trouble getting a job with a major company like RCA.

"Yeah?" Sal pressed him, a bit irritated that he had been interrupted before he finished telling his whole elaborate plan. "So how are we going to put this shit on our resumes? What you going to tell an employer? Hey, I was the communications specialist for a top-secret assassin team in Palestine. You just better hope there're no Arabs who are in charge as they might not appreciate your background." That quieted them all for a few miles as they bounced along the rutted road heading north.

"So," Jacob yelled toward the front seat, "what about you Sammy?" He wanted to keep everyone relaxed and talking as much as possible.

"I guess I'll go back to school. Earn a degree. Maybe go into teaching or something." He looked back over his shoulder toward Jacob. "You won't be the only college graduate." Jacob smiled. That was exactly his plan as well, to go to City College, study pharmacy or maybe even medicine. That had long been his plan.

Although Jacob found it difficult to imagine operating in the future without his partner and best friend, he admitted that he was going to stick around until the very end. He kept thinking of returning home, but as much as he missed his parents and sister and friends, it felt like the life he would resume would be so ordinary compared to what he was doing now. He did not think seriously about remaining in Israel, but he did want to see some more of Europe. Maybe he would spend the month in France.

Rudy, who had overheard snatches of their discussion, chimed in, "Hey, I'll go with you. I hear those French girls are really deprived after all those war years."

"How about you, Sal?" Rudy asked their driver.

"How about me what?" As was his custom, Sal was concentrating intently on his job, not only driving their vehicle but scanning for trouble.

"What are you going to do after we get back?"

"Oh," he grinned. "I go to visit family in Italy. Maybe some of you come with me."

The conversation, even over the sound of the wind and engine noise, continued with all the things they might do in Italy. Morris remained silent, having already decided on his own plan, but unwilling to share it with anyone else. The others found it difficult to separate, even during their time off. They had spent so much time together over the past two years that they felt lost when alone.

"What's that?" Sammy interrupted, pointing ahead. Riding shotgun in front, it was his job to share with Sal the scouting responsibilities.

"I don't see nothin'," Rudy complained. "Just relax. We're almost there."

Since Sammy had the best eyes among them, especially when it came to searching the desert landscape, Jacob leaned forward in the back seat to confirm his sighting. Sure enough, there was some sort of blockade ahead.

"Oh shit. Oh shit. Oh shit." Sammy was muttering to himself, reaching under the front seat for the machine pistol they carried for just this sort of situation. The little Berettas would be useless in a firefight.

"Just be cool," Jacob reassured him. "It's probably just a check-point for reviewing documents. We have perfect papers, so there's nothing to worry about."

Three guards approached the open jeep, one from the front and the other two from the sides. If their intent was hostile, they were doing an excellent job of spreading themselves out for an ambush. Each soldier was armed with MP 40 Schmeisser machine pistols, courtesy of their German suppliers. The weapons, capable of spraying 10 rounds per second, were casually pointed in their direction. There was no way that the boys could draw and fire before they would be cut down.

"Your papers please," the first guard approached Sammy in the front seat, assuming he must be the one in charge. Because he had spoken to them in Arabic, Sammy only shrugged, indicating he did not understand. The guard tried Hebrew next, evoking the same response.

"Do you speak English?" Jacob called out from the back seat. "We're Americans."

"Oh, Americans!" the guard smiled, then lowered his gun. But since that seemed to be the extent of his English, he gestured for papers. Once Jacob handed them over, he laid them out on the front of the vehicle and inspected them carefully. At one point he rubbed his finger across the seal and even held the document up to the light.

At the same time, the two other guards remained in a ready position, their gun barrels pointing toward the ground but their fingers resting on the trigger guards, just close enough that they could spray the entire vehicle if they so chose.

Finally, the head guard returned the papers. "You go now," he said pointing toward the village.

Rather than feeling relieved by their close call, Jacob and the others were increasingly uneasy about what lay ahead. They now realized that they had been very stupid riding in an open jeep like this. If the guards or the villagers had any kind of description about the Jewish team that been operating in their area, then they would know to look for five men riding together in a jeep.

"Sal," Jacob called up to the front. "Do you know any way we could circle back and get the hell out of here? I've got a very bad feeling about this."

Sal just shook his head no. "Once we go through the village we can turn around, but see," he said pointing ahead, "it's too late now."

Sure enough, they were just arriving on the outskirts of the town and there was some sort of assembly going on, hundreds of people milling around the streets. As the jeep approached the town square, Sal began to swerve to the left, looking for an unobtrusive place to park that would make for a quick getaway. Standing directly in front of the vehicle, blocking their path, was a young boy of about 14 years of age. He was screaming something, pointing in their direction, but nothing could be heard over the general sounds of the crowd now making their way over to the jeep.

"Shit Sal, get us the hell out of here!" Sammy screamed, grabbing the wheel with his own left hand to turn them around.

"Can't move. Can't back up," Sal answered in frustration. Behind them, blocking any hope of escape, were a half dozen other teenagers who were now advancing more aggressively.

"It's them! It's them!" could be heard clearly now from the crowd. "They are here!"

Whether the guards at the blockade had somehow announced their arrival or the boys had been recognized from their physical descriptions that had been circulated for some time no longer mattered. The reality was that they were now surrounded on all sides by dozens, then over a hundred villagers. Their screams were deafening, especially the high-pitched calls from the women.

It was the worst nightmare that any of them had ever imagined. If they had thought about being killed at all, it was a swift and sudden bullet to the brain. But this murderous crowd had vengeance on its mind, and a swift execution would be out of the question. Immediately, Jacob remembered a conversation on the ship to Malta when his friends had been talking about all the ways the Arab villagers would torture captives. At the time, the thought of having the bottom of one's feet beaten by pipes seemed like the worst possible fate. Since that time, Jacob had heard a hundred stories of torture and mutilation that were far worse. He had discovered victims of these atrocities himself in which the man's penis had been cut off and stuffed into his mouth. There was some question as to whether he was still alive or not at the time.

The jeep was now being rocked back and forth, side to side, all the while they heard the screams, "Death! Death to the Jews!"

Rudy was on the radio, desperately trying to call for help, while the others drew their weapons hoping to stall the crowd for a little while until reinforcements could arrive. If the crowd even noticed the guns, they gave no indication of fear or hesitance.

"What's going on Rudy?" Jacob yelled over the crowd. "When can they get here? Did you tell them we're surrounded?"

Rudy was still talking into the radio, repeating his request for help again and again, when someone from the crowd snatched it out of his hand and threw it into the outreached hands. There was a roar of approval from the villagers who proceeded to stomp the radio into pieces.

"Did you get a response?" Jacob asked again. "When are they coming?"

"It's hard to tell," Rudy answered. "There's a unit that can get here in a half hour. Maybe. But they weren't sure. It's possible. . ."

Rudy never finished the sentence, nor perhaps ever spoke again, because the next thing they knew the jeep was overturned and the boys were yanked out. The last thing Jacob saw as he was pinned to the ground was his four friends being carried off into the desert, each one in a different direction. He frantically tried to make eye contact with Morris, at least to say goodbye, but by then his friend appeared unconscious, already beaten senseless.

It might have been only a few minutes, or maybe even hours—by then time had lost all meaning—there was only pain. Jacob tried to keep his head covered as best he could, but the kicks would then be drilled into his ribs and back. Each inhale felt like he was breathing fire. The last thing he heard before he passed out was the sound of gunfire.

***

First there was only taste, the most horrible taste imaginable. It was more than sour and bitter; it felt like something had died in his mouth, something that had been dead for some time. The taste had its own putrid odor.

Next there was sound. He heard a machine gurgling, and other indistinct noises that for some reason reminded him of school. There were voices, but they were not Arab voices. Unless he was mistaken, he heard English, but with some strange sort of accent.

For some reason, the thought had not yet occurred to him that he could open his eyes and see for himself what was going on around him. His eyelids felt too heavy to lift. Everything about his body felt heavy as if encased in a stiff wrapping. Even he could not exactly call it pain, there was something about his breathing that wasn't right. It was as if his body was no longer a part of him, as if it was *out there* somewhere while he was *in here*.

Purely as an experiment, Jacob decided to peek open an eye. This was hardly an instantaneous decision, as he spent many minutes, or perhaps hours or days, trying to decide if opening his eye would be an altogether good thing. It wasn't fear exactly that changed his mind each time he considered the option; it was just that he could not concentrate on any one thought long enough to act upon it. His mind kept drifting away to thoughts of home.

It was the voice that decided things for him. He just *had* to see who it belonged to. Once he opened the lid, he was surprised to discover that he had not needed to worry, because whatever was out there was so fuzzy and unfocused that it felt much better to keep the lid shut.

"Where am I?" he croaked in a voice that was not his own. Or at least that was what he meant to say. In fact, the sounds he made more resembled a clearing of the throat.

"You're in hospital," the British voice answered him. Unless Jacob was mistaken, it sounded Cockney. And to further validate that assumption, he was surprised that he noticed that characteristically English way of leaving out the article before the noun. Instead of saying, "in *the* hospital," the limeys act as if there is only one.

"Where are my friends?" Jacob asked, but all that came out were the words "where" and "friends" with the part in the middle garbled. Nevertheless, the British hospital person—a nurse? a doctor?—understood the gist of the message.

"I'm afraid, dear, that it's just you. They brought you in over a week ago, that Jewish lot. None of us thought you were going to make it, all beat up as you were."

Jacob tried to form his next question, but he felt so confused he could not figure out what to ask next. He had been in the hospital a week? None of the others had been brought in with him? What the hell had happened? But Jacob realized that those were questions he did not need to ask, even if this nurse or doctor—she must be a nurse, he decided, since she was so friendly—knew the answers. Jacob was absolutely shocked to discover that he was still alive, but he held out no such hope for his friends.

The nurse must have been speaking to him for some time, but Jacob realized that he had not been paying attention. She said something about his injuries that must have been pretty bad judging from how proud she sounded that he was still alive. If he could take her word for things, he had a broken back, several broken ribs, multiple skull fractures, and internal damage that, as yet, could not be fully assessed. So that was why he felt like he was entombed like a mummy. He must be wrapped up pretty tightly.

He checked out for a minute but then heard her talking about his leg. Apparently it was pretty messed up. "It was broken in so many places dear we almost had to amputate it right about here." As she touched him mid-thigh, he could feel a shiver run up his leg to his groin. Even with all the morphine in him, he still felt aroused.

Jacob wanted to reach down underneath the sheet and feel himself but found he did not have the energy to sustain any one thought for very long. He just kept drifting away, thinking about the past—and the future.

During the next week during which Jacob regained use of his vision and was finally able to get rid of that awful taste in his mouth, he learned that were was no news to report on his team members, who simply vanished. Jacob supposed that the gunshots he heard were the sounds of their executions, but perhaps they actually came from his rescuers, an Israeli commando unit that had delivered him to his present bed.

Because he had no visitors or phone calls, the only news he heard was from the radio or hospital staff. It seemed that Ben-Gurion decided to boot the Egyptians out of the whole Negev Desert while they had them on the run. They might as well enjoy some of the spoils of this war with all the sacrifices that had been made. Apparently in the north, Mordechai's worst fears were being realized as the Lebanese were indeed trying to extend their borders. Unfortunately for them, what Jacob had not been able to take care of, the rest of the Israeli army was completing. They had been able to counterattack and capture the whole Galilee Valley. There was talk they might even drive farther north to capture Beirut.

As he listened to the news, Jacob wondered idly if the villagers who had killed his friends had perished in the invasion. He found it strange that he no longer cared. This war, this country. . . none of it seemed to matter to him anymore. In a way he was grateful that Mordechai had stayed away. But he was also very, very hurt. It was as if he had been cut loose simply because he was no longer useful.

They used me. They used all of us. Where's Mordechai now? How can he just leave me here? Why doesn't someone tell me what happened to the others? I've gotta start taking care of myself now. There's only me left.

It was during the following week that Jacob was finally able to speak with his parents. They had been notified immediately after Jacob had been brought in that their son was in serious condition, wounded in action, and was not expected to recover. Then there was some question as to whether he would ever walk again.

"Are you okay?" his mother's voice asked him from another world. "They told us you were hurt so badly, that you wouldn't. . . ."

"I'll be all right Ma. They're taking good care of me."

"Did they. . . ? Did they tell you when you can come home?"

It was good to hear their voices. It amazed Jacob, though, how little he missed them or needed them. They were acting like everything would be the same, that Jacob would just come home and they would all pick up where they left off. Did they really think that he would hang out at the candy store all day like he used to? Play stickball with the guys? He was no longer a kid.

The people in the hospital had not told him much of anything. He did not know how long he would be in recovery. He did not even know what happened after he passed out. Had the commandos finished his original mission? Had they recovered the bodies of Sal, Sammy, Rudy, and Morris? Had anyone contacted Morris's fiancée and let her know how he died? The guy managed to survive the worst part of World War II, and all but the very finish of the Israeli War of Independence, and then ended up beaten to death by a mob, or worse.

During the next two months, Jacob did nothing but sleep and practice walking again down the hospital corridors. He still had no visitors and, except for the one phone call home, remained alone. In a way, it felt like he was being punished as the only living witness to events that he could never tell anyone about.

He wondered if it had been worth all this. All those guys died. Jacob was probably going to be a cripple. He would never have a good night's sleep again. He could not stop thinking about heads exploding. There was nothing for him in Palestine and nothing to go home to. He had gone to Palestine as a 17-year-old kid, and he felt he had missed the best parts of his life. What was he going to do now?

How could he have anything in common with his friends after all the shit he had been through? They had been going to college, but this was real here, as real as it gets.

But for most of the time during the long days of recuperation, Jacob felt his mind just turn itself off. There was only his pain, waiting for the next dose of medication, waiting to be released. But released into what? The world outside this hospital seemed so remote that he just could not imagine what he would do after he left. Meanwhile, it was only 50 minutes until his next dose of morphine.

***

Two months after entering the hospital, an officer in civilian clothes arrived to announce that Jacob would be going home. In fact, he would be driven to Tel Aviv that very afternoon. The next day he would board a plane for London, then on to New York.

"We know you have a lot of questions about what happened to your friends," the man said to Jacob as his few belongings were packed up, "but I'm not at liberty to say much about that except that they were not recovered. I've been told by certain representatives of our government that as grateful as they are for the work you've done, they would prefer that you not mention anything about it to anyone. And if you do—well, all I can say about that is that you might be putting yourself at great risk. Well, that's enough about that. Let's get you dressed and out of here. You must be anxious to get home."

And that was all Jacob would ever hear from his handlers. As far as they were concerned, he had never existed. Everything that he and his team had done was never officially sanctioned and completely under the radar. It was all a matter of deniability.

At this point, Jacob could have cared less. He was done with all this, ready to get as far away from here as he could, as fast as possible. His most pressing concern was whether he would be able to travel without becoming sick on the plane.

Jacob walked slowly across the tarmac, limping toward the stairs that led up to the plane. He stared straight down at the ground, steadying himself carefully as he negotiated the stairs. He just felt numb.

Chapter **10**

Return
Bronx, 1949

The plane landed at Idyllwild Airport in New York. Jacob walked awkwardly down the stairs on crutches, trying to keep his balance. Once he hit solid ground, he looked up to find his mother crying and his father stoic as ever. There was someone else standing near them, and it took him more than a few seconds to recognize his little sister; he could not believe how much she had grown.

Jacob's family was appropriately welcoming and loving, but what puzzled him the most about his homecoming was how nobody wanted to talk about where he had been and what he had done. He did not exactly expect a parade, but he thought that maybe his family and the whole neighborhood would be proud that he had just spent two years of his life fighting for the Jewish homeland. These people around here always talked about nothing else but news about Israel, and here was one of their own who had just come back from there and they did not say a word about it.

Maybe it was his eyes. Except for the crutches, Jacob figured he pretty much looked the same. He weighed about the same as when he left, about 145 pounds. While in Palestine, he had bulked up with a growth spurt and all the exercise, but after all that time recovering in the hospital, he had become gaunt and listless.

The worst part was that he could not get around very easily. The crutches proved useless because his shattered shoulder had not healed properly and that made it difficult to put any weight on it. So he shuffled along, his eyes to the ground, and practically everyone ignored him. Even his friends acted as if he had never left, or that he had just been upstate for awhile attending school and was home on holiday.

Frustrated with having to hide a past that he had actually been quite proud of, Jacob broached the subject at the dinner table once.

"How come you never ask me about what happened over there?" he announced one evening when there was a lull in the conversation. His little sister looked up immediately from her plate, and then turned her head back and forth between her parents as if she was a pigeon.

"Son," his father said gently, "it's not that we aren't interested. It's just that we figure it's your business."

He abruptly turned away and looked toward his wife. "Are there any more potatoes or did this growing boy of ours polish them off?" He said this as if this was some sort of joke, but it did nothing to cut the tension.

"So," his mother picked up the lead, "When are you going to be starting school?"

This was typically how things went, not only at home but all over the neighborhood. If anybody cared what had happened and how he ended up such a wreck of a human being, they were too embarrassed to ask directly. Eventually, Jacob just decided to join in with the rest of them and pretend that he had never left. As it turned out, this was fairly easy to do because nothing had changed much in the old neighborhood.

The real problem he had was keeping up with things that had happened in the rest of the world while he was gone. His whole universe had been contained in a piece of property, 50 square miles claimed by four different countries. His only concern had been the geography, politics, and weather patterns in Northern Palestine.

While Jacob had been gone, the Yankees had won the pennant twice, once under a new manager, Casey Stengel. A Negro, Jackie Robinson, had joined the Brooklyn Dodgers across town. Chuck Yeager had broken the sound barrier. Jacob also learned that Israel wasn't even the newest country since Korea had been partitioned. And the Communists now had an atom bomb.

Jacob's body healed as quickly as one could expect in someone so young and healthy. He pretty much kept to himself, breaking ties with his previous friends who seemed to be wary of him anyway. Mostly, he missed Morris and the other guys, the only friends who ever understood—ever *would* understand—what he had gone through.

Tired of his parents pestering him to get out of the house more, Jacob enrolled at City College for a semester, setting his sights on a more ambitious plan of attending medical school. He finally decided to devote his life to being a helper, saving people instead of killing them. This was a time when Jews were not welcomed warmly in professional schools, so the first rejection letters stung terribly. Jacob felt the world owed him something for the sacrifices he had made, and he was not prepared for the disappointments.

By the time the dean at Columbia Medical School had offered encouraging news, Jacob had already enrolled in a college of pharmacy. Excelling in his studies, he then went on to complete a graduate business degree.

Jacob met his wife during the last year of pharmacy school, and they set up their home at the same time he opened his own drugstore after borrowing the seed money from friends and family. As he sat behind the counter each day, his partner manning the cash register, Jacob would imagine that Sal might have a pizza parlor down the block. In fact, because it was never confirmed what happened to his friends, he fully expected that one of them might one day walk into the store with a grin on his face.

Whatever satisfaction Jacob might have felt in launching his own business was tempered by the realization that his partner was skimming money. Because this was a time when matters of honor were considered serious crimes, Jacob arranged for the two of them to spend an evening at the steam bath at Silver's on Coney Island. The two of them were wrapped in towels lounging on the wood benches, steam choking the air, making it difficult to breathe. Once Jacob was sure they were alone and would not be interrupted, Jacob pulled out a Beretta wrapped in the folds of the towels. It was just like the one he carried in Palestine.

"Hey, what's that?" his partner cried out in alarm, then started to laugh as if something was funny.

"What do you think it is asshole?" Jacob then stiffened his arm so the muzzle of the small pistol was aimed right at the guy's forehead.

"Jacob, *shlemiel*, what are you doing? What do you think. . ."

"*Sha!*" Jacob answered him in Yiddish. "Please be quiet." He then sat next to his partner, cradling the pistol in his hand, careful to keep it pointing directly at the man's abdomen.

"Do you think I'm stupid?" Jacob asked him in a voice so soft it was far more terrifying than if he had been screaming at the top of his lungs. "I know what you've been doing in the store. You've been robbing me blind."

"But Jacob, let me explain. . ."

"Enough!" Jacob raised the pistol again and pointed it again right between the cowering man's eyes. Neither one of them was sure what would happen next. Jacob thought about pulling the trigger. It would be so easy. After all, he had done it so many times before. Nobody had seen them come in, so he could leave just as quietly.

The silence must not have lasted more than a few seconds, even though it felt like long minutes to both of them. Finally, Jacob made his decision. With his arm rock steady, he said, "I dissolve our partnership." Then he got up, dressed in silence, turned around, and walked out the door.

As he felt the chill on his seared body, Jacob thought about how close he had come to solving problems the way he had been taught in Palestine. He even went out and purchased the Beretta as soon as possible after he returned, a reminder of what he was capable of doing. He would end up keeping this weapon within close proximity for the rest of his life, although he would never fire it again.

Disillusioned with running his own business, Jacob went to work for a pharmaceutical laboratory, first as a salesman and then later as a manager. With his pharmaceutical training, coupled with his business degree and experience, Jacob quickly rose through the ranks from district to regional to Eastern U.S.

manager. Throughout most of his working life, Jacob remained in some facet of pharmaceutical sales, eventually landing on the West Coast to open his own medical supply company.

After Jacob's three children left home and his wife later died, Jacob returned to the kind of risky work that he had so enjoyed as a youth. After training with the FBI and Drug Enforcement Agency, Jacob became an investigator with the State Board of Pharmacy. Working closely with federal law enforcement agencies, Jacob's job was to reduce fraud and substance abuse among doctors, nurses, and hospital employees. In one of his last cases before retiring, he was part of a team that arrested a dozen nurses who were stealing narcotics. They had been shooting themselves with Demerol to maintain their habits and then giving their patients plain saline solutions in the syringes.

At the time these words were written and this story ended, Jacob had just retired. He was working part time as a consultant and expert witness in legal cases for the state and federal government. He and his second wife were looking for property in Arizona where they might spend their last years.

***

After the year we spent together working on his narrative, Jacob had turned 72 years old but seemed much older. He was in very poor health and had recently recovered from open-heart surgery that did not go as well as expected. He was still plagued by nightmares.

Just the previous week, Jacob had one of his worst dreams ever. He had been captured by an Arab mob that had descended upon him. He kept screaming over and over for his friends, but they had quickly disappeared. It was as if they vanished completely into the sand. He was now totally alone.

Six or seven Arab women pinned him to the ground even though he was thrashing with all his strength. He thought he knew what would come next, remembering his conversation on the boat to Malta when he had first heard about them beating his feet into bloody pulp with metal pipes.

To his surprise, one of the women approached him with a huge sword like something from *The Arabian Nights*. It was long and curved into a moon shape, sparkling in the bright sun. Then with a swift motion, the woman brought the sword down onto his shoulder, severing the arm in a clean blow. Blood started spurting in a fine spray, covering everyone within the immediate vicinity. Rather than backing away, the crowd's frenzy seemed to grow with the geyser of blood.

Jacob was most surprised that rather than feeling the expected excruciating pain, he felt only numb. He must be in shock, he thought, until he heard his wife calling out to him.

What is she doing here? He wondered to himself. I did not even meet her until a few years ago.

"Jacob," he heard again. "Jacob! Wake up!"

He awoke startled to find that he was in his own bed looking up groggily at his wife. He noticed that his arm still felt numb and then found that it was pinned underneath him. It had not been cut off after all, merely bent at an odd angle.

Jacob's wife calmed him down as she often did when he had these night terrors. Things had gotten a lot worse in the past year since he told his story to me, and I feel badly about that. We have been stirring up all these memories again after more than a half-century of keeping them under tight lock and key. Jacob reassured me that this was all for the better, that he needed to get this story out. I encouraged him to see a therapist, but he insisted that he was too old for that.

The heart surgery also complicated things. The last thing he thinks about before he goes to bed each night, feeling the long zipper scar down his sternum where they pried open his chest, is that there is a good chance he might not wake up in the morning. Part of him thinks that he does not care one way or the other. Considering the things he had to do in the war, and what he lived through, he considers himself pretty lucky to have lived this long. He feels he should have been buried in that sand dune with his friends.

Afterword

I looked across at Jacob and observed that he was more sad than usual.

"So is this it?" he asked me.

"Is this what?"

"Are we done now? Will I ever see you again?"

After spilling his guts to me for the past year, telling me his deepest secrets, I could tell that he was having a hard time letting go. In a sense, Jacob had been a client of mine for the past year, but this had been a very different kind of relationship from that found in psychotherapy. As deeply as we delved into his life, Jacob and I had been partners and collaborators.

"No Jacob," I reassured him, and I meant it. "I imagine we'll still be getting together at our usual table every once in awhile. But let me ask you one more question."

Jacob groaned, pretending to be irritated, but I knew he had come to love having an interested audience who listened well. This was a man who had kept a lifetime of secrets inside him. Even his own kids did not seem all that interested in what he had done in his life.

It had taken every ounce of my clinical skills to keep Jacob on track. He tended to ramble a lot, especially lately as his health had deteriorated. Usually, I would have to remind him what the question was.

"I was just wondering what you learned from all this. What's it all mean to you now?"

Jacob shrugged, uncharacteristically speechless. If he was waiting for me to clarify further, I did not help him out. I wasn't really sure myself what I was asking.

"I don't know," he said hesitantly. "I just keep thinking. . ."

"Go on," I prompted him.

"I just keep thinking about that guy in prison, the one I told that he was being abandoned."

"You mean the Moroccan Jew who was going to be hung and was hoping you were there to rescue him?"

"Yeah. That's the one."

"What about him?"

"Well, two things. First of all, that was the hardest thing I ever did in my life. Telling him he was going to die after all and there's nothing I could do to save him."

"And secondly?"

"That I feel just like him."

Section II

A Therapist's Story

Chapter **11**

A True Story
Based on a Lie?

The chronicle might seem as though it is over, but in at least one sense, there is another surprising way that these events continued to unfold. There were some complex and profound consequences for me as a result of spending time with Jacob and functioning as his narrator. I mentioned earlier that I ended up in danger as a result. I said this was a true story, but one that was built on a lie.

There were indeed times during the preceding year I met with Jacob that I frequently looked over my shoulder. I was pretty sure it was my overactive imagination at work, but there were still times when I got the impression I was being watched, if not followed. During our weekly sessions at the sports bar, I noticed one of those huge Ford Excursions with darkly tinted windows follow me into the parking lot. Even I knew from watching movies that this was the vehicle of choice among law enforcement personnel (and perhaps terrorists?).

Putting my apprehensions aside, I continued to ignore a series of spooky episodes that ensued during the year I met with Jacob. I had written a true crime book years earlier, delving into the world of serial killers, which resulted in a series of threatening messages from some of their minions. I also had a few close calls that could have been life-threatening—a motorist, for example, almost ran me off the road while I was riding my bike. Still, I wrote these unnerving experiences off to coincidence. Yet a part of me had so completely entered Jacob's story that there were times I felt myself a part of this world of assassination.

Truthfully, I was just so hooked on this story that there was no way I was going to let it go. I could not recall a time when I had been more excited about a book than this one. I lived and dreamed the latest installment of the narrative, as if it was my own story rather than Jacob's life. Sometimes I would awaken in the middle of the night realizing that I had been reliving some of the events, but with *me* running for my life.

I spent hours each week going through history books, accessing archives online and on microfiche, authenticating many of the scenes and specifics of the story. Jacob was an old man, after all. A lot of the details of his story were hazy at best. In order for this narrative to work, for *any* story to be engaging, it must include all the atmospheric scene setting that makes it come alive.

In order to accomplish this task, I had the challenging job of taking Jacob's often sketchy descriptions and filling in the parts that were missing. For instance, Jacob might say something like this in his typical terse style: "So, there we were, all of us together, and we just looked around."

"What do you mean you just looked around?" I would press him.

"You know, I'd check the possible places where there might be a sniper, or surveillance."

"And what did you see in this village exactly?"

Jacob might hesitate for minute or two, going back five decades to retrieve memories that were buried for so long.

"Were there stucco-like structures surrounding the center market?" I might ask. Prior to each of our meetings, I would do my homework, peruse Web pages, history books, and photo archives, so that I might be able to better picture what Jacob was describing.

"Yeah," he would admit after another lengthy pause. "They were sort of like that. The roofs were. . ."

And so we would work as partners to try to recreate events that happened so long ago. I found this part of the writing assignment thoroughly satisfying, bringing out all my skills, both as a psychologist trying to draw out buried material, and as a writer who was attempting to describe the scenes and events with authenticity and veracity.

One other thing you should know is that I was in a segment of my existence that was otherwise unsatisfying. Sure, I was helping Jacob to tell his story, but he was also filling a hole in my life. Truthfully, I was bored with my job and settled into routines that seemed predictable. I lived for our weekly sessions when I could learn more about the story and then totally immerse myself in fleshing out the details.

Shortly before meeting Jacob, I had resigned my tenured professorship at the university after many years as a teacher and scholar. I was tired of the politics, as well as burned out over the petty conflicts and power struggles that so dominate academic life. I had also been teaching the same classes for over 20 years; it seemed at times that I was just repeating the same semester over and over again. I felt stale and frustrated. I walked away from a guaranteed job for life in order to strike out on my own as a writer.

Things had not been going as well as I had hoped so far. I was struggling to make a living. I missed daily interactions with others while sitting alone in my study. Sure, the arguments and conflicts with colleagues had been infuriatingly draining, but at least there had been some interpersonal contact. Now I spent most of my time in solitude.

I have been reading spy novels and watching war movies all of my life, and I could not believe the good fortune that I was privileged to actually write one myself. It felt like I had won the lottery. I could not wait to get out of bed in the early morning (or often in the middle of the night) and write my heart out. I counted the days until our usual Wednesday meetings when I would harvest the next installment of Jacob's incredible story.

I am sure you can see, then, that I was truly the coauthor of Jacob's narrative. Little did I realize this role would take place in more ways than one. But now I am getting ahead of myself, and we will return to this part of the story a little later.

Cold Feet

Once the story you have read was completed, I next set my sights on launching it into the public domain. It was not difficult to find a publisher for the project, and my editor was anxious to get it into print as soon as possible.

I called Jacob to tell him the fabulous news that his story would be sold. There would be foreign translations and perhaps even movie rights. I was so ecstatic that it took awhile before I noticed that Jacob was unusually silent.

"Jeffrey," he finally said, "I don't think I can go through with this."

"WHAAAT?" I screamed involuntarily. "What the hell are you talking about?" Whatever he was referring to, I could already feel my heart pounding. I knew this was too good to be true. I had finally gotten the break of my life and now I could see it all unraveling before my eyes.

"You said. . ." Jacob started out, then stopped to construct carefully what he wanted to say, and how he wanted to say it. He could tell I was about to explode. "You said if I ever got cold feet that we could stop this. And that's what I want to do."

"Jacob," I said as slowly and calmly as I could, "that was a long time ago that we talked about that possibility. I just spent a year of my life writing this damn book and you think I'm just going to put it on a shelf?" I paused to catch my breath. I was so angry I could hardly think straight. "And why are you telling me this now?"

"Jeffrey, I told you that I killed some very important people. These were from the most wealthy, prominent families in the Middle East. Do you think they will ever forget something like this? If this book is published, they will find me. They will find you. And they will seek revenge."

He actually said it in this melodramatic way that made me stifle a laugh. I wanted to ask him if he was really serious, if this was some kind of joke, but I knew he meant what he said.

"Jacob," I pleaded one more time. "Why did you wait until now to tell me?"

"Let me ask you something, Jeffrey. Have you noticed anything peculiar lately?"

"Like what?" There was no way I was going to give the guy the satisfaction of knowing there actually might be some merit to his fears. As I said earlier, there had been times when I felt I was being stalked by some malevolent presence. But I wrote this off as the logical result of being so immersed in the violent story.

"Like anyone following you," he said. "Like the feeling you are being watched."

I could feel this chill down my back. This guy was paranoid, and I wondered how I could have missed it. He seemed so reasonable and convincing all throughout our conversations. I have been in practice a long time. I like to think that my diagnostic and clinical skills are pretty well honed. I made a few mistakes and missed some things, of course, but I spent a year with this guy and more than 200 hours talking to him.

"I know what you're thinking," Jacob interrupted. "I know you think I have an overactive imagination, but I'm telling you that I am genuinely afraid. I've been looking over my shoulder my whole life, fearful that some relative of someone I killed would come to get me. You forget: I was trained to think this way. The last thing the Israelis said to me before they sent me home was to watch my back. They warned me that if I ever told anyone about what happened I would live to regret it. I could never be sure if they were warning me, or threatening me."

"So, what are you saying now Jacob? That the sons of your victims are hunting for you? And now that you've told me what happened they're going to come after me as well?"

"I don't care if you believe me or not," Jacob responded to my tirade, "but I'm not going through with this. I *can't* go through with this. I wish you'd understand." Then he hung up.

Everything Coming Together

I hoped Jacob would change his mind, but he stubbornly maintained his position. For the next two years, every day I would walk into my office and see the damn manuscript sitting on the top shelf of my bookcase. That pile of paper represented one year out of my life. Among all the books I have written, it was the only manuscript I never published.

I was sitting at my desk with my feet propped up, staring out the window watching the students walking through the quad below. I glanced up toward the bookcase and saw the pages stacked neatly on the top shelf. I just shook my head in frustration. Why did I torture myself by having the book so visibly present? Why could I not throw the thing away and move on?

During the intervening years, I reentered academic life full time, seeing a few clients in my spare time, and I loved the work. I felt totally engaged and busy with an assortment of interesting projects. Yet my attention kept being drawn back to this unfinished story, the one I had worked so hard to produce but nobody had ever read. It just seemed so crazy that I had given in to Jacob's irrational fears. This was ridiculous. I decided it was time to assert myself.

Impulsively I picked up the phone and called Jacob to tell him that I had decided to proceed with the book. I had given his concerns a lot of thought and believed that each of them could be addressed. I reassured him I would protect his identity and would send him his fair share of the proceeds upon publication. I started to marshal my arguments for the really hard sell when, to my surprise, Jacob readily agreed. We were finally going to get the story published!

Now I began the final writing touches in earnest. I contacted researchers in Israel who could help me to corroborate some of the names and dates and locations. I began a correspondence with the archivist for *Machal*, the veterans' organization of North Americans who fought in the 1948 War. I contacted a travel agent about arranging a trip to the Middle East in order to visit the villages and towns described in the book and access the archives of the Haganah (now the Mossad).

Perhaps I should not have been surprised that my story was met with skepticism by the archivist in the veterans' organization. He was a man close to 80 who had flown planes during the war to deliver weapons and supplies. He had devoted his life to studying the history of the Israeli War of Independence and especially the pivotal role played by the North American volunteers.

Our communications became quite animated and passionate, the archivist insisting that these events could not have happened as reported.

"Look," I told him, "I'm a psychologist. I spent a year with this guy. You don't think I can tell when someone is lying? Give me a break! These events happened over 60 years ago. The poor man is experiencing nightmares. For God sakes, he wakes his wife up screaming in Arabic! What do you think happened?"

"Calm down," he said. "Just ask the man several questions. Can you do that? If you get me the answers to these questions, then maybe you got something. First, find out the name of his commanding officer. Second, the name of his unit. He should also have an army identification number because he needed that to get paid. With that information I can access some records and find out what's what. Oh yeah, ask to see his travel papers that he would have needed to get home, something that proves he was actually there at that time."

All of this made perfect sense. I was anxious to take care of these small details and move forward with the project. I just needed this final bit of information from Jacob and we would be off and running. Everything was finally coming together.

There Is a Slight Problem

I could not wait to get Jacob on the phone. I called him later that night to tell him how excited I was about everything falling into place. He recited the latest litany of physical complaints as was his custom. He was having trouble breathing and needed some more tests. His gout was bothering him. "So, how's the family?" he finally remembered to ask.

"Good, Jacob, good. Hey, by the way, I just have a few more questions to ask, do you mind? It won't take more than a minute."

"Sure. Yeah. Go ahead."

"Okay, thanks. I was talking to the guy at *Machal*, you know the veterans group that. . ."

"I'm a member. Sure I know them." Ever since we began the project, Jacob had joined the volunteer organization and said he planned to attend their annual reunion.

"Well, anyway, the guy who's been helping me there told me to ask you just a few questions that would help us find the records on your service. He said I should ask you for the name of your unit, your commanding officer, and your army identification number. And it would also be helpful if you could show me your travel papers that you. . ."

Click.

"Jacob? Jacob? Are you there? Hello?"

After we were disconnected (I could not bring myself to imagine he had actually hung up on me), I sent him an e-mail with the list of questions. When after a few days he did not respond, I sent him a fax with the same queries. Still there was no response. I called his house but he would not answer. When he was home, his wife apologized but insisted he would not take my calls.

So, let me ask you: What do *you* make of that?

At first I considered all the reasonable explanations for why these questions could not really be addressed. Team *Gimmel* was off the books, disowned by the Israelis. He may very well have been told to destroy all his travel documents because he was issued forged papers in the first place. And as volunteers who were part of a commando squad that supposedly never existed, it might very well be impossible to supply definitive proof. Yet with all these considerations, my own painful and inevitable conclusion was that Jacob made up the whole damn story. It most likely had never happened. Once I required him to supply physical proof to back up his claims, that was it, the whole incredible tale vanished in a puff of smoke.

To say I was devastated would be an understatement. My whole world collapsed. Everything that I thought I knew and understood was thrown into chaos. How could I not have seen this coming? Why did I not pick up the clues a long time ago that this was all fiction, that Jacob was playing me? Sure, I have been fooled by clients before, lied to, deceived, and manipulated. Who hasn't? But I had experienced nothing like this complete and total fabrication taking place over more than a year.

Parallel Processes a[...]
Reactions: You Feel M[...]

I know from reading comments by those who r[...]
script that some people feel duped and taken in [...]
may not be true. After investing all the time and energ[...]
into this rather extraordinary narrative, then you fin[...]
end that it is not exactly what it seemed. But isn't that the [...]

I wanted you to feel, to really *know* what it was like, to [...]
about the reality of what you read—and experience in your w[...]
This is not an unusual experience for therapists after all: we a[...]
often forced to consider how much of what our clients tell us ever [...]
really happened.

Some of you are saying to yourselves that the twist on this tale
was no surprise to you, that you were skeptical from the beginning. You just *knew* that this could not be true and you wondered
how I could be so gullible. Well, let me tell you that I have been
kicking myself ever since. Now that I look back I can see some
things I missed, and other things I ignored and denied, and still
other things that I overplayed. But the truth be told (and now you
can see that this really is a book about the meaning of truth), I
really did believe Jacob and had very few doubts about the veracity and authenticity of his story. We spent so much time together.
I knew him. I *knew* him. He was not that bright. He was easy
to read, more transparent than most people I have known. He
just was not capable of lying in a way that I would not have seen
through him.

Then I started to think back on things, review each of our interactions, returning all the way to our very first meeting. During
that initial breakfast when I was about to dismiss him as a cranky
old man, Jacob knew that he had lost me. He was lonely and
depressed. He had nobody to talk to, nobody who paid attention to
him, nobody who valued him. And he could see that I found him
boring and was about to write him off. As a last desperate effort,
he seduced me with a fictitious story that he sensed I needed as
much as he did.

During that breakfast, all I had been trying to do was to
extricate myself from the conversation with this self-centered,

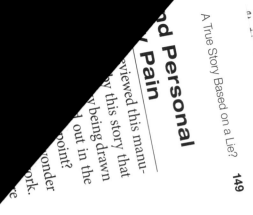

e session, lasting well over
he never asked anything
eetings, the conversation
ising from my seat, about
e dropped the bomb: "I
anyone about it before.
lped down the bait and

ew times that my anten-
ome aspect of his story,
been in a therapist role
id called "evenly hov-
_.. detachment in which I believe

... tells me, and nothing a client tells me. But in this
case, I was seduced by the story and left my objectivity way behind.

I know many professionals, psychologists among them, who go through life skeptical and challenging everything they hear. I always preferred to trust people and see the best in them. I have chosen a way of working in my sessions or classrooms in which I can create an atmosphere in which mutual trust and collaboration are critical to the process. It is not that I am completely naïve, but I prefer to give people the benefit of the doubt whenever possible.

Over time, I grew fond of Jacob and his eccentricities. I knew he was a lonely guy with very few friends and his wife at work all day; he looked forward to our meetings as the highlight of his week. I was so focused on getting what I wanted from the relationship—his story—that I did not stop to consider very often what *he* was getting from the relationship. Like so many people in his position, he just wanted attention. He wanted to be a hero and so he may very well have created a story that had always been his dream. It was a story in which he was everything that he was not in real life: young, fearless, strong, resourceful, and courageous.

Throughout all our conversations, and the whole story that you read, it now appeared to be a work of pure fiction. You may have thought you read a historical account of true events, but I was now convinced this was actually a novel that was cocreated by the two of us, each of us pretending that it all really happened.

My whole world had been turned upside down. How do I know anything that anyone tells me is really true? Every day I see clients in therapy, and students in the classroom, who tell me what disturbs them most and the whole basis for my work is built upon an agreement that they will be honest and I will agree to believe what they tell me.

I went through a period when I began to doubt myself, to question everything that I think I know. Who could I really trust? A client tells me a story about childhood abuse that accounts for feelings of insecurity, but what if it never happened? Yeah, yeah, I know that there are many who say it does not matter as long as the client believes it is true. But it *does* matter on some level.

This revelation so rocked my world that I virtually stopped practicing therapy thereafter. I did not feel like I could trust my judgment about people any longer. I wondered if I could ever tell when someone was putting me on. Before you continue diagnosing my core narcissistic wounds (and you *have* been diagnosing me, have you not?), please understand that I have already been there. I decided it was time to do different work and so devoted myself to administration as a department chair and began writing technical papers and edited books that did not require me to think so much. I needed time to heal.

We Are Not Nearly Done Yet

The story is not over yet, by any means. Maybe it was wishful thinking on my part, but I could not quite let this story go. It was just too simple to say that Jacob made this whole thing up. I still could not quite believe it was possible. Oh, I had by now surrendered to humility and recognized my fallibility (I have made a career writing about failure), but there was still something gnawing at me. I remembered all too well the vivid details with which Jacob would sometimes describe things he had seen and places he had been. By training he was a pharmacist, concrete and methodical. I could not recall any evidence of a vivid imagination (unless he really did make up this story). He just did not seem capable of creating anything this rich and complex.

Every few weeks I would begin to wonder if the story was really true as Jacob reported it. I replayed that last phone call in my mind. Maybe he hung up and would not talk to me because he was so offended that I was questioning his integrity. Perhaps he was still looking for a way to bail out because of his original fears of retribution. Now I was starting to rethink this whole episode in still another light. What if the story really *did* happen as he described it? For those of you who were so certain that you guessed the ending and never believed this story to begin with, what if I told you that I have it on good authority that it really did occur after all?

It was during this latest plot reversal that the phone rang late one night.

"Jeffrey, is that you?"

I had not heard Jacob's voice in many years, but I immediately recognized his thick Bronx accent. "Yes, this is Jeffrey," I said, trying to give myself some time to collect myself. I did not know whether to feel angry or indignant or just hang up on him. But I was also still so damn curious about the end of this story. True or untrue? I so badly wanted to believe him.

"Jeffrey, there's people walking all around. They got white coats on, but it's not cold outside."

"Jacob, where are you? Are you at home?"

"That's why I'm calling you," he said, his voice rising in panic, "I don't know where I am. I think they're taking me somewhere."

I was totally confused. Why was he calling me after all these years? What was he saying? He was not making sense. And then it hit me: Jacob was hallucinating. There went my illusion that he had been telling me the truth. It was clear now that he had been out of it all along. Again I wanted to kick myself for having been so stupid.

"Jacob," I prompted him again after a long silence. "Are you still there?"

"They're taking me away. I don't know where I am. How can they take me away when they don't know where I am?"

"Jacob," I said gently, feeling so sorry for him. "Is Helen there? Is she with you?"

"Helen?"

"Your wife, Helen? Is she there? Can I talk to her?"

When Helen got on the phone, I learned from her that Jacob's health had been deteriorating rapidly in the past year. He had a heart attack, surgery, and was now having memory problems that could have been related to Alzheimer's. Half the time he did not know who she was. The next day she was indeed planning to place him in assisted care because she could no longer handle him.

So here is another end to this bizarre story. Obviously, he must have been delusional all along, right? But how had I missed the symptoms? I had never done a formal mental status examination of Jacob, but I was absolutely positive that several years earlier he had been both coherent and rational, especially for a man of his age.

With another sigh of disappointment, I decided that it would finally be best to just let this story go, resolved that I would never find out what really happened.

***

Several months later I had come to some kind of accommodation, if not acceptance of this situation, when the phone rang late one evening. It was Helen calling to tell me that Jacob died peacefully in his sleep.

"I'm so sorry," I offered. "I know this must have been so difficult for you these last few years."

"Yes, it *was* difficult," she admitted, and then stopped there. In all the years I had known her, Helen never complained about the burdens she carried. And to put it politely, Jacob had always been rather high maintenance.

"Well," she continued after a long pause, "I guess now you can publish the book."

"Publish the book? What are you talking about?"

"Jacob's book. The one you had written about Israel. The one he didn't want to publish."

"But, Helen," I said exasperated, wondering why she was stirring this up again after I had finally found a way to let it go, "it was all a lie. Jacob made the whole thing up. Or rather *I* made the whole damn thing up thinking it was him. He was crazy. You saw that. The guy was hallucinating."

"That was only at the end. Don't you know? It was all true. I should know. I lived with him. I slept with him. I heard those damn nightmares. Don't you think I'd know if he was telling the truth or not?"

I was literally speechless. My heart was pounding so hard I had to force myself to take deep breaths. It was like I was in some kind of alternative universe where things kept getting turned upside down. This made no sense whatsoever. Or actually, maybe it made complete sense. But I was so disoriented I could no longer tell what to believe.

"Helen, let me see if I understand what you're saying because I'm not sure I heard you correctly. Are you saying that this whole story that Jacob told me is absolutely true?"

"Why of course it is! Why would you think otherwise?" She sounded hurt and confused.

I explained how Jacob had been so uncooperative, not helping me to document the facts of the narrative. I told her how skeptical others had been. I described all the fact-checking I had tried to do but could find no way to corroborate the details.

Helen was unbowed, absolutely convinced beyond any doubt that every word in this story was true. We hung up and promised to keep in touch, but soon afterward she moved away and we have not spoken since.

Chapter **12**

Not the End
of the Story

I have gone over the details of this case again and again, and each time I come up with a different conclusion. I have been back and forth so many times I get a headache thinking about it. Sometimes I think it just *had* to be true, most of it anyway. I reassure myself that I just could not be fooled so thoroughly, over such a long period of time, that surely I would have caught Jacob contradicting himself. But then I replay some of our conversations and recall the sketchy plot that Jacob supplied about a particular incident and realize that *I* was the one who filled in the details based on my diligent research. So maybe I wrote this story after all based on Jacob's rough outline of an idea.

After due consideration, I reject that possibility. In so many other ways, in every other context in which we spent time together, Jacob was utterly without guile. He seemed so transparent and predictable that it felt like most of the time I could finish what he was saying; at times it felt like I could read his mind. I could easily anticipate what Jacob's answers would have been had he been willing to address my questions suggested by the archivist. He had been smuggled into Palestine using false papers. He and his team

) the books as official soldiers, and his
He never knew the real name of his
ıai. And as far as travel papers, before
lis, they would have made sure that
·o them after he was sent home. It is
· Jacob's indignant voice explaining

:cept what I heard as the way it is.
ᵤould have been so easily fooled (if I was—
..gain—the lingering doubt), I find solace in the reminder
that one of our jobs as therapists is to exhibit trust. How can we
blame ourselves for being caring, open-minded, trusting, and for-
giving, because that is what we do (Newman & Strauss, 2003)?

If this story is false, or even only half true, points out one
reviewer (Hall, personal communication, 2009), it highlights the
power of the mind to create a story for the sake of an audience, for
achieving some kind of validation and approval, for staying connected to someone with whom one feels a bond. And if it really
is true, then it is just as amazing that the mind can recreate trau-
matic experiences in such minute detail (with help). Was it necessary for Jacob to relive his trauma, to tell his story to an attentive
listener, in order to die in peace? If that is the case, how ironic that
his story has been cast in such doubt.

Hardly the First Time

It is not like I have not been misled or fooled before. It is time to
come clean. I was once director of a psychiatric clinic and super-
vised more than a dozen therapists. It was one big, happy family. My partner and I carefully selected each professional not only
based on his or her professional experience, but on our sense of
what each would be like to socialize with. We had weekly group
meetings, catered by different local restaurants. We had dinners at
one another's homes. We went on weekend retreats. These people
were not only my colleagues but my closest friends.

In the history of poor judgment, there are few blunders more
profound than those I made to recruit and retain this particular group of professionals. It turned out that one therapist had

never graduated from school and had a forged license (the really distressing thing about that is that he was a fabulous clinician). Another therapist was having sex with his clients—*in the office*—and charging money for the extra service. Another on the staff was billing insurance companies for multiple sessions during the same hour. Our consulting psychiatrist was arrested for soliciting sex in a men's room. And in my mind, among the worst betrayals, a colleague and friend was conspiring with her clients to lie to the office staff about how much she was charging so that the therapist could keep a higher percentage of the fees. I guess what I am saying is that I have a certain history of being unduly trusting. Yet I learned some hard lessons from this experience that taught me to be far more cautious about what people tell me, to look at evidence more carefully, to cross-check stories whenever possible, and yes, to be a lot less trusting about what I see and hear. I learned not so much to *mistrust* my judgment as to *withhold* it until such time that I can find corroborating data. I suppose I also developed greater humility, as well as skepticism, which has provided a different kind of challenge to avoid feeling disillusioned.

Being duped by the dishonesty of my colleagues is somewhat different than the sorts of lies that are told by clients, but the effect is the same in that I am far more careful and cautious about whom I trust. I trusted Jacob, and he trusted me. Is it my narcissistic delusion that stopped me from looking more objectively at the facts of the case? That's the thing: there are precious few objective *facts*. With any of our clients, all we usually have to work with are their stories, coupled with our own observations to validate what we see and hear. Once that clinical "crap-detector" (in the words of Ernest Hemingway) goes awry, or we no longer trust its accuracy, then we might as well stop practicing therapy.

If you are now feeling perplexed about what really happened with Jacob, then join the club. Everyone I have ever told this story to, therapists and nontherapists alike, have immediate, visceral reactions as to whether this story is true or not. I am actually agnostic on the subject—I no longer have an opinion one way or the other. I stopped trying to figure this out awhile ago and have accepted, even embraced, a position of not-knowing. I'm actually quite pleased with this state of affairs.

That Which Cannot Be Explained

A few years ago, I spent some time doing research in the Namibia desert on the indigenous healing practices of the Kalahari Bushmen. For the past 10,000 years or longer, they have been practicing the same rituals as their ancestors. I described some of these practices in the context of a shaking ceremony in which I was inducted as a shaman (Kottler, Carlson, & Keeney, 2004). Prior to being lifted off my feet and carried into the dance snaking around the fire, I was sitting on the edge of the circle laughing with my companion about the goings-on within.

As I was being held close to the fire with the shamans dancing around me and poking my belly, I remember thinking to myself that this felt awkward, to say the least. I am not a very good dancer anyway, but here, surrounded by a whole village that was clapping and beating drums, I was more than a little self-conscious. I was frightened by the whole scene—fires lit to keep away the predators, women shamans pressing their fingers into my belly, people singing and chanting in a strange language, and someone bending me over backwards so that I was looking up toward the sky. The last thing I remember was seeing a shooting star cross the sky. Then I passed out.

I awoke in the dark, confused and disoriented, with several of the elder women rubbing their sweat into my chest and arms, cooling me off after my ordeal. Once I regained full consciousness, I half crawled back to my chair where my friend was waiting for me.

"What the hell happened?" he said laughing. He thought the show I had put on was absolutely hysterical. "I thought you didn't dance. I thought you didn't believe in this stuff."

All I could do was shrug.

Later my friend would persistently ask me what happened. Each time he would bring up the subject, I would give the same answer: "I don't know what happened. Let's leave it at that."

I decided after this experience that there were certain things that could not be explained or even described. My whole life I have been an explainer: that is what I do for a living. I supposedly explain how therapy works to readers or my students. I explain why my clients have problems in the first place, or else help them to find their own answers.

After this episode in the Kalahari, I became more comfortable with that which is ambiguous, complex, and inexplicable. I also learned to accept that certain things would forever remain a mystery and perhaps that is a good thing; if not, it is the way it is.

I may have felt more at peace with Jacob's story, but the preceding years had been difficult in terms of the questions it raised about my work. It got me thinking about how many other elaborate fantasies and fabulous lies I might have heard from clients to keep me engaged and entertained. I reviewed all the research projects I had done over the years in which my data consisted largely of the stories I collected from people. You have to admit, it *is* disorienting once you admit that anything and everything a client or research participant tells you could be pure fabrication.

Three Therapists, One Client

All the great philosophers have debated the nature of truth and concluded, as they usually do, that it is a slippery idea. Truth has been conceived and classified as a sense of what feels right, consensual ideas and facts that are part of cultural knowledge, self-evident reasoning, and that which is perceived (Fernandez-Armesto, 1997). We use all of these sources to determine what we can and cannot trust.

Historically, psychotherapy had been conceived as a search for truth, a path to help people sort out their life experiences in such a way that they eventually uncover what is true. Given that this process is predicated on client self-reports and narrative accounts, it turns out that our job is not really to search for truth but rather to discover or create meaning from these experiences (Goncalves, 1994). This has been the basis for contemporary constructivist views of truth-seeking as an individually designed and culturally contextual enterprise. Truth is not something that we arrive at but rather a process of cocreation in the relationship between client and therapist.

The problem with this position for me is that research and therapeutic relationships are based on *mutual* trust. Both participants in the process agree to an implicit contract that they will enter the encounter in good faith. As a therapist, I promise to uphold confidentiality, to behave in an honorable and professional manner, and to demonstrate a certain level of competence. In turn, I choose to believe what clients tell me is a reasonable approximation of their experiences. When someone tells me that he was physically abused as a child, and we make that the focus of our work together, the integrity of the relationship falls apart if this was all a lie.

This lesson really sticks in my mind when I recall a time I was doing a workshop series in New Zealand on the subject of "Working with Difficult Clients." The organizer had scheduled me to do one-day programs in several locales throughout the two islands, ending up in a smaller town where he resided. The workshop was actually misnamed in a significant way because it was not really about difficult clients but rather about difficult therapists. I believed (and still believe) that there really are very few difficult clients but only their professionals who refuse to surrender their own rigid beliefs. After all, the client's main job is to be who he or she is in sessions, demonstrating the same behavior that gets them in trouble in the outside world. It is amazing to me how often we whine and complain to one another about how resistant and difficult clients are being because they do not cooperate with our expectations for how they should be. But I am digressing: the main idea is that if I really advertised the workshop accurately, that it was about therapists being difficult with their clients, then nobody would ever show up.

The heart of the learning experience was to put therapists into small groups of three and share with one another their most difficult client, the one who was giving them the most trouble, haunting their dreams and invading their consciousness. I asked them to talk about the story of the one client who troubled them the most and made them feel most powerless and inept. Then the point was to look at what they were doing that wasn't working and help one another to brainstorm a lot of other options. It was a strategy that usually produced breakthroughs, having been field-tested in a number of other settings.

This particular workshop was a little different because it had been advertised to the whole community (all few thousand of them) as a "Workshop on Difficult Clients." Not only did a few psychotherapists show up, but also physical therapists, sales-people, masseuses, accountants, hair stylists—anyone who had "clients" in their work. I organized the small group work by pro-fession, placing the few psychotherapists together in a triad. Then I wandered around the room listening in on the conversations.

While I was observing a rather eclectic group composed of a veterinarian, a shop owner, and a sheep farmer (only in New Zealand), I heard someone calling my name. Across the room, the therapist group was signaling me to come over and join them.

"We've got a bit of problem, mate," one of the therapists said in a typically Kiwi understated way.

"Oh yeah? What's going on?"

The leader of the group went on to explain that he did as he was asked and talked about his most difficult client, a woman who had been driving him crazy during the preceding few months.

"What's the problem then?" I asked. "That's exactly what you're supposed to do."

Then a second person in the triad chimed in. "What's inter-esting is that when he was describing his challenging client, it reminded me *exactly* like someone I was seeing."

"That's not uncommon," I reassured her. "That's one of the purposes of this exercise—to realize that you all have similar struggles."

"Yeah, we understand that," agreed the third member of the group, "but there's more to the story."

"Sorry. Go on."

"Well, when it was my turn I told them about my most difficult cli-ent and she seemed identical to the client described by my partners."

"Wait a minute," I interrupted. "You're saying that there is an epidemic in this place where each of you is encountering the same kinds of problems that are giving you all the same difficulty?"

"No," the leader explained, "that's not what we're saying at all. We started comparing notes about our most difficult client and then discovered that we are all seeing the same person in therapy."

"I'm not sure I know what you mean."

The three of them looked at me like I was really slow. What they had just realized during their conversation, and were now telling me, is that during this exercise they found out that the same client was simultaneously seeing three different therapists each week and not disclosing to any one of them that this was the case. Furthermore, they all agreed that this was the most difficult client in their practice.

What are the odds of that? What are the chances that three therapists in the same town would get together and compare notes and discover that they were all seeing the same client?

I thought that was one of the strangest, most hilarious things I'd ever heard, although the three therapists did not think it was funny at all. They felt betrayed and even angry. They ended up providing comfort and support to one another after learning that the whole basis of their relationship with this client was a lie. They were being manipulated week after week.

I never forgot that story because it reminded me of how little we really know and understand about what happens in our clients' lives when they are not with us. For all we know, they could be assassins or just taking us for a ride. We are certainly gullible enough targets.

Narrative, Historical, and Artistic Truth

The lessons contained in this book are far different from those I ever imagined. And if you thought this book was just a true-life adventure, you were partially right—it just was not the story you (or I) thought it was.

It turned out that Jacob was an assassin after all, but what he actually killed was my innocence. After all these years listening to people's stories, as a therapist, a researcher, and a storyteller, I enjoyed the illusion that my clinical acumen, diagnostic skills, and long experience could help me determine truth from lies. I suppose good journalists know all too well how important it is to confirm all sources and to mistrust anything that anyone tells them without corroborating evidence. But in our profession, we take people on faith.

I cannot imagine saying to a new client who is in tears: "What do you mean you have been sexually abused? Can you show me a police report to prove this really took place as you say it did?"

Or, to a medical referral: "You say that you have been diagnosed with pancreatic cancer and you are struggling with issues related to your impending death? Before we get into this, I wonder if you have some medical records I could read that substantiate the claim you are really dying?"

So, when someone like Jacob told me he was an assassin, my initial skepticism gave way under the barrage of convincing detail. Every therapist does the same thing when we choose to believe most of what anyone else tells us without demanding irrefutable evidence, supporting documentation, and corroborating witnesses.

Each of us has a story within us—whether it is strictly "true" or not. The details become shaded or even lost over time. We fill in the gaps with fantasies of what we imagined really happened—or preferred scenarios. Eventually, what is real and what is made up become the same thing, especially with older people whose most precious possession is their own life history.

In his classic exploration of the differences between historical and narrative truth, Spence (1982) brings into greater focus the elastic nature of "reality" as it is presented in therapy. A client tells a story that represents the core issue that is to be worked on during sessions. This could be anything from early childhood trauma or a more recently reported loss. These events and experiences are first *perceived* by the individual and then *interpreted* in a particular way as "catastrophic," "devastating," or "just annoying." They are *stored* in memory and then *retrieved* at a later time, and with each *reexamination* of the experience, they are inevitably *altered* and *reinterpreted*. The events are converted into language and organized into a coherent story during the session. So far we have about six different degrees of separation between what originally took place as it might have been recorded, and what the client tells about the experience.

We are not even close to being done, because we also have a *receiver* of the story, the therapist, who *hears* the story as constructed but makes more changes based on how the narrative is *heard, interpreted,* and *understood.* Once the story is encoded according to the therapist's perceptions and interpretations, stored in memory, retrieved, and converted into language, we have another half dozen derivations from the original event. Obviously something is lost, distorted, as well as fundamentally changed during these levels of translation. "Thus the very act of talking about the past tends to crystallize it in specific but somewhat arbitrary language, and this language serves, in turn, to distort the early memory. More precisely, the new description *becomes* the early memory" (Spence, 1982, p. 92). So we have original events (historical truth) recreated and changed as they are told and heard (narrative truth), which is then *re*-reconstructed in descriptions by the therapist in case notes or supervision (artistic truth).

You are already familiar with the dilemma we face in sorting out what is accurate and reality based in client stories. We depend almost completely on what clients report in sessions, as well as what we observe in their behavior. Maybe it does not really matter if the story is "true" or not as long as the client believes it to be so. What about in situations in which the client is deliberately distorting and lying for reasons that actually sabotage therapeutic work? We will come back to this question in subsequent chapters when we explore how we live with the uncertainty and how to work within it in therapy (and in our hearts and minds).

13

What Is Truth and What Does It Really Mean?

Everybody lies, every day; every hour; awake; asleep; in his dreams; in his joy; in his mourning.

Mark Twain

Mark Twain once wrote an essay, "On the Decay of the Art of Lying," for a historical society meeting in which he hoped to win a $30 prize (he lost). With his customary wit and cynicism, Twain (1882/2007) lamented that whereas lying is universal, it had become clumsy, tortuous, awkward, and pusillanimous. We may as well accept that lying is part of human discourse and treat it as a high calling. As Twain said, "Then shall we be rid of the rank and pestilent truth that is rotting the land; then shall we be great and good and beautiful, and worthy dwellers in a world where even benign Nature habitually lies, except when she promises execrable weather" (p. 36).

Twain also observed that unless people are good at fooling themselves, there is little chance of being able to deceive others. In that sense, self-deception is highly functional in that it makes it easier for people to lie convincingly. When you hide something from yourself, you also hide it from others (Smith, 2005).

Apart from what Twain considered the inevitability of lying in every human interaction, we must come to terms with the meaning of truth and deception as they play out in conversations, especially those that take place in helping relationships such as psychotherapy. First we explore the nature of truth in a more general sense before subsequent chapters examine its meaning for the work we do as therapists.

A Confusing Maze

How do we know anything that *anyone* tells us is "true" as reported? Nine out of ten people admit to lying on a regular basis, usually as often as twice per day (Serban, 2001). Politicians lie continually about promises they make only to get elected to office. Lawyers routinely lie for a living to win cases. The media lies in order to promote their particular ideology. Scientists fudge their data. Students make up things to put on their college applications. People fabricate jobs on their resumes or exaggerate their accomplishments. The Internet is filled with lies that penetrate our inboxes every day. Everyone lies about sex, what they are doing or not doing.

Children learn at an early age that the problem is not lying but getting caught. Sometimes people tell a lie so often they come to believe it really happened. Clients tell us things that are complete fiction, just to command attention or enjoy a feeling of power. Oftentimes they are so completely lying to themselves that they really are telling the truth as they know it.

In courts of justice, prospective witnesses are asked to "tell the truth, the whole truth, and nothing but the truth." If only it was that easy. For instance, telling a lie is not the opposite of truth. What if someone reveals what he knows to be a lie, but it really turns out to be the truth? Or what about when someone tells the truth, but by means of a lie? Citing Freud's case of Dora in which she pretended to be innocent of symbolic meaning in a dream as a way to get her therapist to reveal the truth for her, Zupancic (2007) asked how we can possibly define a lie when we do not know what is truth? This has not stopped logicians from attempting to reduce truth to a formula that includes all possible variables (Urchs, 2007, p. 3):

$$L(x,p,t,y) = {}_{df}O(x,p,t) \wedge A.^a(x,p,t,y)$$

Basically, what this suggests (which I am sure is obvious to you) is that a lie (L) occurs when someone internally rejects something that is publicly affirmed.

Rejecting truth as something that is concrete and knowable, Weinshel (1979) enjoyed the task of sorting out what is truth as a "Talmudic exercise," one that "risks traversing a semantic and epistemological minefield" (p. 503).

Philosophers from Socrates and Kant to Russell and Dewey could never agree on what constitutes the nature of truth, so it is no surprise that we are still debating its properties. There is nothing even close to universal agreement on what form reality takes. Reality has generally been defined as seeing the world as it exists, independent of the knower (Chalmers, 1982). Yet there are some indigenous traditions where the belief is that when we are dreaming, that is the true reality, and that when we are awake, that is just a dream.

Just as lying has been so often ignored in therapy, so too has it been mostly avoided by psychotherapists in studying everyday behavior, at least until the last few decades (Komet, 2006). This is all the more remarkable considering how common the practice is in almost every aspect of human interaction. It has been estimated that between 20% and 30% of all human exchanges that last for 10 minutes or more include a lie. When diaries are kept of falsehoods, people admit they lie at least once each day (DePaulo et al., 1996). Among college students, they lie to their parents half the time.

Within the practice of medicine, patient lying has long been recognized as a huge problem in making accurate diagnoses. It was estimated that close to half of those who seek the services of a physician either exaggerate or minimize their symptoms or lie in response to direct questions about their health. Four out of ten patients lie about following their doctor's orders (Ravn, 2009).

Adding to the challenges of understanding the differences between truth and lies, there are over a hundred different words in the English language for deception or lying, including treacherous, sneaky, dishonest, double-dealing, two-faced, devious, fraudulent, untrustworthy, fake, insincere, unprincipled, and my personal favorites, perfidious and mendacious.

Most dictionaries define truth as "the agreement with reality," but as we all know, reality is a very flexible idea, shaped by all sorts of subjective variables, including the perceptions and interpretations of each individual within each cultural context. Enter constructivist and social constructionist interpretations, stage left.

According to more recent postmodern conceptualizations (Gergen, 1991; Mahoney, 1991; Widdershoven, 1992), not only is there no absolute truth, but it can actually never be known (Hansen, 2007). Truth does not represent a series of verifiable facts or events but rather an individual or collective story about what people believe occurred (Anderson, 1990). There are multiple versions of truth, equally valid, and each the product of our own unique experiences, perceptions, and cultural background. Further, we actually *become* the stories we tell, whatever relationship they hold to objective reality; these form our core identities and capture our identities (Parry, 1997).

Mahrer (2004) found that once he dived into the confusing maze of truth and its properties, he began to feel both anxious and frightened. (I know the feeling.) Based on interviews he conducted with therapists, he concluded that most had no interest in the subject of truth; it was just not something they cared to look at too closely. Ultimately, he concluded that theories of truth are not particularly useful in the work we do. We are less interested in whether what clients tell us is "true" than whether it is helpful for them to hold onto those beliefs in terms of achieving their desired goals, reducing suffering, and leading a more satisfying life (Polkinghorne, 1992). I disagree. I think that we miss out on opportunities for helping clients live more congruent lives when we fail to address issues of truthfulness and honesty.

At the very least, we are interested in approximations of truth— that is, an absence of delusions and a reasonable connection between events as they occurred and the story that is reported. It *does* make a difference if the client's report of having been molested, of being in the terminal stages of cancer, or of suffering from posttraumatic stress from having served in combat, really occurred or not. This is the case with respect to what occurs in therapy, just as it is with respect to writing a biography or journal article.

Motivations for Deception, Secrecy, and Lies

Related to our present subject, the following question is asked: Why would someone go to a therapist, physician, lawyer, or any other professional for help, and then not provide the necessary and accurate information that is most needed to produce the supposedly desired outcome?

"Because it works," answers Smith (2005). "Lying helps. And lying to ourselves—a talent built into our brains—helps us accept our fraudulent behavior" (p. 2). Further, he makes the point that "we are astonishingly oblivious to our own duplicity" (p. 3). Thus, at its core, lying is a form of self-protection or image management. Furthermore, the compulsion to always tell the truth is not necessarily a sign of mental health (Stein, 1972).

Lying provides a number of advantages to those who get away with the deception—and the chances of getting caught are pretty remote. People actually tend to underestimate their ability to lie and overestimate their skills at detecting such behavior (Vrij, 2008). The risks are thus well worth the effort, at least if the goal is to achieve control, power, or greater resources. Niccolò Machiavelli counseled way back in the 16th century that it is all but necessary for people to lie and use deception in order to hold on to their positions of power.

Lying is an effective adaptive strategy used by 90% of the population on a daily basis (Serban, 2001). Goffman (1959) likened human existence to a performance on stage in which we carefully control the image we project to others so that they see us in the best possible light. Deception and secrecy are a big part of this process, and to be a convincing actor, it is often necessary that we engage in *self*-deception. Such behavior allows people to seek advantages and leverage when competing for limited resources, whether status, power, food, shelter, or prospective mates.

Within Nature, there have evolved all sorts of biological adaptations that provide ways for an individual to fool others; those that have been most successful at developing camouflage or deception are likely to live long enough to reproduce. Certain plants, insects, reptiles, and animals have developed shapes and colorations that allow them to hide better to protect themselves. Human beings do the same thing but hide in plain sight (or in a therapist's office) by taking on a chameleon-like form, becoming whatever is believed to be most advantageous.

Deception is so much a part of daily life that people routinely use makeup, cosmetic surgery, hairpieces, and artificial fragrances to disguise their actual appearance or essence. "We cry crocodile tears, fake orgasms, and flash phony 'have a nice day' smiles" (Smith, 2005, pp. 1–2). We understand that politicians virtually have to lie in order to be elected to office. Advertising and marketing campaigns also lie so often about their products that we have learned to accept this as normal.

Dishonesty and Deception on the Internet

The question of honesty in the Internet Age is even more curious. "There are only two ways of telling the complete truth," said Thomas Sowell, "anonymously and posthumously." People are far more willing to bare their souls and share their most shameful secrets when they can hide their true identity. They are willing to reveal more information at a deeper level (Joinson & Payne, 2007) and disclose secrets that they would not consider doing face to face, even to a therapist (Whitty & Joinson, 2009).

On the other hand, it is so much easier to lie online without visual cues or even verbal nuances. There is also compelling evidence that without normal social, contextual cues typical of direct contact, people tend to be more self-centered and less controlled. In other words, they are more likely to deceive, lie, attack, distort, manipulate, and control others because there is less likelihood of being caught (Whitty & Carville, 2008).

We have become so accustomed to deception and lies on the Internet that we no longer find it the least remarkable that on any given day you will receive notice that you won a national lottery, inherited a fortune from an unknown relative in Indonesia, are offered a job paying a six- or seven-figure income, are proposed marriage by a supermodel in Russia (who only requires that you send airfare), and have an unclaimed account in Nigeria that only requires your bank information in order to transfer the millions of dollars. We laugh at these obviously fraudulent offers, yet deceit has become so common in cyberspace that the vast majority of online daters routinely lie about their age, height, weight, marital status, profession, and even post fictitious photos of themselves (Hancock, 2007; Whitty & Carr, 2006).

Boundaries Between Fiction and Nonfiction

There was a huge uproar when it was discovered that James Frey's (2003) story of struggling with alcohol and drugs ended up being pure fiction. It was a remarkable, vivid, and powerful memoir of recovery from addiction; the only problem is that it was not true. That does not take anything away from the quality of the writing, but it does lessen the impact of its themes.

Lauren Slater, a psychologist who has made a career of talking about her struggle with mental illness, ignited a huge controversy with the publication of her memoir, *Lying*. She blurred the boundaries between what is real and what is unreal, between facts and fantasy, between confusion and clarity, between fiction and nonfiction, refusing to disclose what she made up and what really happened. She finds narrative truth to be far more "bendable" and interesting than mere historical accuracy. And why should she limit her freedom by sticking to the facts? "When all is said and done," she said to end the book, "there is only one kind of illness memoir I can see to write, and that's a slippery, playful, impish, exasperating text, shaped if it could be, like a question mark" (Slater, 2000, p. 221).

Such question marks are certainly familiar to us as so often we have no idea what is really going on with our clients while they are still in therapy, much less what occurs once they leave. Most of the time we are reliant on what they tell us, reports that are certainly imperfect and distorted to say the least, and sometimes downright deceitful.

With regard to Jacob and his case I presented in this book, my role was not to help him but to tell his story. My obligation and responsibility to him was to make sure that I got the facts and descriptions right, consistent with what he remembered and related. Yet there is also a responsibility I have to you as the reader, as would be the case with any writer or journalist. If this story is a fiction à la Frey or Slater, then it does not really matter if it is true as long as I make the narrative believable. My job is not so much to inform as to entertain.

Ah, but there is the catch. I am no fiction writer and never aspired to be. So what does that mean if Jacob's story is really a novel instead of a biography? Consciously and unconsciously we functioned as coauthors to either record or create a narrative. I take some reassurance from the reminder that the same imperative that makes us so empathic also means a sacrifice of our "critical edge" (Newman & Strauss, 2003) and willingness to challenge clients when we sense something amiss (although I *did not* sense anything of the sort until Jacob stopped talking to me).

Could this happen to you?

Nah, you think. After all, you are not as gullible as I am, right?

Think again. In fact, think back on some of the clients you have seen and review some of the more improbable things they told you to set off alarms that you chose to ignore. I can think of a dozen cases, maybe more, in which I decided not to rock the boat in the interest of maintaining the illusion of trust in our relationship. Since this book was completed, a colleague and I recruited dozens of other therapists to tell stories of being duped by their clients (Kottler & Carlson, 2011).

Vrij (2008) called this the "ostrich effect" in which most people hold their illusions and would prefer not to know when others are lying. For those of us who are members of a profession that offers trust as our calling card, we are even more willing than most to accept what people tell us at face value. Liars get away with their behavior most often because others do not wish to investigate very closely what they have said. That is how ongoing extramarital affairs are possible by half the population who admitted such deception, and it also explains why therapists also do not look as closely as we might at the veracity of client stories. When is the last time a client left your office and you began systematic research to determine what and how much of what you were told was really accurate?

Cultural Contexts for Meanings of Truth

In all other facets of our profession, we continually emphasize the importance of multicultural sensitivity to the particular values, needs, and interests of our clients. If cultural context is absolutely critical in terms of understanding someone's worldview and presenting complaints, not to mention the development of an appropriate treatment plan, why would this also not be operative in making sense of truth in therapy, or any other form of interpersonal engagement?

Certain cultures define lying in terms of being "kind" and "considerate" so another is not hurt or offended. Within many Asian cultures, for instance, people may be concerned with saving face and maintaining cordial relationships at the expense of perfect frankness.

An Afghan woman, training to be a therapist, reflected on the meaning of lies through the lens of Afghan culture. "I was raised to exaggerate often," she explained. "Most of the members in my family are this way. We do not see this as a lie of any kind. I never even saw this as a problem until I moved here [in the United States] when people constantly corrected me. Culturally, things are just not taken literally and we assume everyone sees it the same way."

When I asked for examples, the intern mentioned several that may sound familiar: *I was waiting for my sister for almost an hour* (anything over 15 to 20 minutes is significantly rounded up); *There were hundreds of attendees* (if the event is favorable), *No one really showed up* (if the event is unfavorable); *Suddenly the lady started going crazy in front of the waitress* (this lady could have just sent a meal back or made a criticism but the story is exaggerated to show the disapproval); *Everyone went home hungry after the party* (an abundance of food was not left over—when a host makes just enough food, the host shows guests that they were not worthy of the food and disrespects them). Her point is that within Afghan culture, there is a different definition of what is a lie and what is truth, just as there are in many other cultures.

"When I exaggerate to friends, they would take me literally and tell me I'm lying. This never made sense to me because I wasn't really lying at all; I was just telling a story the way we do in my country and everyone there knows and understands that. Obviously, I've had to learn to change my style."

This admission presents an intriguing reminder to our work with any client. Truth and lies mean such different things to people of various backgrounds. And we had better be able to sort this out considering that our ability to detect truth is not nearly as good as we might believe.

Detecting Truth

There is a myth, if not an illusion, that lying can be detected, especially by professional interrogators, therapists, and poker players. Freud (1963/1905, p. 69) launched this idea with his famous quote: "No mortal can keep a secret. If his lips are silent, he chatters with his finger-tips; betrayal pours out of him at every pore." Supposedly there are "tells" or giveaways such as twitches, averted gazes, flushed coloring, fidgeting, or Pinocchio-like elongated noses that can be identified by trained observers. "What is true, instead, is that there are as many ways to lie as there are liars; there is no such thing as a dead giveaway" (Henig, 2006, p. 1).

You might think that experts in law enforcement or interpersonal relationships can recognize deceit when it occurs, yet many juries, judges, FBI agents, secret service agents, and psychologists are just about as easy to fool as someone without training or experience in lie detection (Ekman, O'Sullivan, & Frank, 1999). Polygraphs, magnetic resonance imagery, brain mappers, thermal scanners, eye trackers, pupillometers, facial recognition systems, breathalyzers (measuring hormonal stress), sodium pentothal, and scopolamine have all been tried—with only limited reliability and accuracy—to ferret out deception. Perhaps we will never have the means to determine whether someone is really telling the truth or not.

The majority of therapists like to think of themselves as pretty skilled at spotting lies when they see or hear them, but only a small percentage can really do so with any consistent accuracy. And technology is not that helpful: lie detectors do not really detect lies as much as they do anxiety. Magnetic resonance images (MRIs) are beginning to show some promise in isolating regions of the brain (parietal cortex, anterior frontal cortex) that are activated during rehearsed and spontaneous lies (Kosslyn, Ganis, & Thompson, 2001), but we can hardly hook our clients up to this machinery during sessions.

There are many reasons why it is so challenging to tell if someone is lying. Different parts of the brain are involved in different kinds of lies—those that are made up on the spot versus those that have been rehearsed over and over; lies to protect oneself (image management) as opposed to those that safeguard others (altruistic); lies of omission versus exaggeration; casual lies compared to lies with strong emotional arousal; lies out of the mouth from a practiced sociopath versus someone who feels apprehension and guilt; and lies about the past versus those planned for the future (Henig, 2006).

When a lie has been rehearsed, it only has to be retrieved from memory. For example, a client relating to a therapist an often-told tale about a family incident that never happened but always elicits sympathy in the listener: "My parents once left me alone in a shopping mall for half the day because they forgot about me and that's why I've learned to take care of myself." By contrast, in a spontaneous lie, not only does the person have to make up a response or story on the spot, lighting up one part of the brain, but then he or she has to keep thinking about the lie, distinguishing it from truth so as to not make a mistake and accidently reveal what really happened (or did not happen). For example, a client is asked by a therapist, "Did you talk to your parents the way we discussed?" The client does not want to disappoint the therapist—besides, he "forgot" to do the assignment—so the simplest solution is just to lie.

To complicate the matter of lie detection further, besides the different parts of the brain involved—with corresponding neural activation and behavioral responses—people often feel ambivalence about their lies. Sometimes they desperately want to keep certain things private or engage in deception for huge personal gains; other times there is an unconscious desire to reveal secrets that may manifest more observable cues.

In spite of advances that have been made in "facial recognition coding systems" (Ekman, 2009) that supposedly allow trained professionals to recognize nonverbal cues, microexpressions, and "leakage" of even practiced liars, when people have learned to believe their lies, it is virtually impossible to distinguish truth from deception. So often clients come to us with stories that may not bear much resemblance to what actually occurred in their lives, but they may insist that they are true—even in the face of contradictory evidence—because they have *become true* in their own minds. This may, in fact, be one of the possible explanations for Jacob's story that made it so difficult for me to determine facts from fantasy.

Chapter **14**

What Is Truth in
Psychotherapy?

I was supervising a blind therapist who was completing his internship prior to graduation. He had been assigned to work in an inner-city school where many of his clients were gang members who were referred because of behavior problems. Even with his visual handicap, the intern was remarkably effective with the kids he worked with, earning their trust and confidence. At the end of one long day, his supervisor came into the office, and said, "Whoa, what happened here?"

The office furniture had been "tagged" with gang signs. Apparently, one of his clients had picked up a magic marker that had been sitting on the table and sneakily drawn the name of his gang, and his own gang name, on one of the chairs. He seemed to take some special pleasure in doing this literally under his therapist's nose, knowing he could not see what was going on. Later in the day, a client from a rival gang tagged other parts of the furniture with his own gang signs, again without his therapist being unable to detect the defacement.

As he was telling the story, the therapist laughed about the incident and actually thought it was pretty funny. Both boys were confronted about their behavior, apologized, but said they could not resist the temptation.

This story got me thinking about how blind we all are to certain aspects of what clients do right before our eyes.

Paradoxes Within the World of Therapy

Before we can ever hope to get a handle on the meaning of truth in therapy, it is helpful to review the intrinsic complexity of the work we do, as well as the many paradoxes that are part of the unique relationships that we develop. There are few absolutes in our thinking and less than perfect agreement about the best way to proceed. It is not surprising that the subject of truth is one that we would prefer not to examine too closely, especially considering the paradoxical nature of some of our most cherished assumptions.

Let's face it, doing therapy is a peculiar way to earn a living. We are paid to listen to people because they feel so rarely heard and understood, yet we are not always fully present but drifting elsewhere into our own personal journeys. We hear the most incredible stories every day, plots that make television dramas or situation comedies pale by comparison, yet except during supervision, we cannot talk about them to others.

We pretend a degree of modesty and transparency yet appear to be able to read minds and see into people's souls (or at least differentially diagnose their various maladies after a single conversation or two). We say to others, with more false modesty, that we are nothing special, yet deep down inside we really do see ourselves as privileged if not extraordinary.

We claim to be nonjudgmental but have a running critical voice inside our heads, often seeing the worst in people. We help clients deal with issues that we have not yet resolved; there are some professionals among us who are seriously impaired yet still seem to do solid work. We devote ourselves to helping others but often learn as much, or more, from our clients during sessions; sometimes it is not clear whether we are the mentor or the student.

We practice a profession that is solidly steeped in evidence-based practice and empirical research, yet if pressed to be completely honest, we do not really understand how the process works—and probably never will. And speaking of research, we all say that it is critical for the advancement of our profession, but most clinicians either cannot critically evaluate studies they read, or more often than not, do not bother reading them in the first place.

We say we trust the process and believe in the power of relationship, yet clamor for new techniques and strategies that we think will produce miracles. We claim to have discovered the one true path to effective treatment (our favored approach), yet there are more than a dozen other styles that appear to do things very differently which are just as helpful. If truth be told, sometimes we are frauds, failures, and hypocrites. We question whether what we are doing really matters or even whether the people we believe we helped are really fundamentally different after they leave our care.

And the most compelling paradox relevant to one theme explored in this book: The whole premise of psychotherapy is based on the idea that people are telling us things that they believe happened to them, but could very well end up being exaggerations, fabrications, or outright lies. To complicate things even further, psychotherapy has traditionally been conceptualized as a search for truth, a mission that has all but been debunked in light of cultural and individual differences, postmodern reconceptualizations of differing realities, subjective experiences, linguistic challenges, and problems of ever finding or discovering or identifying absolute truth in any stable form (Hansen, 2007).

Even when clients are absolutely convinced that what they are telling us is the absolute truth, memories are so inaccurate and skewed that the stories could actually have little resemblance to what actually took place (Birch, 1998; Newman & Strauss, 2003; Spence, 1984; Akhtar & Parens, 2009). Narratives take on a kind of artificial coherence that does not, by any means, reflect actual events (Adler, Wagner, & McAdams, 2007). If that is not unnerving enough, postmodern paradigms tell us that "truth" may not be that important or relevant because the *perception* of experience makes it real. These are the stories that each of us live by, create meaning in our lives, and construct the sense of self (Bruner, 1990; McAdams, 1993, 2006).

Stories are the lifeblood of our work. We hear client stories all day long, sorting through long, rambling monologues to identify material considered significant. We help people to flesh out their stories, fill in missing gaps, and elicit crucial information. We focus on plotlines and thematic elements. We coauthor stories with our clients to reconstruct alternative narratives that are far more empowering (White & Epston, 1990). We use stories to teach and enlighten, share healing tales, construct metaphors, and self-disclose relevant anecdotes. We also use them to cement trust and intimacy in the therapeutic relationship.

I already mentioned the point that trust in therapy goes both ways. Not only do clients have to trust us for things to work well, but we also have to trust them. I am not saying that the people we help can hurt us in the same ways that we can betray their trust (although they can get some solid licks in if they are interested in doing so). But clients can—and do—lie. They deceive themselves, and they unconsciously (and quite deliberately) mislead us as well.

Most therapists take what their clients say as a reasonable approximation of "truth." It is not that we believe completely whatever people tell us, but in one sense anyway, it does not much matter: if a client remembers events in a particular way, and operates as if they actually occurred as recalled, then this becomes a kind of reality for that person which is just as influential as any other experience. For this reason, we do not tend to interrogate our clients in the same ways that criminal investigators or journalists might do. If someone comes in and tells me that he was abducted by aliens, I may not take the story at face value, but I do respect that person's perception of reality until such time as we can explore events more deeply.

Traditional Conceptions of Discovering (or Creating) Truth in Therapy

One question we are exploring in this book is what meaning truth has in the context of psychotherapy. For the first century of our profession, truth has been conceptualized as some absolute entity that can be captured through persistent and dedicated hard work. Freud likened the therapist's role to that of a detective whose job is to help solve the mysteries of the unconscious mind or an archaeologist who excavates buried memories to identify the true core issues. For Freud, the foundation of psychotherapy was embedded in the notion that absolute truth was possible: "We must not forget that the relationship between analyst and patient is based on a love of truth, that is, on the acknowledgment of reality, and that it precludes any kind of sham or deception" (Freud, 1937b, p. 266). The possibility of pursuing truth and acknowledging reality was great in theory, but Freud eventually recognized that patients would not only deceive their therapists because of unconscious defenses but may also outright lie as a manifestation of their neuroses or transference reactions (Gediman & Leiberman, 1996; Akhtar, 2009).

Classical psychoanalytic interpretations of lying in therapy understand the phenomenon as a reenactment of the oedipal conflict (Weinshel, 1979), primitive sadomasochistic gratification (O'Shaughnessy, 1990), maintenance of repression (Blum, 1983), psychopathic transference (Kernberg, 1992), or maintenance of perversions (Gediman & Leiberman, 1996), to mention a few. Other therapists might interpret the deceptive behavior as an act of aggression toward the therapist, a distancing defense, an avoidance of humiliation, attention- or sympathy-seeking behavior, an expression of power, an adaptive response to a perceived threat, a learned manipulative interpersonal style, or evidence of a personality disorder.

If transference or relational phenomena are strong factors in the reasons why clients lie, the therapist's own countertransference or personal responses tend to be part of the picture. You can no doubt identify that some of the feelings that I have been experiencing in reaction to Jacob's story, with all the evolving different interpretations, bear a strong similarity to what many therapists have reported when they discover that a client has been deceiving them—confusion, frustration, anger, shame, sadness, hurt, self-doubt, regret, guilt, and, ultimately, betrayal.

Storytelling Effects

The process of therapy is one in which clients are helped to tell their story. Yet the very act of telling any story means that there is a certain "bending of the facts" or "slippage" that make the sequence of events and details more coherent and comprehensible. The "evidence is stretched to conform to the contours of a relatively simple skeleton theme" (McGregor & Holmes (1999, p. 403). Lying is, therefore, inevitable, because facts that do not fit the main theme are deleted and other details are invented to make the plot more interesting (Schank & Abelson, 1995). We never make direct contact with any client's memory, but only its filtered description. And we never deal with truth until it achieves a status of plausibility to the client (Bohleber, 2007).

Lying is often understood to mean some form of deliberate falsification. The person intentionally sets out to mislead or misdirect another person for some personal gain or form of self-protection. But what about self-deception when a client actually believes what he or she is saying? "If self-deception is a lie that one tells to oneself, then paradoxically the deceived is also simultaneously the deceiver" (Kirby, 2003, p. 99). There is a significant difference between conscious deceit and objective reporting of events—even if the latter was possible (Birch, 1998).

I may never know whether Jacob's story was strictly true or not, but I have not the slightest doubt that he believed what he was saying. In part, that is what made him so convincing. When someone lies or deceives himself or herself, it creates considerably less dissonance and greater internal consistency, making the story much more believable (Wiley, 1998). We witnessed many times in our sessions how what clients wish or believe to be true *becomes* true for them.

There is evidence that a "storytelling effect" shapes the way memories are formed and leads people to believe that their stories are true after a period of time (McGregor & Holmes, 1999), unable to distinguish between fiction and reality (Birch, Kelln, & Aquino, 2006). I am convinced that Jacob could have passed a polygraph test.

It is obvious that deception and lying in therapy occur as a *relational process*, an interactive effect in which the clinician's responses to the lies become part of the ongoing phenomenon (Gediman & Leiberman, 1996). All storytelling takes place in an interpersonal context with an audience in mind. This is especially the case in therapy in which one stated goal is for the client to present a life narrative that explains the current predicament. Clients present themselves to us in particular ways—as hapless victims, heroic protagonists, misunderstood, or misinformed—and their stories tend to consistently portray those images. Jacob's story was narrated (or created) for an audience of one: me.

There are all kinds of complications and confusion surrounding this struggle with making sense of truth and reality as they are presented in therapy. Yet the veracity and sincerity of the client's story are hardly the only parts of the complete picture that we struggle with every day.

Lying and Deception in Psychotherapy

Therapists often hold certain assumptions that are at the core of the work we do. We see ourselves as honest, transparent, and forthright professionals who value cooperation, trust, openness, and candor as much as possible. We start every new relationship with a client by assuming that what we are hearing is based on good faith—that the client really wants to get better and has a much better chance of doing so if he or she provides the most accurate picture possible of events that led to the presenting complaints. "Under this cloak of naiveté," Wiley (1998, p. 869) noted, "we consider deception to be so rare as to not be important."

In surveys of therapists, almost all practitioners admit that they have been lied to on occasion, so this is hardly a rare occurrence. Likewise, most clients report that they lie to their therapists as a way to avoid shame and embarrassment about issues they would prefer to avoid (DeAngelis, 2008). Even a significant number of therapists who seek help for their own problems kept secrets that would have been important for their own therapists to know (Pope & Tabachnick, 1994).

As online counseling and e-mail consultations by therapists become increasingly common, along with videoconferencing, synchronous communication, instant messaging, blogging, texting, and twittering, issues related to truth and deception become even more challenging. In one sense, clients might be more willing to reveal things that they would ordinarily hide or disguise in face-to-face encounters. Clients would also find it much easier to shade the truth without concern that they would be caught (Whitty & Joinson, 2009).

We have seen that there are all sorts of ways that clients lie to us, just as therapists are prone to such untruths in their supervision sessions. There are lies that involve deliberate falsification and elaborate stories that are completely made up. There are lies that represent exaggerations or mixing facts with fiction. There are lies of omission, lies of misdirection, lies of concealment, lies of inaccuracy, and lies that are inadvertent or unconscious. Then there are lies that are not really lies but are rather multiple versions of truth (such as what we often hear in family therapy).

There are people who believe their own lies because of rampant narcissism and grandiosity. Manifestations of psychotic behavior are another example in which lies become real for people. Schizophrenia is a kind of "lie" in the sense that the person walks around in the world spouting fantasies ("There are alien implants inside my brain"), reporting ideas ("I am Napoleon in disguise"), and hearing or seeing hallucinations ("Squirrels speak to me") that are clearly not true. There are organic conditions such as Korsakov syndrome (thiamine deficiency) that results in memory impairment and making up all sorts of stories that never happened. Ganzer syndrome or Munchausen syndrome are just a few of several factitious disorders in which people will manufacture or create mental or physical illnesses as a way to seek attention. Then there are all the personality disturbances (like borderline, histrionic, and sociopathic) that routinely use deceit as a form of life support (Serban, 2001).

Less extreme in nature, we often encounter "little white lies" that come up in client stories, the kind that represent slight exaggerations or omissions that are not intended to be harmful either to oneself or anyone else. They are designed to spare hurt of oneself or others. Then there are "big lies," the kind of whoppers that are pure fantasy. A client says: "I had sex with my sister. It's been going on for a long time." Then later we learn, "Did I say my sister? Well, she isn't *really* my sister, more like a friend, but I still think of her that way."

While searching the literature on this subject I was relieved to find a name for what I could have encountered with Jacob: *pseudologia fantastica*, first described a century ago (Healy & Healy, 1915). Although what I may have faced with Jacob does not yet qualify for inclusion in the *Diagnostic and Statistical Manual of Mental Disorders (DSM)* because the behavior is not considered delusional, this condition may describe the usual symptoms consisting of a believable, fantastic story; enduring and developing plot lines; an aggrandizing, heroic quality; and the possibility of underlying neurological disease (King and Ford, 1987). Although the condition is considered rare, it is most commonly found in those who falsely confess to crimes or those who claim they have been kidnapped by aliens (Birch, Kelln, & Aquino, 2006). Far more hurtful are instances when people make false accusations of abuse that were, in fact, either fantasies or deliberate attempts to inflict harm.

I do not believe that Jacob qualifies for inclusion in the Pseudologia Fantastica Hall of Fame. There was no evidence that he had any kind of previous history of lying or exaggeration, as is usually the case. I spent a lot of time with him in a number of different settings, socialized with him and his wife, observed him in the company of friends, and watched him interact with others, and I cannot recall ever being struck by inaccuracies or distortions. But then, it is entirely possible that the deceitful behavior was specific to our relationship and this was one whopper of a story.

I have been presenting two possible explanations for Jacob's story in absolute terms that either it was all true or all made up. Another possibility is that part of the story could have been true and the rest fabricated. For instance, the early part of the story relating to Jacob's relationship with his rabbi, his experiences in the neighborhood, being beaten up by anti-Semitic gangs, could have all been true, whereas his story of revenge for these injustices could have been a complete fantasy.

Given the nature of fragmented memories, especially in someone as old and ill as Jacob, it is no wonder there were holes in his remembrances that were filled in with content to give the story greater coherence. Jacob and all of our clients have their secrets, many of which we will never know. But therapists have their own secrets as well.

A Therapist's Secrets

One of the main reasons that therapy often stalls is because of secrets that have not yet been revealed. Sells (2004) referred to client secrets as those undercurrents within the family that provide critical clues as to what is really going on. These can range from outright lies to whole stories that have been completely fabricated.

Whether deliberate or unconscious, it is clear that such untruths make it far more difficult to be helpful. It would be as if a patient reported to his doctor that the pain was in his leg when the problem was really in his chest. Even more frustrating is when this same patient, providing inaccurate information on the nature of the problem, then complains about why he is not improving.

But what of *therapist* secrets that can be just as inhibiting to the process?

It turns out that once upon a time, while still naïve beginners, therapists were far more transparent, honest, and forthcoming about their doubts and fears. Over time, we learn to be more secretive and withholding. In supervision, therapists are known to fabricate notes, distort reports, exaggerate outcomes, and lie about what occurred in sessions (Hantoot, 2000).

Whereas novices tend to talk out loud about their confusion and experiences of not-knowing, veterans are inclined to keep such doubts to themselves (Williams, 2003). There are all kinds of taboos and secrets that we keep private—the fantasies we have about our clients, the self-serving or economically driven motives for clinical decisions, the lies we tell clients when we say that we can help them, the mistakes that we cover up, and the failures that we deny, to mention a few (Kottler, 2010; Pope, Sonne, & Greene, 2006).

It is not surprising that new therapists would have heightened self-awareness during sessions, continually asking themselves how they are doing and second-guessing themselves. Because of increased anxiety and inhibition, experience teaches us to shut down such self-talk that can be distracting. But one side effect of this is that some of our most secret concerns and questions are buried. We learn not to question certain things that might lead to other queries for which we are not prepared.

By definition, psychotherapy is supposed to be the place where people go to talk about things they never revealed before. It is a sanctuary for that which has not been said—or sometimes ever been considered. Clients share their deepest secrets, darkest fantasies, and most closely guarded vulnerabilities. They take huge risks and often suffer immeasurably as a result, at least until such time that they reach some accommodation with the "truth."

Therapists are experts at exploring this forbidden territory. We know just when to push, how much force to exert, and when to back off when things become too tough to handle. We probe deeper and deeper. We dig at those spots that appear to be most productive, all the while sifting through layers of accumulated memories and reflections. That such remembrances and reports are subjective, skewed, biased, and imperfect is acknowledged but not often to the point that it bothers us very much.

You would think that with this practice of delving into the realm of the forbidden, we would be quite accomplished at revealing our own doubts and uncertainties. Yet in many ways we have been trained to avoid talking about our own issues and discouraged from admitting our fears and foibles. We work mostly in isolation. We are continually warned to be careful of boundaries that could be crossed. We are admonished to keep secrets. We are used to being caretakers and rescuers of others. We fear being judged critically, of surrendering our image of invincibility, and of revealing our characterological flaws (Sussman, 1995).

Well into his seventies, Carl Rogers (1980) looked back on his life as a therapist and confessed one of his own secrets: "I recognize how much I need to care deeply for another and to receive that kind of caring in return. I can say openly what I have always recognized dimly: that my deep involvement in psychotherapy was a cautious way of meeting this need for intimacy without risking too much of my person" (p. 83). How many of us can say the same?

There are many things that contribute to our reluctance to speak about the unspeakable. Fear is a huge part of the problem—fear of being revealed as a fraud, fear of having our mistakes uncovered, fear of admitting what we do not really know and understand, fear of opening up a can of worms that we can never close again. There is also the quite reasonable suspicion that if we were to be honest, really, really honest about what we do not know and understand, we would be drummed out of the profession as traitors. A pervasive atmosphere of political correctness in the field dictates what we are allowed to say and how we are allowed to say it (Pope et al., 2006; Zur, 2005).

Cummings and O'Donohue (2005) believed that many of us have surrendered our integrity to the forces of conformity and compliance, defining what is permissible, dictating what is considered appropriate discourse, labeling offenders who speak out of turn, and punishing transgressors through ostracism and sanctions, even when the behavior has not breached ethical codes or laws but merely strayed from what is considered by "authorities" and those in power to be most suitable. The authors believe that such political correctness reflects a degree of rigidity, intimidation, dogmatism, narcissism, and absolute morality that makes it even more difficult to talk about matters of professional interest in more transparent, honest, open ways. Members of the guild who speak their minds, but in contrast to prevailing norms, are branded heretics for exploring new territory. The authors suggest that such oppression of diverse points of view is antiscientific and prevents the sort of critical inquiry that leads to advancement of knowledge.

Therapists Lie Too

Clients are not the only ones who lie.

The most influential and famous recording of psychotherapy in history was a lie. I am referring, of course, to the *Gloria* film produced by Everett Shostrum (1965) in which Carl Rogers, Fritz Perls, and Albert Ellis saw the same client for a 20-minute interview each. This was revolutionary at the time, one of the first times that actual therapy sessions were documented in recordings, much less by three of the most prominent practitioners of the era. If you recall (and almost every generation of therapists has seen this film during the almost five decades since it was made), Gloria first worked with Rogers and found him warm, charming, and a father figure. Then she saw Perls who beat her up pretty good, calling her phony and stupid, and after the session actually used the palm of her hand as an ashtray. Finally, Ellis worked with her in the third session doing a fairly accurate but rushed demonstration of his theory in action. As Rosenthal (2005) pointed out in his investigation of the lingering mystery surrounding this landmark film, anyone who has ever watched the sessions leaves feeling bewildered by Gloria's assessment afterward that Perls did the best job and he is the therapist who could help her the most. This was especially confusing given how rude, inappropriate, and adversarial Perls was during the session, essentially inspiring viewers to use these same overly confrontative techniques in their own sessions.

It turns out this whole episode was a sham: Gloria lied! In fact, Shostrum was both a passionate disciple of Perls and Gloria's therapist for the previous four years. He used his influence to persuade his client to lie on camera and tell the viewing audience that Perls was the best therapist. Years later, Gloria confessed that she felt "small, belittled, unimportant, confused, and lacking wholeness. In a sense then, I felt a bit of myself destroyed in that short session" (Dolliver, Williams, & Gold, 1980). In other words, the most significant therapy training session ever made was a hoax that had been carefully edited by the producer to make his own mentor look good. Rosenthal (2005) pointed out that it is the most important therapy artifact of the 20th century, yet it was also a lie.

It is hardly surprising to hear that therapists would resort to deception and lies, being as human as anyone else. Most of the time, the lies we tell are little, white lies, shades of truth, that, ultimately, are designed for the client's own good. Here are just a few of the most common lies we tell (Kottler, 2010):

- *"I know I can help you."* Research and clinical experience has led us to understand that positive outcomes are far more likely when positive expectations are planted early in the relationship. Placebo effects are intensified when we instill confidence in our ability to be helpful. Imagine what would happen if we were completely truthful at the start of a new therapy relationship: "Gee, you really have a lot of terrible stuff going on in your life and I don't have a clue as to what is going on. In fact, I've never seen or heard anything quite like what you are presenting and right this moment I am on the verge of panic myself about what I could possibly do to help you. But, what the hell, let's give it a try."

- *"Our time is up."* There are all the little tricks of the trade that we use to enhance our magic, persuading clients that we really do have healing powers beyond mortal beings. Among them is the way we always seem to know when the 50-minute session is up—without looking at the clock. Of course, we have devised sneaky ways to check the time periodically without getting caught, among them surreptitiously checking the client's watch. My favorite trick was a colleague who arranged his office in such a way that the only clock in the room was located next to him on the table, but out of his sphere of vision. He never wore a watch, just to add to the effect. Yet from his vantage point he could look at the reflection on a picture hung on a side wall, which in turn reflected the image of the clock on another picture, giving him a clear view of the time. I once overheard two of his clients talking in the waiting room about how mystified they were that he always knew when the session was over without ever consulting a clock or watch.

- *"That's a very good question. What do YOU think?"* Of course we do not really know the answer and we are stalling until we can think of something, or at least deflect the question back, hoping that we can avoid answering altogether.
- *"Of COURSE I like you."* There comes a time in many therapy relationships when clients ask directly how we feel about them. It is entirely reasonable that we do like some of our clients, but there are others with whom we find it challenging to deal with them on any level—and those are usually the ones who ask the question (because they already know the answer).

Maybe you object to calling any of these "lies" because they are really just evasions or relatively harmless attempts to avoid inflicting any harm. Hopefully, the intent is to do whatever is needed in order to benefit our clients. Technically speaking, placebos are lies, just as paradoxical directives deliberately "trick" clients into solving their own problems. Usually the motives are altruistic rather than self-serving when such manipulation or deception is employed.

Nevertheless, our field also attracts those with darker purposes related to exploitation, power, or meeting their own needs for attention, adulation, and control. There are few other professions that give professionals so many ways to manipulate others.

"Sure there are lunatics in the field," Smith (1993, p. 113) readily admitted in his discussion of therapist dishonesty, "but I can assure you that the majority of abuses perpetuated in psychotherapy are committed by ordinary people like you and me." He is not referring necessarily to ethical lapses or exploitive behavior but rather to the situations we find ourselves in with so little definitive and disciplined guidance. "We are all cast adrift," he says, struggling to make sense of experiences that are often so complex, confusing, and ambiguous.

In its modern solution-focused permutations, psychotherapists resort to all kinds of lies and deceptions that are justified for the client's own good. We are wizards of Oz, magicians who use sleight of hand and hide behind curtains in order to increase our powers of influence.

Raise your hand if you ever "tricked" clients into doing something for which they did not feel ready but you thought it would be good for them. How about instances of exaggeration ("I know I can help you") or deception ("Don't worry. It doesn't really matter") in which you were planting hope and capitalizing on placebo effects? What about using paradoxical directives in which you asked or told clients to do things that were actually the opposite of what you really hoped and intended? How often have you heard yourself tell a familiar story but adapted and embellished it a bit to fit the client and context? How about working the system to benefit a client or yourself—using benign diagnoses that were not strictly accurate but minimized stigma? And what about the ultimate lie—the hypocrisy that comes from asking clients to do things that you cannot—or will not—do yourself?

My training years took place in rather traditional mental health settings such as an inpatient psychiatric unit, outpatient hospital clinic, and community mental health center. Each week we would have case conferences and group supervision in which the interns like me would take turns presenting our cases, and then the senior staff would discuss the nuances of what we missed, offer feedback, reformulate diagnoses, and construct treatment plans for us to follow. Most of the time it was a fairly humiliating process in which the supervisors would interrogate us with questions we could never answer, compete with one another to determine who really understood what was going on, and who could ridicule our cluelessness with the most incisive wit. Over time, we learned *never* to present any cases that confused us but only those about which we felt confident we could answer the inevitable questions from the staff. It was almost never acceptable to admit we did not know something; most of the posturing that took place in the conference rooms was about sounding as convincing as possible about what we did know.

It struck me as rather strange at the time (much more so now) that it was somehow possible to spend an hour or two during an intake with a new patient and be able to identify all the presenting complaints, hone in on the "core" issue, collect all necessary background information on past history and family of origin, formulate a multiaxial diagnosis, and plan a detailed treatment strategy. Oh yeah, and also get the person to return for another appointment.

Among all these assigned tasks that we were expected to report during case conferences, the one that perplexed me most was how we were supposed to figure out what was "really" going on. I do not know about you, but I have been living with myself for most of my life, close to six decades, and I *still* do not know what is really going on with me. I spent a zillion hours in therapy, supervision, journaling, workshopping, going on retreats, and exploring and analyzing every aspect of my behavior, motives, and central issues, and I cannot say with any confidence that I really know what is going on or why I do the things I do.

So here is my question: How on earth are we supposed to *know*, I mean really, really *understand*, what is happening with any given client at a moment in time, much less as a representation of their essence?

It has been one of my secrets, one of the things that I have been most reluctant to admit, that most of the time I'm just winging it in therapy. Sure, I have a plan. I also have a working hypothesis of what I *think* is going on with a client, what *might* be most useful, and what *could* be effective as a strategy or intervention. But on a 1-to-10 scale in which I am required to rate my degree of certainty in this conceptualization, or confidence that the direction we are headed is the "right" one, I'd be fortunate to hit a five.

I just think that people in general, and therapy clients in particular, are far too complex to ever understand what is really going on. I also believe that the process of psychotherapy is so complicated and multidimensional, so layered in phenomena we will never identify, much less understand, that it is impossible to really get a handle on what happens. We can have ideas, conjectures, hypotheses, theories, diagnoses, and treatment plans, but what it all comes down to is that we have access to about 10% (maybe less than 1%) of all the data we really need to make truly accurate and robust predictions about what is unfolding, much less comprehensive descriptions of what already occurred.

All of the above is absolutely unacceptable. We cannot possibly face our clients and the public, much less ourselves, by admitting that our science is not only inexact, but mostly an illusion. We need some semblance of certainty, if not faith, that what we do is not only helpful but that we can replicate the effort again and again. I do not quibble with the research that demonstrates, more than conclusively, that psychotherapy is incredibly effective with most people most of the time. Our success rates rival the most time-honored medical procedures. Even when the results do not measure up to what was expected, most clients still leave satisfied customers, happier with the ways they learned to reframe their problems or live with their conditions.

I am not sure it matters that it is important—or even matters that we know where we are going. The most interesting adventures, most memorable explorations, and most transformative experiences are those in which we ended up somewhere quite different from where we intended. It is good to have an itinerary, to make reservations and plan ahead, to do research about the anticipated destination, but also to go with the flow and take advantage of opportunities that emerge along the journey. Time after time, it is when you get off the tour bus and depart from the agenda that the real action begins.

I do not deny that it is important to *pretend* there is a plan when therapy begins. Clients certainly appreciate it when we reassure them that not only do we know what their problems might be but we also know how to best address them. I do not think we would have many clients left if we ended the first session with the following confession:

"How should I know what the hell is wrong with you? I just met you. You've been struggling with these issues all your life and you don't know what is going on—how could I? I have no clue what is happening and I'm as confused as you are. There is a lot of stuff for us to sort through and I'm not sure how long this will take. Right now I'm feeling pretty apprehensive about the whole thing, but then I always feel that way when a new relationship begins. I'm reasonably confident that if we spend enough time together—a few weeks, months, years—who knows?—we'll make some good progress. But then a lot of that depends on you. So far

I don't know you well enough to make any kind of predictions. But I'll let you know when things start to come into better focus. How's that sound?"

I fully recognize that many professionals have a very different experience of what it is like to conduct a first session. I used to use structured intake forms, checklists, assessment instruments, and standardized questions designed to efficiently hone in on presenting problems, diagnostic categories, and the best empirically supported treatments that match the results. All of this can be very helpful. But do not think too hard about whether these instruments and structures are really serving the client or are rather appeasing the therapist's own discomfort and intolerance for complexity and ambiguity. Ultimately, so much of what we do can be reduced to an issue of trust.

Chapter **15**

What Do We Believe and Whom Do We Trust?

Caitlin had been referred by her physician because he could find no organic cause for her symptoms. She had complained of a variety of medical problems that led to being run through a gauntlet of tests, scans, and diagnostic procedures, all negative. Yet her problems, regardless of their origin, seemed to worsen over time.

Caitlin was hardly the most expressive or verbal client I'd seen. Although in her mid-twenties, she reminded me of some adolescents who would rarely speak; in her case she was virtually mute.

"What can I help you with?" I asked to begin our first session. Shrug.

"You're not sure?"

Another shrug.

Was she playing a game with me? Was I being tested? Did she have laryngitis or a mental handicap? I could not be sure.

After five long minutes of silence in which she stared at the floor, seemingly fascinated by the weave of the carpet, I had finally had enough. "Look Caitlin, I'm not sure what you expect of me or why you're here. The only thing that I know is that your doctor sent you to me because he couldn't help you. I understand you are having a lot of problems, and, apparently, he thinks it might be helpful for you to talk about them. But I can't help you unless you tell me what's going on."

Incredibly, Caitlin shrugged again but this time offered a wry smile.

Now I was determined to wait her out. There was something going on here that I did not understand, but I sensed that pushing her further was not going to work. I just wanted to get through the hour and send her on her way. Obviously, she was not ready for therapy.

We sat silently for the rest of the session, Caitlin alternately staring at the floor and some undetermined spot over my left shoulder. I checked a few times, just to see what was so interesting, but it was one of the few blank spots on the wall. Maybe she was projecting her own images. At this point I did not know or care; I was already thinking about my next client and what I could do to make up for this disaster.

Imagine my surprise when the session finally ended and Caitlin said to me, "Same time next week?"

I was taken by such surprise that all I could do was nod my head. Now I was the one who was rendered mute.

The second session repeated the pattern of the first—Caitlin took her seat but would not speak. She just sat there, apparently comfortable and unconcerned with the silence. Even though I was prepared for this eventuality, and had rehearsed several things I might do to draw her out, each overture was met with a shrug or ignored altogether. By the time the second session ended, I was resolved that I'd had enough: no more "same time next week."

I was just about to call for an end to this charade, pretending to be therapy, when Caitlin abruptly stood up, handed me an envelope, and exited, stage left. I was dumbfounded, frozen in place, holding this offering in my hand, unsure what to do next. I told myself that I should just put it aside for now—it could not be good news—but my curiosity got the better of me. I ripped open the envelope to find a five-page single-spaced letter in which Caitlin had outlined the sorry state of her life. It included all the things that a client would normally reveal in the first few sessions, talking about her early history, her family situation, her living arrangements, employment, and cogently reviewing all her various physical symptoms. She ended the self-report by stating that she hoped I understood how difficult it was for her to talk about these things and asked if I could be patient with her. She said she would return the following week if I'd still be willing to see her.

What could I say to that? I just shook my head, eager to resume this "conversation" during our next meeting. Oh, did I mention that I assumed that the structure of our communication might change?

No such luck. It was more of the same: continual and unremitting silence. In response to everything I brought up from her letter, Caitlin would smile or shrug or sometimes frown and shake her head. I was so desperate, that seemed like progress: at least now I could get a tentative yes or no in response to a question.

"Caitlin," I tried again, "you wrote in your letter that you live with your brother. How's that working out?"

Shrug.

"Just okay? You mentioned in your letter that you were close."

She nodded her head.

And so it went, another frustrating, laborious, tedious (did I mention frustrating?) hour.

Fast forward five months. I have now seen Caitlin every week at our appointed weekly time. We are talking now. Or at least I am mostly talking and she occasionally rewards me with an actual verbal yes or no response, and sometimes she even utters a whole sentence. But basically she does not say much—until she hands me a letter at the end of the session that basically answers every question I asked the previous session and even a few things I wondered about but had not yet broached. I have certainly never done therapy quite like this, and it sure is hard work, but I tell myself that she is coming back, so she must be getting something out of the experience.

Another few months go by and I eventually learn a lot about Caitlin's life and her predicament. Her physician has been increasingly concerned because of abrasions in her vagina and burns on her breasts, wounds that appeared to be self-inflicted. When I asked her about this, Caitlin immediately clammed up and would not talk about them at all, even in a follow-up letter.

The doctor called a week later to tell me that he "fired" Caitlin as a patient, refusing to see her any longer. I assumed this was because she was playing the same kind of silent treatment games with him that she was acting out with me, but I was wrong. Apparently, Caitlin had been left alone in an examining room when a nurse unexpectedly entered and found her holding the thermometer that had been placed in her mouth underneath the flame of a lighter to artificially raise the temperature and fake a fever. All of a sudden things started to fall in place, and the doctor realized that he was dealing with a case of Munchausen syndrome in which Caitlin had been manufacturing various disorders and diseases all along as an excuse for attention. This was clearly a case for psychological treatment, way out of his domain—and firmly back into mine.

But this called into question everything that she had thus far told me in her letters. How much of this was really true? How much could I trust anything that she had related to me? If she had been willing to fake her various ailments, and lie about her symptoms, what was to say that *anything* about her history was true? How could I work with a client who was now identified as a chronic liar?

I'm hardly the first therapist to work with someone with Munchausen syndrome, or a factitious disorder, or a sociopath, or any other client who *knowingly* lies, but once these fabrications and deceit are uncovered, what are we to do with them?

After so many months invested in our relationship, I initially felt betrayed, just as I had with Jacob. But in Caitlin's case, I quickly realized this was one very vulnerable, terrified, disturbed young woman who was doing the best she could to hold things together. If she was willing to go to such extremes for attention and self-protection, what did that say about anything she would tell me in therapy? And how and when is it appropriate and safe enough to confront this issue directly?

I decided that I really did need to confront the issue of truth with Caitlin, not for my own satisfaction, but to make it possible for us to have a truly trusting relationship, maybe the first one in her life. I had by this point learned that there were all sorts of weird things going on in her family, lots of secrets and lies that had been kept hidden.

It was during the middle of one of our silent conversations that I took a deep breath and told Caitlin that I had a few things that I wanted to bring to her attention. One of the advantages of having a client who does not talk is that it is very easy to carve out time to say whatever I want and expect a fairly compliant audience. She cocked her head and actually made eye contact, signaling that she realized that something important was coming.

I told her everything that I had recently learned, that she had been making up her various ailments and faking the symptoms in order to visit the doctor, perhaps for attention and sympathy, or perhaps for other reasons that she might reveal. I presented specific, irrefutable behavioral evidence, complete with witnesses, so there would be no sense denying the "charges." Furthermore, I shared with her my concerns that all along she had been playing games with me, just as she had with the doctors—giving me the silent treatment and refusing to talk (except in carefully constructed letters). She seemed to be taking this with relative calmness, so I went further and talked about how this made it difficult for me to trust her. I told her how much I cared about her, how much I wanted to know her better, how important it was for me to help her if she would let me, and how I was bringing all this up because it felt like we could never go much further unless we were more honest with one another. Maybe this is coming across as harsh, but I tried to be as gentle and loving as I could while bringing the deceit into the open. And I insisted on thinking about this as an issue of honesty in our relationship rather than as a pathological condition named after an obscure German baron.

Caitlin looked at me thoughtfully after I finished what I had to say. I fully expected complete silence and so was surprised—and delighted—that after close to nine months we had our first real face-to-face conversation. It was as if a door had been opened and she had decided to walk through and meet me, if not halfway, then a few tentative footsteps in my vicinity. For the rest of that session, and the few that followed, she told me about the sexual abuse she had experienced since she had been a child—by her brother, the same brother who was still living with her, and still sneaking into her room at night. She admitted that she had been hurting herself, sticking objects in her vagina and burning her breasts with lit cigarettes, in order to discourage her brother from continuing to have sex with her. She talked about all the guilt she had been feeling and how she understood the meaning of the self-punishment. She even understood that her silence in her relationship with me was a way for her to maintain control, to take care of herself while in the room with a strange man who might hurt her the way she had been betrayed before.

Yes, I know what you are thinking: Was this true?

This time I can say, unequivocally and without reservation, yes, I am convinced that Caitlin did eventually trust me to risk revealing herself in a more honest and authentic way. How do I know that? Well, for one thing her symptoms disappeared. She moved out of the apartment where she had been living with her brother. She became functional in a whole host of other ways related to her work and other relationships. She confronted her brother, finally, and told him to never, ever come near her again or she would call the police. (I was able to get corroboration that this, in fact, did take place, and I was prepared to testify on her behalf.)

Yet would I be surprised if I ever learned that I had been scammed, that she made the whole story up, that she was still playing me—but simply changed tactics once I caught on to the previous game? Yes I would. I will never know of course. Most of the time we can never really know what is true and what is not. We have to live with this uncertainty and give people the benefit of the doubt. To do otherwise, we could never do this work or function at all.

Maybe you are not very surprised that there would not be much neat closure to our topic. You already knew there is no certainty in what we do, given the complexities and ambiguities or the territory in which we operate.

Clients Who Lie and Deceive

It is the client's job description in therapy to tell us what is going on as fully, completely, and honestly as possible, providing the most detailed and robust descriptions of complaints, life history, contextual features, and innermost thoughts and feelings. The reality of what we actually get from clients is less than ideal for a number of reasons. There are unconscious distortions and imperfect memories. Defense mechanisms operate to protect the client against pain, discomfort, and perceived attacks. Character traits may compromise trust and intimacy.

In a blog (psychcentral.com), psychologist John Grohol (2008a) asked people why they would ever lie to therapists. This was a question that he could never really understand. "If you lie to your therapist," he pointed out, "especially about something important in your life or directly related to your problems, then you're wasting your time and your therapist's time." He cites lies of omission as an example, such as a client saying he is depressed and uncertain why, yet failing to mention that his mother recently died. Or another example in which someone complains about low self-esteem but neglects to say that she binges and purges after every meal.

When Grohol first wrote his essay, musing about the ridiculousness of lying to the person who is paid to help you, he was completely unprepared for the barrage of clients who would respond on his blog. Here are a few representative reasons posted why people lie to their therapists:

> I don't yet trust my therapist, partly because I'm not confident that this therapist has the skills or experience to handle my problems in the first place. (Adrivahni, January 9, 2008)

> i lie to my therapist about what i'm feeling towards her. i'm embarrassed about these feelings, and when i do try to share them, they come out wrong. those are that i feel too dependent, that i want more than what she can give me, and that i find these feelings to be a sort of weakness in me. (Cameron, January 9, 2008)

> We all lie to our shrinks, just like we lie to our dentists (Sure, I'll floss twice a day) and our mechanics (It's not so much a click as a drum roll). But the point of repeat visits to our shrinks is to allow for the time necessary to figure out what's a lie, what's a misconception, and what the truth (for that day) is. (Gabriel, January 10, 2008)

Dozens of other confessions led Grohol (2008b) to write a follow-up essay about common reasons to lie to your therapist.

Contributions from him and from other sources (DeAngeles, 2008; Gediman & Leiberman, 1996; Kelly, 1998) identified several of the most common reasons for deception in therapy sessions.

Some Reasons Why Clients Lie

We have seen how lying is a natural and normal part of daily life, a practice that first begins about age 3 or 4 when we first learn we have choices about what we tell others, each presenting different consequences. Biologist Lewis Thomas once observed that if people stopped lying, the world would end—politicians would be arrested, media would be cancelled, and people would stop talking to one another. Lies, or at least half-truths and other fractions of complete honesty, allow trust to build. In therapy, deception is just another in a series of defenses that clients use to remain in control and to protect themselves.

Many, if not most, clients keep certain things from their therapists in order to present themselves in the best possible light. Whereas previously it was believed that lying or deceiving a therapist would only sabotage the treatment, it would appear as if clients may actually benefit by keeping some things private (Kelly, 1998). People lie to their spouses and partners, their family and friends, especially to coworkers and others in which favorable impressions are critical to continued success. It should come as no surprise that clients also lie to their therapists—a lot.

Fear of Shame and Humiliation

Let's face it: it is hard to talk about secrets, about sex, about mistakes and failures, about shortcomings, about feeling helpless to take care of one's own problems, about almost anything that people bring to sessions. It *hurts*.

Many clients lie to their therapists to avoid feelings of shame, embarrassment, and what they believe will be critical judgment by their therapists (DeAngelis, 2008). We may think of ourselves as neutral, accepting, and nonjudgmental, and advertise ourselves as such, but that does not mean that people actually believe us. And they aren't far wrong. The reality is that we *are* sometimes critical and judgmental (at least inside our heads) when clients do or say things that seem stupid, even as we keep the poker face in place, nod our heads, and pretend we do not care one way or the other.

Much of the content of therapy involves talking about things about which people feel most ashamed and embarrassed, and most reluctant to admit. It takes awhile for clients to warm up, to feel safe enough, in order to broach the subjects that are most sensitive. It is during this period in which the therapist is on probation that clients will take any steps necessary to risk greater vulnerability. When we think about it, it is absolutely ridiculous for us to anticipate anything different—that is, to actually expect a new client during the first few weeks to spill his or her guts and come clean with anything and everything that has been previously disguised or hidden. Lying during the initial (and subsequent) stages of therapy is not only normal but highly adaptive and healthy.

Disappointing the Therapist

Whether clients are afraid of disappointing their therapists, or whomever he or she represents as an authority or parental figure, there is often concern (or perception) that the naked truth will result in a loss of respect. One client explains why she lied: "For myself, one of my biggest problems has been worrying that I was letting my therapist or psychiatrist down in some way. I try to hide when I feel depressed, fearing that my mood is somehow going to wreak havoc on others. My therapist is a cognitive behaviorist and I used to fret that she'd think I hadn't been doing my homework. Also, she was so clearly concerned for my well-being that it upset me to come in when I was feeling lousy!" (MacNamarrah, 2008).

It is ironic, but all too often the case, that clients do not talk about what is really bothering them, or even cancel sessions when they need help the most. They believe that others—even someone who is paid to be helpful—cannot really handle their deepest secrets and innermost selves.

In addition, therapists are required by law to report suspected (or confessed) cases of physical, emotional, or sexual abuse. We are also forced to act when there is a risk of harm to self or others. Then there are other illegal or moral transgressions that may have been committed in the past, or are still currently going on. It behooves such an individual to be less than completely forthcoming with anyone, much less a professional who is mandated to contact authorities.

Ignorance

Some clients, who are relatively unsophisticated about therapy, or about how change takes place, leave out all kinds of important stuff because they did not know it was particularly important. It wasn't exactly that they were lying as much as choosing to ignore, deny, or otherwise gloss over things that did not seem all that important—and besides, they are uncomfortable to mention.

Physicians are able to run all kinds of diagnostic tests—blood work, magnetic resonance imaging (MRI), electrocardiograms (EKGs), ultrasound, urine analysis, biopsies, X-rays—because they do not fully trust self-reports as accurate data. We are left with what clients choose to tell us based on their beliefs about what is relevant, awareness of what they know and understand, and willingness to share information selectively. It is no wonder that we are operating with imperfect, flawed, and incomplete data.

Even in cases of clear success, how confident do you feel that you *really* understood what was going on? How certain are you that the results reported were truly accurate? If you answer, unequivocally, that you are *very* confident, perhaps you should consider your own degree of honesty.

Living Alternative Realities

For those with personality or factitious disorders, lying is a way of life. It has become so habituated that the person actually comes to believe the fantasies that are spun; they become an alternate reality.

When Meghan first contacted me, it was in a letter she had written after discovering one of my books at a garage sale (the first book I ever wrote that she purchased for a dollar). At the time she was a teenager and we struck up a correspondence that lasted for 20 years. Meghan struggled with depression throughout most of her life, had contemplated and attempted suicide many times, never deciding on the best method to end her life.

I'm still not sure what role I played in her life, but I always responded to her letters with support and caring, encouraging her to stay in therapy and continue to work on herself. She ended up reading many of my books over the years and, each time, would send her comments and reactions. Over the years she also told me a lot of things about herself, sent photos, brought me up to date on her family and relationships, and occasionally asked for advice. Even though she was not a client, and I never actually met her, I felt a certain responsibility to be as kind as I could; there was obviously some kind of transference going on and I wanted to be careful.

Eventually I learned that much of what Meghan had told me over the years were lies. I believe the part about her depression and suicidal thoughts, but I discovered that the photos she sent me were of someone else, the stories she told me were fictions, and that she had even sent me e-mails masquerading as other people. It was a bizarre case that I did my best to extricate myself from, although every few years Meghan will contact me again in some other disguised form.

There are other people like Meghan in the world and you have met them, perhaps worked with them. Sometimes you recognize them before you are sucked into their fantasy worlds; other times (most of the time in my experience) you do not realize the level of deception until it is far too late. One of the reasons it is so difficult to detect such mendacity is because the individuals have managed to confuse lies from truth; they cannot seem to tell the difference.

Unlike Jacob, I did have the chance to confront Meghan directly (and repeatedly) about the games she had played over the years. After each instance of discovering a lie, she would first deny it, then apologize profusely and beg for another chance. I gave up trying to negotiate a more honest form of communication with her soon after she sent me a draft of her autobiography, which she claimed would soon be released by a major New York publisher (another lie). It was titled: "I Will Tell You No Secrets and Tell You All Lies."

As with Meghan, some clients are not really lying to "us" but to individuals we represent, whether transference objects or surrogate authority figures. When all is said and done, therapists are never going to be very good at detecting client lies. It is just not part of our constitution, or our training, in which so much of what we learn to do is build trust.

Given the uncertainty and doubt we must accept and live with related to our work, the question remains: How do we work with issues of deception and lies in therapy?

Chapter **16**

Clinical Implications Related to Working With Lying in Therapy

It might seem that you could write off my experience with Jacob as a fluke. I have it on good authority that there are a number of instances in which clients have constructed elaborate hoaxes to fool or mislead their therapists (Kottler & Carlson, 2011). One such case involved a woman who reported over several months that her mother was dying of cancer. At the point at which therapy was about to end, she informed her therapist that her mother had finally died and she was grief stricken. The therapist suspected something was wrong with this story and so confronted the woman who insisted it was true. It wasn't until the therapist asked her to bring in an obituary to prove it that the woman finally confessed her lie. When pressed she admitted that she was afraid her therapist would abandon her, and this was the only way she could think of to be allowed to continue the sessions. Yet Billig (1991) saw this as an opportunity to deal with the issues related to abandonment, as well as deceit. With compassion and new understanding, he realized that the client was trying in her own way to protect herself and also deal with feelings of anger and mistrust that were difficult for her to express in more direct ways.

It is not a matter of what you will do *if* your clients lie to you, but *when* they do so. Once recognized, such behavior must be examined and analyzed—not just within the context of that single deception but within the larger sphere of the relationship, and all other relationships. Clients often report that once they have revealed secrets and come clean with their deceptions and lies, they experienced significant benefits working through the deception (Farber, Berano, & Capobianco, 2006).

There is even reason to believe that a certain degree of strategic deception in the first place—or at least selective secrecy—may be of benefit. Clients who kept things from their therapists (roughly half of those surveyed) reported that this allowed them to feel some degree of control in the early stages of the relationship before trust had fully developed. They were able to hide undesirable things about themselves until such time that they felt ready to bring them into the open (Kelly, 1998).

To Whom Does the Story Belong?

One of the possible explanations for understanding Jacob's story is that it was a cocreated phenomenon. Whether deliberately or unconsciously, therapists help to shape what clients tell us by what we selectively probe and prompt, what we reinforce and ignore, and what aspects of the story we focus upon. Clients watch us closely to see what interests us the most and what commands our attention—after all, they want an attentive audience; they want to please us, to entertain us, and even to titillate us.

In cases where memories are a little hazy, we often fill in the gaps through suggestions and interpretations. Here is an extreme example of "leading the witness," so to speak.

Therapist: So, when you say you felt uncomfortable with your father coming into your room at night, do you mean that he touched you inappropriately?

Client: That depends if kissing me goodnight counts as inappropriate.

Therapist: Where did he kiss you?

Client: Where do you think he kissed me?

Therapist: When he touched you like that, how did you feel? It must have been awfully frightening to be sexually abused like that.

Client: Sexually abused? What are you talking about? All I meant is that I felt uncomfortable when *anyone* came into my room—my mother, my sister, even the housekeeper. I've got this thing about my privacy. Actually my father was much more respectful of my space than anyone else.

Without delving into all the controversy surrounding recovered memories and their validity, I only wish to make the point that the ways we ask questions, the choices we make about what to explore, and how we fill in gaps with our paraphrases and interpretations, end up not just fleshing out the client's story but *cocreating* it.

How to (Maybe) Tell When Clients Are Lying

In a survey of therapists asking them how they know when their clients are lying to them, several respondents spoke with authority about their favorite methods for uncovering truth. Excuse my skepticism, but throughout my whole career I have heard colleagues (and supervisors) speak with complete confidence and authority about their flawless abilities to accurately diagnose client problems or design the perfect treatment plan to resolve the difficulties. My own experience has been far more cautious and tentative, almost always concerned that my impressions may not be accurate.

With that said, therapists mentioned that they could catch lies "when her story didn't make sense," or "their cognitive dissonance comes across in subtle ways." I mentioned previously that professional lie-catchers like forensic psychologists, secret service agents, CIA interrogators, judges, customs officials, drug enforcement personnel, FBI agents, and police officers find that even with their specialized training and years of experience, they are often no more skilled at ferreting out truth than others. Yet, there are certain professionals—lawyers, mediators, law enforcement personnel, and therapists—who have been able to develop extraordinary lie-detecting skills. One stated reason for this ability is that it was based on motivation and need: "Many came from difficult or unusual early childhoods, when the stakes were high for learning to read people" (Cooper, 2009, p. 14).

Ekman (2009) offers several explanations as to why it is so difficult to tell when people are lying, foremost among them that, evolutionarily speaking, this had never been that important of a skill. Until relatively recently in our history, there was little privacy and few secrets that could be hidden because everyone lived pretty much within community view in the ancestral environment. Nowadays, there are all kinds of privacy and secrecy that are possible that have never been possible before. In addition, being caught in a lie does not result in disastrous consequences the way it would have long ago, "for one can change jobs, change spouses, change villages. A damaged reputation need not follow you" (Ekman, 2009, p. 342).

Acknowledging the virtual inevitability of client deception, Yalom (2002) used what he calls "here-and-now rabbit ears" to identify possible lies in client stories. He starts out with the assumption that all clients are hiding something: "There is always some concealment, some information withheld because of shame, because of some particular way they wish me to regard them" (p. 74). It is precisely the discussion of these lies that he believes can lead to important breakthroughs in the quality of the relationship, to "fine-tune" it in light of this deeper level of trust and disclosure.

The name escapes me, but some philosopher once said that within every lie there is a grain of truth. More to the point, Weinshel (1979, p. 524) remarked that most distorted memories or deliberate lies in therapy hold within them some "trace of historical truth." The therapist's job, according to this view, is "liberating the fragment of historical truth from its distortions" (Freud, 1937b, p. 268). Both authors see lies not as moral issues but rather as a form of resistance to prevent further suffering. Weinshel (1979, p. 529), in particular, found lies to be "extremely helpful in revealing data" that would otherwise not have become evident. What clients choose to lie about and how they present this material are revealing in their own right.

Exploring the Relationship

So often, deception and lying in therapy occur as a relational process in which the clinician's reactions are part of the phenomenon (Gediman & Leiberman, 1996). We are coconspirators in a sense, coauthors of the lie. Just as there are systemic factors operating in almost any individual's difficulties, so too is deception often (but not always) the product of two or more people engaged in communication.

The big question, of course, is what does the lie mean within the context of the relationship with any client? As with many other instances of incongruity, evasion, and discrepancy that might emerge in a conversation, the most direct response is to name what is felt, sensed, or observed: "I'm confused. You are saying that your wife neglected you and that's why you decided to end the marriage. Yet for the past several minutes all you've been talking about are the ways she took care of you."

If the client is not ready yet to accept responsibility for a more accurate version of truth, we will see evidence of that immediately: "No, you don't understand. What I meant was. . ." Depending how the client chooses to respond to confrontation, or even the labeling of discrepancy, we have sufficient feedback on whether it is best at that point to back off or push a little harder.

There is often an assumption, if not a pretense, that therapists are scientists when often we are intuitive practitioners. If there are not reliable cues that betray fibs, lies, and deception, we are left to monitor our own internal reactions and lived experience within the relationship. It is by learning to pay closer attention to the physical sensations within our bodies, especially as things start to "tingle," that we are able to "reclaim our body's ability to speak to us clearly and directly" (Napier, 2009, p. 36).

Acknowledging and Working Through Feelings of Betrayal

Nobody likes to be fooled or manipulated, a therapist least of all because of our belief (arrogance) of having specialized training and skills that allow us to see through charades. Yet feeling helpless, angry, and frustrated are sometimes to be expected in such a situation in which trust has been breached. This can reflect strong countertransference reactions with the given client, but far more than that, it can spark a crisis to question the meaning of truth in any and all relationships, therapy or otherwise.

Billig (1991) learned a lot from his encounter with the client who fabricated her mother's death. Afterward, he viewed deception as just another kind "of unusual data which may contribute to the reconstruction of early history and conflicts as well as our understanding the transference relationship and more recent crises" (p. 352). In other words, lies represent information from the client about how things are progressing.

Yet it is hard not to take deception personally. Once discovered, questions immediately come to surface: How could I have missed that? Where did I go wrong? How could I have been so gullible? What does this say about my competence? What have I done, or not done, that makes it so unsafe for my client to confide in me?

These are valid questions to a certain extent, conveying the feelings that somehow, some way, you have been fooled and misled. The assumption is that only if you were more alert, more skilled, more experienced, sensitive, attentive, or careful, you would have caught the lie. There is a belief that to be fooled is a reflection of your own misjudgment—with the corresponding feelings of betrayal.

The progression of my own reactions to Jacob's story—over a period of 10 years—followed a series of stages that began with denial and progressed through feelings of frustration, anger, doubt, *self*-doubt, and finally curiosity, if not amusement. It was betrayal that stuck with me most, not only with Jacob but with others who have deceived me.

I remember seeing a couple for marital therapy and things seemed to be going pretty well. I heard the door open in my waiting room, signaling that my clients had arrived for their appointment.

I prepared to greet them when I saw the husband waiting alone; apparently his wife had not yet arrived.

"Oh," I said surprised. Usually they came together. "I'll check in with you again after your wife gets here."

Just as I started to close the door, I heard the husband yell out, "Wait!"

"Yes?"

"There's something I have to tell you."

A loud warning started wailing inside my head, just like a siren, but I was frozen with indecision. Because the couple was my client, we agreed that I would not see them for individual sessions but only together. As such, I neglected to explain or impose any sort of rules about communication outside of our scheduled sessions. But there wasn't time to think about this, or even what the husband could possibly tell me with the door half open and my head stuck outside. I figured he was just going to change our next appointment. Or maybe I was just stupid. In any case, I just stood there.

"There's something I've been wanting to tell you for some time," the husband repeated. "You see, I've been having an affair and my wife doesn't know. She can't know. You can't tell her because what I'm telling you is confidential. But I just wanted you to know because it might help you to understand things a little better. The only reason I'm doing this is because my wife and I, well, we haven't been having physical relations, you know, sex, for a long time."

All I could think to do was close the door. I probably should have sought consultation about this, but I felt trapped and embarrassed. As I sat in my office waiting for the wife to arrive, I realized that this was useful information that did explain a lot about why we had reached an impasse in our sessions. I needed to find a way to bring the secret out in the open so that we could deal with it. I also resolved in the future to make the ground rules a lot clearer that *anything* that the other partner tells me outside of session belongs to the therapy.

Maybe getting the secret off his chest was a breakthrough for the husband, but in that session, and the ones that followed, he was more conciliatory and less obstructive than he had been previously. We made significant progress and I thought the time was almost right for me to invite the husband to talk to his wife about his still ongoing affair (at least I assume it was continuing). But then, maybe it wasn't my place to do this? Before I could come to a decision, there was a major breakthrough in their relationship and both partners expressed delight that their marriage was once again on solid ground and they would not need to return for any more sessions.

I wondered if the husband was still seeing his girlfriend on the side, and still felt very uncomfortable holding the secret, but I did not think it was my place to stir this up as long as both of them were reporting such significant progress. I agreed that this would be our last session and presented the husband with the final bill that included three months of accumulated charges that he had been postponing payment for until he received a commission check. We shook hands. I wished them well. And the husband said he would put a check in the mail.

I followed up with the husband a few weeks later to find out why he still had not taken care of his outstanding balance, and he promised once again he would take care of it. A few days later I received a threatening phone call from him saying that he was consulting a lawyer to sue me and also filing a grievance with the ethics board. Before I could figure out what he was talking about, he blurted out that his wife had found out about his affair and it was all my fault.

"What are you talking about?" I said, feeling both defensive and angry. I had sure wanted to tell the wife, but obviously he had slipped up and she had discovered the truth.

"My wife knows what's going on," he told me. "And I admitted to her that you know about the affair as well and didn't say anything about it because you thought it was okay. After all, if it wasn't, you would have told her, right?"

"Excuse me? I didn't say anything to honor your confidentiality. . . ."

"Doesn't matter," he interrupted. "Someone called her anonymously and told her what was going on. I know it wasn't you, Doc, but I told her it was. Anyway, she's furious at you, more so than at me right now, so that's pretty good, huh?" He started to laugh. "Anyway, those invoices you keep sending me? Forget it. I won't be paying you a dime and if you keep bothering me, you'll hear from my lawyer."

Click. He hung up the phone.

I'd been set up. Later I realized that it was my own fault for mismanaging the case, at least with respect to the disclosure of secrets, but I felt so betrayed. The husband had been lying not only to his wife, but to me. He never intended to pay his bill, and this was just the excuse he had selected. I'm convinced that if his wife had not discovered his affair, he would have manufactured some other reason.

I had worked hard for this couple and done solid work. I had been pleased with the outcome we achieved. They had come to me for help and I had offered the best I could do. After I came to terms that I would never be paid for my work, after I held my breath for months waiting for a nuisance lawsuit or ethics complaint, after I realized that the husband had manipulated me and compromised the trust in our relationship—just as he had done with his wife—I was left with feelings of betrayal. How could I have been so stupid and trusting? Why did I believe him when he said he would take care of his bill? After all my dedication and effort, how could he be so ungrateful?

Ah the things we learn from such tough lessons. I accepted that I really had been betrayed and manipulated. Looking back, I realized this was just part of this man's style, the way he lives in the world. If it was only money I lost, then I paid for my mistakes with fair compensation. But I no longer feel like he betrayed me, but rather betrayed himself. I could have lost my innocence after an experience like this, although I did learn to work differently with couples. I could have become a lot more suspicious and mistrustful with the people I work with. But instead I learned that this supposed betrayal was really just another opportunity for me to work on my own clinical skills, as well as my own unresolved issues related to meeting unrealistic standards for perfection. Whether I messed up or not, whether I had been more careful, suspicious, and vigilant, there are still people in the world (many who end up in our offices) who live by different rules and enjoy the power that comes from knocking an authority figure off the pedestal.

This process of working through feelings of betrayal is best done in supervision or consultation with trusted colleagues. What I have described as my own process took many months of work to accept, forgive, and move on. I wished I had the chance to talk to the husband about the ways he handled the situation and our relationship. I wish I could have done a few things differently myself. Ideally, it is desirable to be able to confront the dishonesty and work through it.

Confronting Issues of Deception and Dishonesty

Ongoing deceit or "big" lies (the kind that go on for some time) continue because the victim (in this case, the therapist) helps maintain the fabrication by giving the client the benefit of the doubt and actually colluding with the dishonesty. This could involve neglect (such as the husband described above) or could be a more protracted and complex case such as Jacob's story that took place over a year.

Once deception and dishonesty are suspected or discovered, the next question is what to do about it. Ignoring this situation for any length of time is probably not an option but neither is rushing to judgment before the client is prepared to "own" the lie.

If you should choose to confront instances of dishonesty, there are several relatively diplomatic ways to proceed that were specifically developed with substance abusers who are prone to lying and deceit (Beck, Wright, Newman, & Liese, 1993; Newman & Strauss, 2003). I have added several other considerations to this list.

Ask Yourself Why the Client Is Lying

Deception has particular meaning for a client at a given moment in time. What are the goals and motives of the behavior? What are possible hidden agendas? Is this about avoiding shame or exhibiting power?

If Jacob was lying in his story, what was that really about? I have offered several possible explanations, most of which are connected to our relationship—wanting attention and affirmation. It did not strike me that his lies/exaggerations/faulty memory (choose one) would have been malicious.

I never had the chance to talk to Jacob about my concerns and what it meant for his life and for our relationship, but one lesson learned for me was to explore these issues with others. Because many of my "clients" these days are graduate students or interns, the nature of the lying I might encounter is somewhat different, yet parallel.

Karla turned in an assignment that I recognized as the most blatant case of plagiarism I'd ever seen. She had literally copied whole pages from an article and pasted them into her research paper. The really strange thing about this dishonesty is that she actually included the citation for the article from which she had stolen the material. Did she want to get caught, I wondered?

When confronted about her behavior, Karla claimed that she did not know that what she had done was unacceptable. Considering she had already completed a bachelor's degree in the social sciences and was in her last semester of graduate school, this excuse hardly seemed reasonable—but she stuck to it no matter how compelling the evidence. I met with her alone and virtually begged her to fess up so that some therapeutic/educational remediation could take place, but she insisted it was just a harmless mistake. Unfortunately, because she would not accept responsibility for her behavior, judicial proceedings were initiated that resulted in her being dismissed from the program. She had been caught in a lie and found herself backed up so far against a wall that she felt she had no other option except to stick with her story: she sacrificed her degree and future career for the sake of preserving the illusion that she did not cheat.

Years went by and I always wondered what really happened with Karla. Is that not so often the case that we continue to mull over the unfinished business with those we help, the ones whose stories leave us hanging? She wrote a letter, finally apologizing, admitting her wrongdoing, and asking to be readmitted. Alas, by then it was too late. As much as she suffered from the lapse in judgment, I spent more time than I ever should have trying to make sense of the behavior and its aftermath.

It Helps to Have Supporting Evidence

It is highly likely that the client will deny any accusation that he or she is being less than truthful. An adolescent who was referred because of skipping school and causing disruptions insisted each session that things were improving. We negotiated a condition of our relationship that I would not speak to his parents or school authorities without his consent, or at least presence, during the conversation (probably my mistake). I only learned by accident from another student in the school that his problems were more pronounced than ever.

I could easily anticipate that if I confronted him with this, he would not only deny the accusations but would most likely accuse me of betraying him by going behind his back to talk to others without his consent. Still, it seemed the alternative was to continue to listen to his fake reports of progress while knowing that our conversations were a sham.

I informed the boy that I had inadvertently met someone who knew him in school and told me, without prompting, about all the troubles that were continuing.

"Not true," he said, crossing his arms defiantly.

"I guess I knew that's what you'd say," I answered, and pulled out copies of his truancy reports that had been part of his school records and to which I had been granted access when his parents had signed a release.

Not surprisingly, he went after me with all his anger blazing, accusing me of reneging on our agreement, betraying his trust, and everything else he could think of to distract us from the issue at hand. I just listened until he talked himself out. Then I calmly reviewed our agreement that the condition stipulated that he would be honest with me so I did not have to check up on him. Once he had violated his pledge, I had no choice but to consult other sources because I could no longer trust what he told me.

"But all that is beside the point," I told him, "you are coming to see me because of these problems at school—during those rare times you ever show up—and nothing much seems to have changed." I still held the evidence in my lap which I held up to him.

This is the point of the story when you are anticipating that the boy finally admitted to his lies, apologized for deceiving me, and made a commitment to be more forthcoming in the future—not to mention attend school regularly.

In actuality, he walked out and never returned. He would not return my phone calls, so I had to tell his parents that, for now at least, I could not do much for him until such a time that he was prepared to be honest. I could now recognize that there were all kinds of things I wished I had done differently—family therapy for one—but I still do not think that would have made much difference.

I was pleased that I had done my homework and was prepared to counter his continued deception, but I had not done a very good job of helping him to preserve his dignity.

Help the Client to Save Face

Nobody likes to be caught in a lie (see example above). It is not all that uncommon for therapists to be "fired" when their clients are confronted with too much vigor and no way to preserve their dignity. As with any confrontation, it is usually best to casually point out discrepancies: "I'm a little confused because what you are saying now is quite different from what you said earlier. Maybe you could help me to understand this."

Of course, this could also be interpreted as an invitation to dig into the hole even deeper. The client might respond with, "What I really meant. . ." or "I think you misunderstood me earlier."

Regardless of the way the deception or exaggeration is handled, we do not want to be in a position in which we are arguing about what was really said or meant, but instead to talk more openly about the difficulties of sharing on a really honest level.

Name and Honor the Reluctance

It is one of the most important strategies whenever at an impasse to stop doing what is not working and try something else. In situations where the client persists in denial or deception, rather than pushing harder, it may be best to back off for the time being: "It seems like it is difficult for you to tell me about what is really going on so let's move on to something else that does feel safe to talk about."

Demonstrating patience and respect for the client's pace is ideal but may not be possible in time-limited treatment plans. Like any other form of resistance in therapy, it is almost always helpful to examine the interactive effects that are operating—that is, what the therapist might be doing, or not doing, that makes it difficult for the client to be more honest and open. It is often the case that it is not a matter of clients being resistant, but they are cooperating in ways that are different from what their therapists expect and prefer. You ask a direct question, for example, and the client provides an evasive, less than honest response. Perhaps this interaction reflects the way the question was asked—its timing and phrasing—rather than the client's intent to deceive.

Of course, these approaches, or any others, are not going to be very successful if the client is determined to maintain a false front and avoid authentic engagement on an honest level. I never got the chance to broach this with Jacob before he died, perhaps in part because of my own fear of what I would hear.

Chapter **17**

When a Therapist Catches Despair

This is the parallel story of an assassin and a therapist, how each of us was involved in a narrative that may or may not have been factual, but that represents a window into the nature of truth and what it means for the work we do. We began with the therapist's story, followed by roughly one half of the story told to me by Jacob. After exploring some of the meanings, implications, and applications of the issues raised, we return to my story once again, especially as it relates to the lessons learned.

A Lapse Back Into the Past

On one level I was horrified by Jacob's story. He was a trained killer, an assassin. If his story was indeed true, then he walked up to people, supposedly designated as enemies, and murdered them in cold blood. Moreover, he did not seem to show the slightest remorse or guilt, claiming he was just a soldier following orders. We have heard that excuse before.

If Jacob made up this story to entertain me, or keep me engaged with him, I just feel sad about the whole sorry mess. Rather than betrayed or victimized, I feel like I coconspired with him to keep the fantasy going. I wanted this story to be true. I *needed* it to be true and so did not press as hard as I could have to get some definitive answers.

When we were together, I did not want Jacob to stop talking—and that says a lot because that guy could talk. I am not the most patient listener in the first place, and it would take him hours to get to the point he was making. I'd ask him a simple question: "What was it like to kill someone for the first time?"

Jacob would shrug. "What can I say? The guy deserved it. I gotta tell you one thing, though, I sure don't deserve this pain in my side. I've been to the doctor early today, before I saw you, and he ran the usual tests. He can't figure out what's wrong. None of them can. I got this dull pain right here and sometimes it just starts to burn. First they think its colitis. Then maybe gallstones. They run more tests. They tell me it might be Crohn's disease. Do you know what that is?"

I nodded my head in the affirmative, not because I knew the answer but because I was trying to get him back to his story. This is how it went because Jacob was so easily distracted. And because this is a book about truth, I might as well admit that I was doing anything I could think of to avoid going back to work. I was tired of listening to my clients whine and complain. I was bored with my work and even more bored with myself.

Jacob, on the other hand, was a character. And I just hit the jackpot: he had a story to tell that was literally like something I'd read in the history books or seen in the movies. And I could be part of this—I would be the one to tell his story. This would be my escape from the tedium and stress of my other jobs. I could reinvent myself.

I thought back to other times in my life when I had been feeling this way, and it almost always ended up with me back in therapy as a client or, more often, making a dramatic change in what I do or how I do it. I was thinking about the last time I felt so discouraged and wished to change my work.

Loss of Hope

Rewind the story about 20 years or so. Angie was depressed. Not just ordinary, run-of-the-mill a little bit sad, but profoundly, disturbingly, chronically, hopelessly depressed. This was the kind of depression that I could see at a glance, that I could hear in an instant, and that I could feel seeping into my pores. It was depression that represented utter despair.

Angie had already seen a half dozen other therapists. She had tried a number of medications without improvement, the side effects only making her worse. She had been referred to a neurologist and a host of other specialists looking for an organic origin but again without success. By the time she saw me, she was beyond caring. In fact, the only thing I got out of her in our first session is that her parents made her come but she did not see the point. Angie was 15 and felt her life was over.

During the first few sessions I tried to sound as upbeat as I could, suggesting that we really could make a difference if we put our heads together. I could not tell how well this went over because Angie hid behind a cascade of hair falling forward over her face. She sat hunched over on the couch, grasping her knees, sobbing wordlessly throughout the whole session. Sometimes I might see a slight nod of her head, acknowledging some question I might ask or comment I might offer, but it may have just been wishful thinking. About one thing I was totally certain: I had caught her despair.

Over the course of the next 18 months that we spent together, meeting once a week, sometimes more often, Angie spent virtually all of our time together crying. She spoke in a language of tears that inspired me to write a book of that name trying to make sense of what she was trying to communicate. I felt helpless, impotent, and worthless as a therapist because I could do nothing to help her; I could not even get her to speak. She would sit with me throughout the whole hour crying behind her shield of hair. I would watch her shoulders rise and fall in synchrony with her sobs, waiting for a sign that she was ready to talk.

During this period of time, I went to a dozen workshops to study different techniques that I might employ with my most resistant client. Each time I would return to our next scheduled session with renewed hope that I might finally break through Angie's despair. I tried at least a hundred different strategies during our time together. After exhausting my usual repertoire, I experimented with hypnosis, then psychodrama (with me playing all the roles because she would not speak). I sought consultation with a dozen different supervisors and twice as many colleagues, asking for advice, feedback, and support. Most of all, I kept the frustrations and feelings of ineptitude to myself. It was one of my most deeply guarded secrets that I had begun to lose hope in the power of my ability to heal.

Then, like almost everything that happens in my life, I decided to write a book about all of my clients who were so stubborn, resistant, obstructive, and ornery. Quick. Who comes immediately to mind?

I bet you would think about that surly adolescent who will not talk, who tells you to go screw yourself every time you try to break through his shell. Or you might nominate the client who rambles endlessly, never listens, and will not let you talk. Or the one who's got your number, knows your weak spots, and exploits them every chance she's got. The chronically mentally ill, drug addicted, manipulative borderline, overly anxious OCD—they all get chapters too. I had an endless catalog of incredibly difficult clients, each of whom would get due recognition, but Angie was at the top of the list, the one who worried me most.

Caring a Little Too Much

I became a therapist in the first place because of my own sense of worthlessness. I believed that by devoting my life to helping others I might somehow redeem a life that, until then, had felt wasted. I lived for the validation I felt knowing that I made some kind of difference. It gave some meaning and purpose to the suffering in my early life. But it also left me vulnerable to those times when I felt like a failure. I'm a good therapist, but there were times I still felt like a fraud, especially when clients like Angie did not improve.

I often wished Angie would just go away, that her parents would give up and take her to someone else who specialized in lost causes. I was supposedly an expert on hard-to-treat cases, having done research and a book on difficult clients, so it was nothing new for me to work with such challenges. But there was something about *this* case—no, not the case, but Angie as a person—that struck terror in my heart and soul. By this time I cared so deeply for her that I convinced myself I could save her, that I could do what nobody else had done before me.

We had settled into a routine after so much time together. Angie would come in, take her accustomed seat (on the right side of the couch next to the Kleenex box on the table), nod at me once, and then lean forward so that she could slip behind a curtain of hair.

"How are you doing?" I'd begin.

Angie nodded, at least I *think* there was a slight head movement, but otherwise silence.

I'd wait her out for as long as I could—two, three, five, sometimes ten agonizing minutes with her sitting as still as a statue.

"So," I'd try again, "what would you like to talk about today?"

Then I'd see a slight tremor, the hair waving just a bit, before the tears would start falling. I'd see them falling, little droplets that were so weightless they would settle on top of the delicate hairs of her arm. I'd watch them evaporate as a way to keep myself occupied during these interminable silences.

"I know this is agonizing for you," I'd reflect after awhile, "coming in here week after week, letting yourself feel the full brunt of your pain, but nothing really changes." I wasn't sure if I was speaking to myself or to Angie.

And so it would go for close to an hour, Angie crying, sometimes sobbing, sometimes so still she seemed frozen solid. I would stare out the window and wait. I'd offer deep interpretations or empathic reflections of feelings. I'd share my own feelings of helplessness or talk about times in my life when I felt out of control and misunderstood. I told her stories. I created metaphors. I'd say out loud (even if I did not believe it) that it was perfectly fine for her to do whatever she was doing.

On some level, I knew that this was the one place in her life where she felt safe to cry and let herself go—a number of colleagues and supervisors had already pointed out that this, in itself, was invaluable help. After all, she *was* still functioning in school and performing in ballet recitals, doing quite well in both arenas.

And she had not yet killed herself, or even made a serious effort to follow through on threats. So maybe I was doing something right.

Crossing a Boundary

During one of the rare times when Angie was willing to throw me a few bones, she told me about an upcoming ballet recital in which she would be dancing a lead role. Without consciously thinking about it, I made a mental note of the time and place that coming weekend. I showed up at the auditorium, mostly out of curiosity. The only time I had ever seen Angie was when she was in the throes of despair. I wondered what she looked like in the "other" world. I told myself this was a research venture, but I knew all along that I was crossing a boundary. My only defense was desperation—not only to save my client but myself.

In the darkness of the auditorium I found a seat toward the back, at the end of a row so I could make a fast getaway if I needed to. When the curtain came up, and the performance began, I completely forgot everything else except Angie's incredible grace and beauty on stage. She danced like an angel, like someone with passion and *life*. I had never seen anything so beautiful and I was dumbfounded by how much this meant to me. I was crying out of control, trying to contain myself so I did not make a scene. This was an Angie I had never known existed, and it was moving beyond anything I could possibly explain.

It was at that moment that Angie met my eyes. It seems improbable that she could actually see me in that darkened room, one among hundreds in the audience, but she saw me and she knew that I saw her recognition. There were times throughout the rest of the performance that I saw her glancing in my direction as if to reassure herself that I wasn't an illusion. I slipped out before the lights went on.

When Angie visited for her next session, neither of us said a word about the performance and my presence there. It was like it had never happened. But there was something different from that time onward. There had been some kind of breakthrough—for both of us.

Stories like this are often told as if there was a transformation that occurred all at once; this was far more gradual. For the first time, Angie began to speak to me with words, giving voice to what her tears had been saying all that time. If this sounds like this is all it took, I assure it was not. In some ways, things were even worse for a little while because now she was actually *talking* about how awful she felt most of the time (except when she was on stage). If it had been difficult to "hold" her despair before, now it was even more challenging in some ways. I still felt her helplessness and hopelessness.

Eventually, Angie did grow out of her despair. From ages 15 to 17 that I was privileged to know her (and it did seem like a privilege by the end), Angie blossomed into a mature young woman. She would most likely struggle with depression in some form most of her life, but it seems that she did learn a thing or two from our work together.

Because this final chapter is about the therapist's own struggle with despair and reluctance to own and talk about it, the ending of the story is less relevant to the theme we are exploring. I actually heard from Angie recently; she tracked me down on the Internet after more than 20 years had passed since I had last seen her. She has a family now, works in a helping profession herself, and seems to be quite successful. I did not ask her how she was doing with her despair: I did not want to know.

Hope and Despair

If there is one thing that therapists must confront on a daily basis, it is the sense of hopelessness that clients bring to sessions. Doing therapy can crush the spirit, if not the psyche, of its practitioners. Although there have been some investigations of burnout related to our profession (for example, Edelwich & Brodsky, 1980; Maslach, 2003; Skovholt, 2001), more generalized, accumulative despair has not often been raised with the exception of a few sources (Chessick, 1978; Fine, 1980; Kottler, 2010; Sussman, 1995). It is perhaps not that surprising, then, that one quarter of practitioners do not much enjoy their work, being classified as either "disengaged" from their clients or outright "distressed" (Orlinsky & Ronnestad, 2005).

Whether depressed, anxious, lost, or frustrated, people come to us in the first place because they cannot find a way out of their struggles. Furthermore, they do not honestly believe that anyone else can help them either. Therapy often represents a last desperate chance before all hope is surrendered. To add to the challenges, often the ways they present themselves, especially in the beginning, are less than forthright and honest.

It is a paradox that while despair springs from an absence of hope, it is also the consequence of reaching for expectations that are beyond one's grasp. The British novelist Graham Greene (1948) claimed that despair is the price we all pay for setting grandiose goals. It is, he wrote, "the unforgivable sin," but one that could never be practiced by someone who is corrupt or evil; such individuals always embrace hope. "He never reaches the freezing point of knowing absolute failure. Only the man of good will carries always in his heart this capacity for damnation" (p. 60).

Hope and despair are a therapist's constant companions. The price we pay for our optimism, our hope for the future, our belief in our own powers to help others, is that we must also live with the limits, disappointment, and failures of our best efforts. We must maintain optimism even as we recognize the depths of our own discouragement with some clients who do not improve no matter how hard we work, and those clients who lie to us no matter how much we invite their honesty.

Therapists are virtually required to keep a smile on our faces. We are in the business of selling hope. Hope is our mantra, our reason for existence. Everything we understand about the way therapy works is that if we can convince clients that what we have to offer them is useful, and we believe this, then they will more likely respond to our interventions. The placebo effect is all about capitalizing on these positive expectations.

Yet in the privacy of our own minds and hearts resides an assortment of doubts. Do we *really* make a difference in anyone's life? Do the effects really last? What sort of impact can we really have on people who are wracked with such intractable, chronic problems? And what can we do for those who will never really recover from traumas, illness, or disorders from which they suffer?

One answer is that we believe our own myths and illusions that we present to others. We deny our own sense of despair, disown our failures, and pretend as if we have everything fully under control. We believe our lies when we tell clients that everything will be fine, that we have the answers, that we can cure their suffering or relieve their pain. Oh, we reassure our colleagues and supervisors that we understand our limits and acknowledge our failings. But deep down inside, we really do want to save people; on a good day, we actually believe this is possible.

And what of our personal despair, that which emanates from our own disappointments and failures? Apart from anything depressing that our clients bring us, we each have our own demons. Some of us suffer from chronic depression, and all of us from the kind of existential angst that comes with being alive. Let's face it: as therapists, there is no place to hide.

Every day, we must square off against precisely those same issues that terrify us the most—the fears of mediocrity, of failure, loneliness, meaninglessness, losing control, and being responsible. Countertransference does not begin to cover the territory: we must not only live with our despair but also shoulder the burdens of all those who come to us for help.

A client confesses she has no reason to live, and a part of me agrees with her. I wonder if she will ever experience anything resembling happiness, or even numbness. Another client suffers from a chronic disease for which there is no cure and I am only applying psychological compresses to ease a bit of the pressure. Another client has been so traumatized by a host of early experiences that I have serious doubts about whether I can put a dent in what is needed. Still another pilgrim crawls into the office seeking an end to pain, only to display a bewildering array of chronic addictions, mood disorders, and florid personality disorder.

Then there are those who come for the most pedestrian of reasons, to lose a few pounds, quit smoking, find another job, make a life decision, recover from a lost love, or stop drinking so much. Sure, the success rate in our work seems pretty high, approaching eight in ten among those who seek our services. But during moments of our own despair, we wonder whether these changes really matter much to the person, much less to the rest of the world.

How can we *not* feel despair when looking at the poverty, the starving, the indigent in the world? How can we ever feel satisfied with the small efforts we make when confronting how much there is to do? How can we avoid despair when spending our working days with people who are miserable, conflicted, dissatisfied, depressed, despondent, addicted, suicidal, or sometimes even actively hallucinating?

Rekindling Hope

Despair has been such a neglected, taboo subject in our field, just as has dishonesty. Certainly, there is plenty written about depression, but almost nothing about the more amorphous, intangible despair; most of the major contributors have been the likes of Mark Twain, Albert Camus, Jean-Paul Sartre, and those with an existential bent.

Despair, writes another English novelist, George Eliot, is "the painful eagerness of unfed hope." There can be no despair without yearning, without thoughts for the future. This point is only too obvious when attending any conference or gathering of therapists. In any staff room or meeting, you hear tales of discouragement and disillusionment, of desperate searches for the latest therapeutic technique or magic cure.

Therapists complain that managed care has taken much of the pleasure out of our work or, at the very least, robbed us of freedom and choices. There is too much paperwork and too little control. More and more clients want instant cures, if not from our efforts then from Prozac and other medications. "They just don't want to take responsibility for their own change," one therapist complained. "We are working with a generation of whining narcissists."

Yet hope and optimism can only be rekindled if therapists are given permission to admit the despair we sometimes feel. In some ways, despair is our friend that heightens our empathic attunement and our ability to truly understand a client's experience. It also means that we live with such uncertainty and ambiguity about the nature of our work and its actual impact.

It seems peculiar that anyone who needs to feel validated and useful would ever choose a profession in which we are often unsure whether we helped anyone. Our clients lie. At times even they are not sure what is real and what is imagined. Those who appear to deteriorate the worst in sessions may actually be making great strides outside the sessions; likewise, those who respond spectacularly well to every intervention may not be changing a single thing in their lives. Even more confusing is that lack of ongoing feedback after they leave: Do the changes they appear to make really last?

There are times when therapists feel such despair at what it is we do, even if it is rarely acknowledged, much less spoken aloud. Some of the people we all attempt to help have problems that are so long-standing, so chronic and unremitting, so severe, that whatever we do seems like nothing but a token gesture. The kids leave the session and return to their gangs or abusive homes. Those with impulse disorders, hallucinations, personality disturbances, chronic drug abuse, major depression—the list goes on and on— sometimes seem impervious to the most powerful interventions. When some of our most challenging cases do show definite signs of progress, we are left to wonder how much of these changes will persist over time, especially with toxic families, limited resources, dysfunctional environments, addictions, medical conditions, abject poverty, or crime-filled neighborhoods.

We are all forced to confront our own sense of powerlessness and not-knowing, our confusion and uncertainty about what we do and what our clients bring to us in sessions, and our uncertainty about what is truth and what is a lie. This exploration may be part of the same motive that led us on this path in the first place, yearning to make a difference in the world, wanting to help people who are suffering, and searching for some semblance of truth—if not for our clients' sake, then for our own.

It starts with despair, with the acceptance of everything that is outside our control and power to change. We feel an impossible yearning to really understand our clients and what they bring to us, to help them discover their own truth. Yet we must accept in the end that what they seek, what *we* seek, is ultimately inaccessible. We will never find certainty or truth, and somehow, we must learn to live with that.

The opposite of hope is not despair, or even acceptance as the thesaurus might suggest. "Relinquishing hope hurts," Omer and Rosenbaum (1997, p. 227) counsel, "but it can also be a turning point." Surrendering hope, they say, is not nearly the same as resignation but rather of accepting that which we will never know.

Embracing the Unknown and the Uncertainty of the Untruth

There is the enduring, stubborn myth that therapists really do know and understand what is happening most of the time, that the analytic, evidence-based approach leads to absolute, reliable diagnoses and empirically supported treatments supported by clear data. Cayne and Loewenthal (2007) prefer to think of therapy as a journey into the unknown. They advocate much greater tolerance for uncertainty, ambiguity, doubt, confusion, complexity, and that which is unknowable. This is what Rogers (1951) meant when he talked about being at his best as a therapist when he allowed himself to get in closer contact with the unknown in him and in the relationships with his clients. Freud used different language, but his idea of the unconscious was about recognizing that everything that we think might be going on is just what lay on the surface. Indigenous healers from around the world, as well as contemporary therapists who practice Ericksonian or metaphorical methods, also avoid reducing experiences into simplistic explanations and instead value the primacy of direct experience. Shamans and other healers do everything they can to encourage greater mystery rather than promoting insight and understanding. Their rituals and therapeutic tasks do not logically follow from the presenting complaints but rather are designed to be as ambiguous as possible, often involving tasks and homework that further preserve mystery (Kottler, Carlson, & Keeney, 2004). They would also find it ridiculous that we are even concerned about what is truth because they do not trust words or care much for what the client says in the first place.

This returns us to the central question of the book and the zigzag path we have been navigating through the wilderness. Among the dozens of reviewers who read this manuscript, and the hundreds of others to whom I have told Jacob's story, there almost always follows the insistent query: "So, come on Kottler, is it true or not? Stop the equivocating and explaining and tell us what you *really* think. Bottom line: did this really happen or did he make it up?"

I have thought about this over and over again, perhaps a thousand times, and in doing so it used to drive me crazy to not be able to provide a definitive answer. I have switched back and forth, taken positions that Jacob's story definitely was true, or that it was most certainly a hoax. I have experienced the despair of not knowing what really happened with Jacob, or any of my other clients, to the point that I quit practicing therapy for awhile until such time that I could learn to live with the uncertainty.

Most recently since I began to explore the nature of truth—in therapy and in life—I have come to the conclusion that it is over-rated. Here is the honest truth—*my* honest truth this moment: if Jacob's wife sent me a letter with the answer (and I do expect her to contact me again someday), supplying the proof one way or the other that Jacob's story was fictitious or real, I would be reluctant to open the envelope. I really do not want to know, if for no other reason that it allows me to keep my wishful thinking alive. I have learned to so enjoy and embrace not-knowing. Hope for me springs from giving people the benefit of the doubt.

Go ahead and press me. Hold a gun to my head and force me to decide, one way or the other: Do I think Jacob lied or told the truth?

I honestly do not know. And neither do you.

Epilogue

A few weeks after I finished writing this book, I was going through the attic of our home, sorting things for the annual spring cleaning. At the bottom of a stack of boxes was a blue storage tub filled with old files that I had removed from my file cabinet to make room for documents that were needed more immediately. There were newspaper clippings and research articles from previous books I had worked on, as well as material for other projects that I had never gotten around to writing and now realized that I would never begin.

I went through the pile with just a glance, dumping the papers into trash bags, until I discovered a file marked "To Do Such Things." This was the original title of the book about Jacob the assassin, the original version that chronicled his story. Just out of curiosity, I started looking through the documents and found just what I expected: maps of Palestine, articles about the war, correspondence with people in Israel who had been doing research for me, and a contract Jacob and I had drawn up between us.

Tucked into the papers was also an envelope, lightly sealed, and containing a one-page, single-spaced letter that Jacob had sent to me dated 10 years earlier. He had written along the bottom in his distinctive handwriting: "Jeffrey, I hope you can use this for an Epilogue."

The really strange thing is that I did not ever remember receiving this letter, nor did it seem familiar as I read it for what seemed like the first time. I could feel a chill, almost like Jacob was talking from the grave. These are his last words:

> What are you thinking of me as you read this book? I can tell you that I am a good person, well read, knowledgeable in the Bible and Torah, and I received a good moral background from my parents between right and wrong. I believe very strongly that what I accomplished for Israel was right. I am not a believer in becoming a martyr or a saint by what I accomplished. I did what was asked of me and what was in my heart and mind. I did not commit murder. In war for a true purpose that affects millions of people, tough decisions must be made. I can assure anyone reading this that this type of activity was not frivolous. I care about what you think of me. I want you to feel as I did during that time. We were fighting for the rights of many. Some lives were sacrificed in order to save many others.

> Believe me when I tell you that assassination is tough, but living with the remembrances afterwards is even tougher. For over 50 years I have lived with the effects, now known as post-traumatic stress. There was not much known about this during those years. I have suffered all my adult life with symptoms and nightmares.

> As this book explained, I lived in a world of secrets. I kept everything to myself. I have recently spoken with a number of people about my experiences in this book. Everyone was unanimous that they were concerned about some "crazies" trying to get even with me or members of my family. I have taken their advice and used different names and changed some details of the story. I am afraid of paying the penalty for what I did.

> Enough said about my feelings. Now I would like to give you a glimpse of my life after those momentous occasions [described in this book]. I grew up in the middle class areas of the Bronx. I participated in all the normal activities of a boy my age. After

coming home from my activities in the Middle East, I went on to pharmacy school and became a registered pharmacist. I married and had three children of whom I am very proud. I was married for 43 years when my wife suddenly died of a massive heart attack. I remarried a few years later. At the present time I am living in one of the Western states of the United States. I am relatively happy and content and expect that my remaining years will be content.

My family members, and everyone who knew of my activities, have passed away. I now think that it is time for my children to know what I have done in the past and let them make their own decisions as to whether or not I was one of the good guys.

References and Sources Consulted

Adler, J. M., Wagner, J. W., & McAdams, D. P. (2007). Personality and the coherence of psychotherapy narratives. *Journal of Research in Personality, 41,* 1179–1198.

Akhtar, S. (2009). In S. Akhtar & H. Parens (Eds.), *Lying, cheating, and carrying on* (pp. 1–16). Lanham, MD: Jason Aronson.

Akhtar, S., & Parens, H. (Eds.) (2009). *Lying, cheating, and carrying on.* Lanham, MD: Jason Aronson.

Anderson, W. T. (1990). *Reality isn't what it used to be.* San Francisco: HarperCollins.

Avner, P. (1959). *Memoirs of an assassin.* New York: Thomas Yoseloff.

Barnett, M. (2007). What brings you here? An exploration of the unconscious motivations of those who choose to train and work as psychotherapists and counselors. *Psychodynamic Practice, 13*(3), 257–274.

Bauer, Y. (1970). *From diplomacy to resistancy: A history of Jewish Palestine.* Philadelphia: The Jewish Publication Society.

Beck, A. T., Wright, F. D., Newman, C. F., & Liese, B. S. (1993). *Cognitive therapy of substance abuse.* New York: Guilford.

Bell, J. B. (1969). *The long war: Israel and the Arabs since 1946.* Englewood Cliffs, NJ: Prentice Hall.

Ben-Yehuda, N. (1993). *Political assassinations by Jews: A rhetorical device for justice.* Albany: State University of New York Press.

Bermak, C. E. (1977). Do psychiatrists have special emotional problems? *American Journal of Psychoanalysis, 37,* 141–146.

Billig, N. (1991). Deceptions in psychotherapy: Case report and considerations. *Canadian Journal of Psychiatry, 36,* 349–352.

Birch, M. (1998). Through a glass darkly: Questions about truth and memory. *Psychoanalytic Psychology, 15,* 34–48.

Birch, C. D., Kelln, B., & Aquino, E. (2006). A review and case report of pseudologia fantastica. *Journal of Forensic Psychiatry and Psychology, 17,* 299–320.

Black, I., & Morris, B. (1991). *Israel's secret wars: A history of Israel's intelligence services.* New York: Grove Weidenfeld.

Blum, H. (1983). The psychoanalytic process and analytic inference: A clinical study of a lie and a loss. *International Journal of Psycho-Analysis, 64,* 17–33.

Borys, D. S., & Pope, K. S. (2008). *Dual relationships between therapist and client.* Retrieved September 11, from http://kspope.com/dual/research2/php

Brice, R. (2008). King of the hill. *Outside,* March, 120–122.

Bride, B., & Figley, C. (2007). The fatigue of compassionate social workers. *Clinical Social Work Journal, 35*(3), 151–153.

Brown, L. S. (2005). Don't be a sheep: How this eldest daughter became a feminist therapist. *Journal of Clinical Psychology, 61,* 949–956.

Bruner, J. S. (1990). *Acts of meaning.* Cambridge, MA: Harvard University Press.

Cayne, J., & Loewenthal, D. (2007). The unknown in learning to be a psychotherapist. *European Journal of Psychotherapy and Counselling, 9,* 373–387.

Chalmers, A. F. (1982). *What is this thing called science?* Brisbane: University of Queensland Press.

Chessick, R. (1978). The sad soul of the psychiatrist. *Bulletin of the Menninger Clinic, 42*(1), 1–10.

Collins, L., & LaPierre, D. (1972). *O Jerusalem!* New York: Touchstone.

Cooper, G. (2009). Can therapists spot liars? *Psychotherapy Networker,* May/June, 14.

Cummings, N. A., & O'Donohue, W. T. (2005). Psychology's surrender to political correctness. In R. H. Wright & N. A. Cummings (Eds.), *Destructive trends in mental health: The well-intentioned path to harm* (pp. 3–27). New York: Taylor & Francis.

DeAngeles, T. (2008). An elephant in the office. *APA Online, 39*(1), 33–36.

DePaulo, B. M., Kashy, D. A., Kirkendol, S. E., & Epstein, J. A. (1996). Lying in everyday life. *Journal of Personality and Social Psychology, 70,* 979–995.

Deutsch, C. J. (1984). Self-reported sources of stress among psychotherapists. *Professional Psychology: Research and Practice, 15,* 833–845.

Dolliver, R. H., Williams, E. L., & Gold, D. C. (1980). The art of Gestalt therapy or "What are you doing with your feet now?" *Psychotherapy, 17,* 136–142.

Dorris, M. (1998). *The yellow raft in blue water.* New York: Warner.

Dyer, W. W., & Vriend, J. (1973). *Counseling effectively in groups.* Educational Technology Publications.

Edelwich, J., & Brodsky, A. M. (1980). *Burnout.* New York: Human Sciences Press.

Ekman, P. (2009). *Telling lies: Clues to deceit in the marketplace, politics, and marriage.* New York: W.W. Norton.

Ekman, P., O'Sullivan, M., & Frank, M. G. (1999). A few can catch a liar. *Psychological Science, 10,* 263–266.

Farber, B., Berano, K. C., & Capobianco, J. A. (2006). A temporal model of patient disclosure in psychotherapy. *Psychotherapy Research, 16,* 463–469.

Felder, L. (2005). I gave at the office. *Psychotherapy Networker,* September/October, 60–64.

Fenichel, O. (1939). The economics of pseudologica phantastica. *Collected Papers* (pp. 129–140). New York: W. W. Norton.

Fernandez-Armesto, F. (1997). *Truth: A history and guide for the perplexed.* New York: St. Martin's Press.

Figley, C. (2002). *Treating compassion fatigue.* New York: Routledge.

Fine, H. J. (1980). Despair and depletion in the therapist. *Psychotherapy: Theory, Research, and Practice 17*(4), 392–395.

Flowers, J. V., & Frizler, P. (2004). *Psychotherapists on film.* Jefferson, NC: McFarland & Co.

Ford, C. V. (1996). *Lies! Lies! Lies! The psychology of deceit.* Washington, DC: American Psychiatric Press.

Freud, S. (1905/1963). *Dora: An analysis of a case of hysteria.* New York: Simon & Schuster.

Freud, S. (1937a). Analysis terminable and interminable. *Standard Edition, 23,* 209–253.

Freud, S. (1937b). Constructions in analysis. *Standard Edition, 23,* 256–269.

Freudenberger, H. J., & Robbins, A. (1979). The hazards of being a psychoanalyst. *Psychoanalytic Review, 66,* 275–296.

Frey, J. (2003). *A million little pieces.* New York: Random House.

Gediman, H. K., & Lieberman, J. S. (1996). *The many faces of deceit: Omissions, lies and disguise in psychotherapy.* Northvale, NJ: Jason Aronson.

Gergen, K. (1991). *The saturated self: Dilemmas of identity in contemporary life.* New York: Basic Books.

Goffman, E. (1959). *The presentation of self in everyday life.* New York: Doubleday.

Goncalves, O. F. (1994). From epistemological truth to existential meaning in cognitive narrative psychotherapy. *Journal of Constructivist Psychology, 7,* 107–118.

Good, G. E., Thoreson, R. W., & Shaughnessy, P. (1995). Substance use, confrontation of impaired colleagues, and psychological functioning among counseling psychologists: A national survey. *The Counseling Psychologist,* 23(4), 703–721.

Greene, G. (1948). *The heart of the matter.* New York: Penguin.

Grohol, J. M. (2008a, January 9). *Why would you lie to your therapist?* Retrieved from www.psychcentral.com

Grohol, J. M. (2008b, February 6). *10 common reasons to lie to your therapist.* Retrieved from www.psychcentral.com

Guy, J. D. (1987). *The personal life of the psychotherapist.* New York: Wiley.

Hall, L. (2009). Personal communication as reviewer of manuscript.

Hancock, J. (2007). Digital deception. In A. N. Joinson, K. McKenna, T. Postmes, & U. Reips (Eds.), *Oxford handbook of internet psychology* (pp. 289–301). Oxford, UK: Oxford University Press.

Hansen, J. T. (2007). Counseling without truth: Toward a neopragmatic foundation for counseling practice. *Journal of Counseling and Development,* 85, 423–430.

Hantoot, M. S. (2000). Lying in psychotherapy supervision. *Academic Psychiatry,* 24, 179–187.

Healy, W., & Healy, M. T. (1915). *Pathological lying, accusation, and swindling: A study in forensic psychology.* Oxford, UK: Little Brown.

Heckelman, A. J. (1974). *American volunteers and Israel's War of Independence.* New York: KTAV Publishing.

Heller, J. (1995). *The Stern gang: Ideology, politics, and terror.* London: Frank Cass.

Henig, R. M. (2006). Looking for the lie. *The New York Times,* February 5, Online, 1–16.

Henry, W. E., Sims, J. H., & Spray, S. L. (1973). *Public and private lives of psychotherapists.* San Francisco: Jossey-Bass.

Hynan, D. J. (1990). Client reasons and experiences in treatment that influence termination of psychotherapy. *Journal of Clinical Psychology, 46,* 891–895.

Joinson, A. N., & Paine, C. B. (2007). Self-disclosure, privacy, and the Internet. In A. N. Joinson, K. McKenna, T. Postmes, & U. Reips (Eds.), *Oxford handbook of internet psychology* (pp. 237–252). Oxford, UK: Oxford University Press.

Karsh, E. (2002). *The Arab-Israeli conflict: The Palestine War 1948.* New York: Osprey.

Kelly, A. E. (1998). Clients' secret keeping in outpatient therapy. *Journal of Counseling Psychology, 45,* 50–57.

Kendall, P. C., Kipnis, D., & Otto-Salaj, L. (1992). When clients don't progress: Influences on and explanations for lack of therapeutic progress. *Cognitive Therapy and Research, 16,* 269–281.

Kernberg, O. F. (1992). *Aggression in personality disorders and perversions.* New Haven, CT: Yale University Press.

King, B. H., & Ford, C. V. (1987). Pseudologica fantastica. *American Journal of Psychiatry, 144,* 970.

Kirby, S. (2003). Telling lies? An exploration of self-deception and bad faith. *European Journal of Psychotherapy, Counselling, and Health, 6,* 99–110.

Kirschenbaum, H. (2009). *The life and work of Carl Rogers.* Alexandria, VA: American Counseling Association.

Komet, A. (2006). The truth about lying. *Psychology Today,* May/June 2007.

Kosslyn, S., Ganis, G., & Thompson, W. (2001). Neural foundations of imagery. *Nature Reviews Neuroscience, 2,* 635–642.

Kottler, J. (1982). Unethical behaviors we all do and pretend we don't. *Journal for Specialists in Group Work, 7*(3), 182–186.

Kottler, J. (1987). *On being a therapist.* San Francisco: Jossey-Bass.

Kottler, J. (1990). *Private moments, secret selves: Enriching our time alone.* New York: Ballantine.

Kottler, J. (1991). *The compleat therapist.* San Francisco: Jossey-Bass.

Kottler, J. (1992a). Confronting our own hypocrisy: Being a model for students and clients. *Journal of Counseling and Development, 70*(4), 475–476.

Kottler, J. (1992b). *Compassionate therapy: Working with difficult clients.* San Francisco: Jossey-Bass.

Kottler, J. (1993). Facing failure as a counselor. *American Counselor, 2*(4), 14–19.

Kottler, J. A. (1995). *Growing a therapist.* San Francisco: Jossey-Bass.

Kottler, J. A. (Ed.). (1996). *Finding your way as a counselor.* Alexandria, VA: American Counseling Association.

Kottler, J. (2006). *Divine madness: Ten stories of creative genius.* San Francisco: Jossey-Bass.

Kottler, J. (2008). When a therapist catches despair. *Psychotherapy in Australia, 15*(1), 14–18.

Kottler, J. A. (2010). *On being a therapist* (4th ed.). San Francisco: Jossey-Bass.

Kottler, J., & Blau, D. (1989). *The imperfect therapist: Learning from failure in therapeutic practice.* San Francisco: Jossey-Bass.

Kottler, J. A., & Carlson, J. (2002). *Bad therapy: Master therapists share their worst failures.* New York: Routledge.

Kottler, J. A., & Carlson, J. (2003). *The mummy at the dining room table: Eminent therapists reveal their most unusual cases and what they teach us about human behavior.* San Francisco: Jossey-Bass.

Kottler, J. A., & Carlson, J. (2006). *The client who changed me: Stories of therapist personal transformation.* New York: Brunner/Routledge.

Kottler, J. A., & Carlson, J. (2007). *Moved by the spirit: Discovery and transformation in the lives of leaders.* Atascadero, CA: Impact.

Kottler, J. A., & Carlson, J. (2009). *Creative breakthroughs in therapy: Tales of transformation and astonishment.* New York: Wiley.

Kottler, J. A., & Carlson, J. (2011). *Duped: Lies and beyond deception in therapy.* New York: Routledge

Kottler, J. A., Carlson, J., & Keeney, B. (2004). *An American shaman: An odyssey of ancient healing traditions.* New York: Routledge.

Kottler, J. A., & Hazler, R. (1997). *What you never learned in graduate school.* New York: Norton.

Kottler, J. A., & Marriner, M. (2009). *Changing people's lives while transforming your own: Paths to social justice and global human rights.* New York: Wiley.

Kottler, J. A., & Parr, G. (2000). The family therapist's own family. *The Family Journal: Counseling and Therapy for Couples and Families, 8*(2), 143–148.

Kurzman, D. (1992). *Genesis 1948: The first Arab-Israeli war.* New York: Da Capo Press.

Lacoursiere, R. B. (2008). Freud's death: Historical truth and biographical fictions. *American Imago, 65,* 107–128.

Layton, M. (2005). Facing darkness: The limits of empathy. *Psychotherapy Networker,* March/April, 33–35, 58–60.

Lazarus, A. (2006). Forward. In K. S. Pope, J. L. Sonne, & B. Greene (Eds.), *What therapists don't talk about and why* (pp. xi–xii). Washington, DC: American Psychological Association.

Lebow, J. (2005). The messenger is the message. *Psychotherapy Networker,* May/June, 91–93.

Lilienfeld, S. O., Fowler, K. A., Lohr, J. M., & Lynn, S. J. (2005). Pseudoscience, nonscience, and nonsense in clinical psychology: Dangers and remedies. In R. H. Wright & N. A. Cummings (Eds.), *Destructive trends in mental health: The well-intentioned path to harm* (pp. 187–218). New York: Taylor & Francis.

Lionels, M. (2006). What happened really matters. In M. I. Good (Ed.), *The seduction theory in its second century* (pp. 141–156). Madison, CT: International Universities Press.

Luchner, A. F., Mirsalimi, H., Moser, C. J., & Jones, R. A. (2008). Maintaining boundaries in psychotherapy: Covert narcissistic personality characteristics and psychotherapists. *Psychotherapy: Theory, Research, and Practice, 45*(10), 1–14.

Lucock, M. P., Hall, P., & Noble, R. (2006). A survey of influences on the practice of psychotherapists and clinical psychologists in training in the UK. *Clinical Psychology and Psychotherapy, 13*(2), 123–130.

Lutz, W., Lambert, M. J., Harmon, S. C., Tachisaz, A., Schurch, E., & Stulz, N. (2006). The probability of treatment success, failure, and duration: What can be learned from empirical data to support decision making in clinical practice? *Clinical Psychology and Psychotherapy, 13,* 223–232.

Lynn, S. J., & Nash, M. R. (1994). Truth in memory: Ramifications for psychotherapy and hypnotherapy. *American Journal of Clinical Hypnosis, 36,* 194–206.

MacNab, S. S. (1995). Listening to your patients, yelling at your kids: The interface between psychotherapy and motherhood. In M. B. Sussman (Ed.), *A perilous calling: The hazards of psychotherapy practice* (pp. 37–44). New York: Wiley.

MacNammarah, D. (2008). *Lying in therapy.* Retrieved from http://danomacnamarrah.blogspot/2008/06/lying-in-therapy.html

Mahoney, M. (1991). *Human change processes: The scientific foundations of psychotherapy.* New York: Basic Books.

Mahrer, A. R. (2004). *Theories of truth, models of usefulness: Toward a revolution in the field of psychotherapy.* London: Whurr.

Maslach, C. (2003). *Burnout: The cost of caring.* Los Altos, CA: Malor Books.

McAdams, D. P. (1993). *The stories we live by: Personal myths and the making of the self.* New York: Morrow.

McAdams, D. P. (2006). The problem of narrative coherence. *Journal of Constructivist Psychology, 19,* 109–125.

McGregor, I., & Holmes, J. (1999). How storytelling shapes memory and impressions of relationship events over time. *Journal of Personality and Social Psychology, 76,* 403–419.

Miller, S., Hubble, M., & Duncan, B. (2007). Supershrinks: What's the secret of their success? *Psychotherapy Networker,* November/December, 26–35.

Milstein, U. (1996–1998). *History of Israel's War of Independence* (Vols. I–III). Lanham, MD: University Press of America.

Moss, J., & Kottler, J. A. (1999). *The last victim: A true-life journey into the mind of the serial killer.* New York: Warner Books.

Napier, N. (2009). Finding the pulse. *Psychotherapy Networker,* January/February, 35–38.

Natterson, J. M. (2003). Love in psychotherapy. *Psychoanalytic Psychology, 20*(3), 509–521.

Newman, C. F., & Strauss, J. L. (2003). When clients are untruthful: Implications for the therapeutic alliance, case conceptualization, and intervention. *Journal of Cognitive Therapy, 17,* 241–252.

Norcross, J. C. (2005). The psychotherapist's own psychotherapy: Educating and developing psychologists. *American Psychologist,* November, 840–848.

Omer, H., & Rosenbaum, R. (1997). Diseases of hope and the work of despair. *Psychotherapy, 34*(3), 225–232.

Orlinsky, D. E., & Ronnestad, M. H. (Eds.). (2005). *How psychotherapists develop: A study of therapeutic work and professional growth.* Washington, DC: American Psychological Association.

O'Shaughnessy, E. (1990). Can a liar be psychoanalyzed? *International Journal of Psycho-Analysis, 71,* 187–196.

Parry, A. (1997). Why we tell stories: The narrative construction of reality. *Transactional Analysis Journal, 27,* 118–127.

Polkinghorne, D. (1992). Postmodern epistemology of practice. In S. Kvale (Ed.), *Psychology and postmodernism.* London: Sage.

Pope, K. S., Sonne, J. L., & Greene, B. (2006). *What therapists don't talk about and why.* Washington, DC: American Psychological Association.

Pope, K. S., & Tabachnick, B. G. (1994). Therapists as patients: A national survey of psychologists' experiences, problems, and benefits. *Professional Psychology: Research and Practice, 25*(3), 247–258.

Ravn, K. (2009). Body of lies: Patients aren't 100% honest with doctors. *Los Angeles Times,* June 8.

Ringstad, R. (2008). The ethics of dual relationships: Beliefs and behaviors of clinical practitioners. *Families in Society, 89*(1), 69–77.

Rogers, C. (1951). *Client-centered therapy.* Boston: Houghton Mifflin.

Rogers, C. (1980). *A way of being.* Boston: Houghton Mifflin.

Rosenthal, H. (2005). Lessons from the legend of Gloria: Were we duped by the world's most influential counseling session? *Counselor: The Magazine for Addiction Professionals, 6*(6), 60–66.

Rothschild, B., & Rand, M. L. (2006). *Help for the helper: The psychophysiology of compassion fatigue and vicarious trauma.* New York: Norton.

Schank, R. C., & Abelson, R. P. (1995). Knowledge and memory: The real story. In R. J. Wyer, Jr. (Ed.), *Advances in social cognition* (Vol. 8, 1086). Hillsdale, NJ: Lawrence Erlbaum.

Schwartz, B., & Flowers, J. V. (2006). *How to fail as a therapist.* Atascadero, CA: Impact.

Sells, S. (2004). Undercurrents. *Psychotherapy Networker,* November/December, 75–80.

Serban, G. (2001). *Lying: Man's second nature.* Westport, CT: Praeger.

Shostrum, E. (1965). *Three approaches to psychotherapy* (Film). Orange, CA: Psychological Films.

Shub, N. F. (1995). The journey of the characterologic therapist. In M. B. Sussman (Ed.), *A perilous calling: The hazards of psychotherapy practice* (pp. 61–80). New York: Wiley.

Skovholt, T. M. (2001). *The resilient practitioner: Burnout prevention and self-care strategies for counselors, therapists, teachers, and health professionals.* Boston: Allyn and Bacon.

Slater, L. (2000). *Lying: A metaphorical memoir.* New York: Random House.

Smith, D. L. (1993). Psychoanalysis, lies and videotape: The problem of dishonesty in psychotherapy. *International Journal of Communicative Psychoanalysis and Psychotherapy, 8,* 109–113.

Smith, D. L. (2005). Natural born liars: Why do we lie, and why are we so good at it? *Scientific American Online,* May 18, 1–4.

Smith, E. W. L. (1995). On the pathologization of life: Psychotherapist's disease. In M. B. Sussman (Ed.), *A perilous calling: The hazards of psychotherapy practice* (pp. 81–88). New York: Wiley.

Spence, D. P. (1982). *Narrative and historical truth.* New York: W. W. Norton.

Sprang, G., Clark, J., & Whitt-Woosley, A. (2007). Compassion fatigue, compassion satisfaction, and burnout: Factors impacting a professional's quality of life. *Journal of Loss and Trauma, 12*(3), 259–280.

Stein, M. (1972). A clinical illustration of a moral problem in psychoanalysis. In S. C. Post (Ed.), *Moral values and the superego concept in psychoanalysis* (pp. 226–243). New York: International Universities Press.

Stewart, R. E., & Chambless, D. L. (2008). Treatment failures in private practice: How do psychologists proceed? *Professional Psychology: Research and Practice, 39*(2), 176–181.

Sussman, M. B. (Ed.). (1995). *A perilous calling: The hazards of psychotherapy practice.* New York: Wiley.

Sussman, M. B. (2007). *A curious calling: Unconscious motivations for practicing psychotherapy.* New York: Jason Aronson.

Tal, D. (2000). The forgotten war: Jewish-Palestinian strife in mandatory Palestine, December 1947–May 1948. *Israel Affairs, 6*(3–4), 3–21.

Twain, M. (1882/2007). On the decay of the art of lying, In *Alonzo Fitz and other stories* (pp. 31–36). Bibliobizaar.

Urchs, M. (2007). The logic of lying. In J. Mecke (Ed.), *Cultures of lying* (pp. 31–46). Madison, WI: Galda.

Vilhjalmsson, T., & Kottler, J. A. (2000). The pig's butler. *Talk,* December, 130–135.

Vrij, A. (2008). *Detecting lies and deceit* (2nd ed.). New York: Wiley.

Wang, S. S. (2008). Ethics lapses usually start small for therapists. *Health Blog, Wall Street Journal.* Retrieved from http://blogs.wsj.com/health/2007/10/17/ethics-lapses-usually-start-small-for-therapists/ Accessed September 18.

Watkins, C., & Schneider, C. (1991). *Research in counseling.* Hillsdale, NJ: Erlbaum.

Weinshel, E. M. (1979). Some observations on not telling the truth. *Journal of the American Psychoanalytic Association, 27,* 503–532.

Wheeler, S. (2002). Nature or nurture: Are therapists born or trained? *Psychodynamic Practice, 8,* 427–441.

White, M., & Epston, D. (1990). *Narrative means to therapeutic ends.* New York: W. W. Norton.

Whitty, M. T., & Carr, A. N. (2006). *Cyberspace romance: The psychology of online relationships.* Basingstoke, UK: Palgrave Macmillan.

Whitty, M. T., & Carville, S. E. (2008). Would I lie to you? Self-serving lies and other-oriented lies told across different media. *Computers in Human Behavior, 24,* 1707–1723.

Whitty, M. T., & Joinson, A. N. (2009). *Truth, lies, and trust on the Internet.* London: Routledge.

Widdershoven, G. (1992). Hermeneutics and relativism: Wittgenstein, Gadamer, Habermas. *Theoretical and Philosophical Psychology, 12,* 1–11.

Wiley, S. D. (1998). Deception and detection in psychiatric diagnosis. *The Psychiatric Clinics of North America, 21,* 869–893.

Williams, E. (2003). The relationship between states of therapist self-awareness and perceptions of the counseling process. *Contemporary Psychotherapy, 33*(3), 177–186.

Williams, E. (2008). A psychotherapy researcher's perspective on therapist self-awareness and self-focused attention after a decade of research. *Psychotherapy Research, 18*(2), 139–146.

Wittine, B. (1995). The spiritual self: Its relevance in the development and daily life of the psychotherapist. In M. B. Sussman (Ed.), *A perilous calling: The hazards of psychotherapy practice* (pp. 288–301). New York: Wiley.

Wright, R. H. (2005). The myth of continuing education: A look at some intended and (maybe) unintended consequences. In R. H. Wright & N. A. Cummings (Eds.), *Destructive trends in mental health: The well-intentioned path to harm* (pp. 143–151). New York: Taylor & Francis.

Yalom, I. (1996). *Lying on the couch.* New York: Basic Books.

Yalom, I. (2002). *The gift of therapy.* New York: HarperCollins.

Zupancic, A. (2007). Lying on the couch. In J. Mecke (Ed.), *Cultures of lying* (pp. 155–168). Madison, WI: Galda.

Zur, O. (2005). The dumbing down of psychology: Faulty beliefs about boundary crossings and dual relationships. In R. H. Wright & N. A. Cummings (Eds.), *Destructive trends in mental health: The well-intentioned path to harm* (pp. 253–282). New York: Taylor & Francis.

Index

About the Author

Jeffrey A. Kottler is one of the most prolific authors in the fields of counseling, psychotherapy, and education, having written 75 books about a wide range of subjects during the past 30 years. He has authored a dozen texts for counselors and therapists, which are used in universities around the world and more than a dozen books each for practicing therapists and educators. Some of his most highly regarded works include *On Being a Therapist* (Jossey-Bass, 1987); *Bad Therapy* (with J. Carlson, Routledge, 2002); *The Client Who Changed Me* (with J. Carlson, Brunner/ Routledge, 2006); *Divine Madness* (Jossey-Bass, 2006); *Changing People's Lives While Transforming Your Own* (with M. Marriner, Wiley, 2009); and *Making Changes Last* (Brunner/Routledge, 2001). He has also written several narrative accounts of people's lives (from which the present story evolved) including the best-selling true crime book, *The Last Victim*.

Kottler has been an educator for 35 years. He has worked as a teacher, counselor, and therapist in preschool, middle school, mental health center, crisis center, university, community college, and private practice settings. He has served as a Fulbright Scholar and Senior Lecturer in Peru and Iceland, as well as worked as a Visiting Professor in New Zealand, Australia, Hong Kong, Singapore, and Nepal. Kottler is currently Professor of Counseling at California State University, Fullerton. He also cofounded the Madhav Ghimire Foundation (www.ghimirefoundation.org) that provides educational scholarships for lower-caste girls at risk in Nepal.